Mary Parker Follett— Prophet of Management

Joan C. Tonn and the Urwick Management Centre

Mary Parker Follett— Prophet of Management

A Celebration of Writings from the 1920s

EDITED BY PAULINE GRAHAM

PREFACE BY ROSABETH MOSS KANTER

INTRODUCTION BY PETER F. DRUCKER

A Harvard Business School Press Classic

Harvard Business School Press
BOSTON, MASSACHUSETTS

Library of Congress Cataloging-in-Publication Data

Mary Parker Follett—prophet of management : a celebration of writings
from the 1920s / edited by Pauline Graham ; preface by Rosabeth Moss
Kanter : introduction by Peter F. Drucker.
    p. cm. — (Harvard Business School Press classics)
    Includes index.
    ISBN 0-87584-563-0
    1. Management.
    2. Psychology, Industrial. I. Graham, Pauline.
    II. Series.
    HD31.M3326   1994
    658—dc20   94-19675
                                                       CIP

Contents

Editor's Note

THIS book completes the task I set myself almost three decades ago: to bring Mary Parker Follett to the attention of the large and rightful audience she deserves.

First and foremost a political scientist, Follett successfully applied her original ideas in the field of social work, where she spent some 25 years. Later, she used the same concepts in her lectures on management at the prestigious annual New York conferences of the Bureau of Personnel Administration (BPA), at which she was invited to speak in the mid-1920s. (Follett was nothing if not consistent.)

Follett was profoundly interested in the individual in the group and society; she described how, through democratic governance, we can fulfill our potential and in the process strengthen and develop the groups to which we belong. But Follett's brand of democratic governance cannot be achieved by the mere transfer of formalized powers or by passive acquiescence to what is done in our name. It can be created only through the decisions of the individuals directly involved in a situation. Bureaucratic institutions with hierarchical structures are not appropriate for the purpose and should be replaced by group networks in which members can analyze their problems and produce and implement their own solutions. In a true democracy each individual takes part in the decision-making process and accepts personal responsibility for the overall result.

This approach, according to Follett, applies to any group—small or large, private or public, national or international.

These fundamental ideas—of individual commitment through direct and responsible participation, and all that this entails—are emerging as critical issues in the modern workplace. Our most forward-looking management thinkers and business leaders are looking for the forms of organization best likely to allow these ideas full play. Follett, with her insights on democratic governance, shows us ways and means. We can now catch up with her thinking and learn from her teachings.

How best to encapsulate Follett's thinking so that her management lectures can be set in their proper context? I wanted Follett to speak to the readers in her own words, as no paraphrasing can replicate the immediacy and subtlety of her writing. Therefore, after a preface by Rosabeth Moss Kanter and an introduction by Peter Drucker, two devotees of Follett and her work, the book contains extracts of Follett's own writings on specific subjects—conflict, authority, power, the place of the individual in the group, and the place of the individual in society—with commentaries by the foremost relevant experts on those subjects. All the lectures have been left unchanged, as she gave them in 1925 and in 1933. I did not want to tamper with them and thereby break in any way the continuity of her thought as she unravels it before her audience. I also kept, without explanatory footnotes, the cases and examples she used to illustrate her arguments, as they can be adequately understood within the context of what she writes.

I, of course, had the most enjoyable task: rereading Follett was a pleasure and an invigorating renewal. The other commentators, all distinguished experts, were delighted to contribute. Some of them already admired Follett; others were rediscovering her. Everyone assesses Follett in the same way: ahead of her time in the 1920s, still ahead of our time today: in Drucker's compelling phrase, "the prophet of management."

In Part I, The Psychological Foundations of Business Organization, I start with Chapters 3 and 4 of Follett's book *Creative Experience,* which examine circular response and integrative behavior. These chapters, in my view, reflect her most important psychological contribution to our understanding of behavior: we react not only to the other party but also to the relationship that exists between us, thus creating in part our own response. The nuances here are subtle; they need careful reading.

With this knowledge in hand, Follett's lectures can be enjoyed that much more effectively. Next in order are "Constructive Conflict" and "Power" (from *Dynamic Administration*), two of the papers she presented at the Bureau of Personnel Administration in New York in January 1925. Then, culled from *Freedom and Coordination,* are five lectures she gave in January and February 1933 to inaugurate the Department of Business Administration at the London School of Economics (University of London). These were chosen over earlier lectures on the same subjects because they reflect Follett's definitive views on the giving of orders, the bases of authority, and the essentials of leadership, coordination, and control.

In Part II, we move to the bigger picture, The Individual, the Group, and Society, with excerpts from *The New State* on the individual in the group and the individual in society. This makes exciting reading indeed, with Follett sounding clarion calls about the individual's rightful and responsible place in groups and in society.

Part III, Business—The Way Ahead, is Follett's lecture "Business in Society" (originally "How Must Business Management Develop to Become a Profession?"), which she presented in November 1925 at the BPA. This too makes inspiring reading, with her injunctions to be proud of "our business integrity" and to manage "with style."

Paul Lawrence's Epilogue summarizes Follett's special qualities as a management thinker.

Lyndall Urwick, doyen of the British management establishment for many decades, recalled at 80 his first meeting with Follett: "In two minutes flat, I was at her feet and remained there till the day she died." Like Urwick, all who have contributed to this book—men and women from different cultures and diverse occupations—are to varying degrees in the thrall of this exceptional woman. With sense and sensibility, with generosity of heart and mind, Mary Parker Follett bequeaths us her insights and her wisdom and illuminates our way. She helps us become, each in our uniqueness and in however small a measure, a better person, a more effective manager, a more responsible citizen.

More than other books, this volume would not have been possible without the dedicated cooperation of a large number of people. I am profoundly grateful to those who started the ball rolling and kept it going: first and foremost to Paula Duffy, director of the Harvard Business School Press, who patiently and persistently untangled and resolved the obscure copyright problems, who had the vision to suggest combining writings and commentaries, and who continued to advise how best to put the book together; to Peter Drucker for his blessings, enthusiasm, and impetus; to Rosabeth Moss Kanter for her careful attention and advice; to Garry Emmons and Natalie Greenberg for their expertise in editing and writing; and last but not least to my own editor, Alistair Williamson, for his knowledge of the subject, his empathy and understanding, and his ability to get things done with unfailing discretion and courtesy, in the manner of Follett herself. Thanks are due also to Yoko Nakano, my friend in Tokyo, who skillfully bridged the language gap with our eminent Japanese contributor.

I am also extremely grateful to the expert contributors who, through their commentaries, have given the book that topicality and zest that make it unique. In one of his letters, Drucker calls us "conspirators." We have indeed, from our different corners of the globe, conspired together to present to a worldwide audience this comprehensive, albeit compressed, selection of Follett's writings.

I have no doubt that readers will be enriched by this book and will return to it again and again for refreshment and renewal. Nor do I doubt that some will want to read Follett in her entirety, to get the full import of the subtlety of her thought and the help she can offer as we move toward the twenty-first century striving to bring about a more inclusive, more productive, fairer society.

Pauline Graham
London, England
May 1994

Preface

ROSABETH MOSS KANTER

"If I have seen further, it is by standing upon the shoulders of Giants."

—Sir Isaac Newton, 1675

Rereading Mary Parker Follett is like entering a zone of calm in a sea of chaos. Her work reminds us that even in our fast-paced world—in which 18 months can constitute a high-tech product life cycle and "15 minutes" a person's assigned allotment of fame—there are truths about human behavior that stand the test of time. They persist despite superficial changes, like the deep and still ocean beneath the waves of management fad and fashion.

Follett penned her observations six and seven decades ago, before the computers-and-communications revolution. Six decades, however, is a barely noticeable blip in human evolution. Managers still struggle with the problems of organizations and society that she illuminated. They can still draw inspiration from this insightful giant. Peter Drucker calls her "superbly relevant," especially in her concept of management as a function or process, not a tool box of engineering techniques.

Consider how many Follettian ideas will appear fresh and timely to new readers, how many will serve as philosophic foundations for currently popular concepts. Follett's espousal of mutual problem solving foreshadows employee involvement, participative management, quality circles, and other team-based approaches to involving the workforce in diagnosis, analysis, and solution finding. Her identification of the importance of "horizontal authority," which she described in terms of cross-functional committees and "conferences of parallel heads," fits exactly a shift many companies are making toward recognizing the importance of cross-functional collaboration and peer networks in running flatter, leaner organizations. Indeed, many managers are shifting their orientation from the vertical dimension—obsessed with chains of command and hierarchies of rights and privileges—to the horizontal "boundaryless organization" heralded by Jack Welch at General Electric. Follett would applaud (and perhaps be amused by) the new fashion in American organization charts: circular and oval.

Her ideas about leadership are equally timely. Strip away the name and date, and she could make the best-seller lists. It is not surprising that Warren Bennis, an outstanding advocate of the importance of leadership, finds Follett a fount of inspiration, calling her a "swashbuckling advance scout of management thinking." Follett proposed that a leader is one who sees the whole situation, organizes the experience of the group, offers a vision of the future, and trains followers to be leaders. Many decades and hundreds of how-to-be-a-leader books later, her definition cannot be improved upon. Her advice to leaders seems right out of discussions of empowerment: formal authority is not the same as operative power. It is futile to retain over/under assumptions about the power superiors wield simply because of their role. "Power conferred" always fails, because power is self-developing; it comes from interactions among people, in which respect is earned. The most effective way to exercise authority is to depersonalize the giving of orders, emphasizing the importance of a task rather than the rights one person has over another.

Follett's view of business as a social institution, not just a financial or production vehicle, is a prelude to a variety of contemporary managerial issues. She addressed career issues, such as the difference between professionals and managers vis-à-vis loyalty, and the need for professionals to find meaning in the work itself, not in administrative ladder climbing. Questions of identity and career loom large for managers displaced by downsizing, who must maintain their identification as professionals, with depth in a discipline, longer in their careers, as Peter Drucker urged in "The New Organization" in the *Harvard Business Review*. Today's quest for corporate social responsibility can be informed by Follett's notion of the integrated life, in which a person's work itself becomes community service. Similarly, she provided a philosophic basis for corporate ethics: morality is social; it stems not from inside a person in relation only to self, but from membership in the group. Indeed, she argued presciently that the professions are ahead of business in having "group codes," which make it easier for people to speak up about issues.

So many so-called new management ideas are previewed in Follett's work. Before Jim Heskett's *Managing in the Service Economy* helped put service management on the general management map, Follett held that customer service means more than "service with a smile." Long before those of us studying strategic alliances and joint ventures, as I did in *When Giants Learn to Dance,* discovered the virtues of cooperation with competitors, Follett had analyzed when competition can turn into a kind of cooperation—for example, the formation of trade associations, in which competitors join forces to build an industry and provide the highest quality goods and services to ultimate customers; cooperative credit systems; trades linking to form apprentice schools; conferences between managers in the same industry; and professional associations such as the Employment Managers' Association, formed as she was writing. The formation of alliances is not a new idea derived from heightened global competition; it is a Folletian idea in new form. And decades before David Osborne and Ted Gaebler exhorted America to "reinvent government" through privatization and grass-roots entrepreneurship, Follett urged leaders to replace bureaucracy with empowered group networks with a common purpose.

Throughout her diverse commentaries on so many matters of concern to today's managers, Follett sent one principal message: *relationships matter.* Underpinning all of her work is the importance of relationships, not just transactions, in organizations. She pointed to the reciprocal nature of relationships, the mutual influence developed when people work together, however formal authority is defined. She applied general systems theory to organizations, demonstrating the intermeshing of cause and effect, arguing that actors and activities cannot be examined in isolation, but only in relationship to other actors and activities. Her ideas about the dynamic nature of organizational processes are well suited to the world of constant motion my co-authors and I portray in *The Challenge of Organizational Change.*

Follett's ideas are timely and insightful, and this volume helps us climb onto her intellectual shoulders to see the tasks of managers more clearly. Still, as we do, we should ask ourselves the question posed by so many commentators here. If Follett is so good, why were her ideas ignored for so many years? Why do so many leading figures in the management field confess to having read her work after they developed similar ideas, not before? Or, to put it another way, what can we learn from the neglect of this pioneering management philosopher?

Drucker, whose insight and experience must be respected, argues in his introduction to this book that her ideas did not fit emerging trends. He blames her obscurity on her era, which rejected her ideas but embraced exceptional women. He explicitly rejects sexism as an explanation, pointing to prominent American female leaders of Follett's era, a stark contrast to the environment in Europe, from which he came.

But it is hard to disentangle the person from the ideas. Contemporary feminists such as Carol Gilligan would argue that Follett spoke "in a different voice," a female voice. It is hard to untangle the kinds of ideas she espoused from the gender of the person espousing them. With the 20:20 hindsight of decades later, and the experiences of the first or second high-ranking woman in many corporate and academic settings (which I captured in *Men and Women of the Corporation* and the video, *A Tale of "O": On Being Different*), I am convinced that Follett's gender did indeed play a role in her neglect. It is hard to found or build a discipline without disciples. It is hard to attract disciples if one is very different from traditional authority figures. For every Frances Perkins who Drucker saw rise to leadership in the 1930s, there were thousands more women who were not given the opportunity to have even Rosie the Riveter's well-paid World War II factory job. Sprinkled throughout Follett's observations are clues to how rare she was in management circles. The leaders in her examples are entirely male; women appear as "shop girls."

Moreover, it was undoubtedly just as true then as it is now that powerful women and their ideas were more readily accepted the greater the geographic distance and, therefore, the lesser the immediate threat. Follett's ideas were embraced in Japan, a continent and an ocean away, where people could accept her expertise because they did not deal with her personhood. Follett's work was kept alive in Britain, another ocean away, not America. Across the water she was the star from America; at home in Boston, it was harder to be "one of the boys." Furthermore, she was neither an academic who could build a cadre of devoted students nor a chief executive who could create a model organization, so she lacked two means for ensuring lasting impact.

Still, there is clear truth to the proposition that her ideas were ahead of their time or even wrong for their time. Mary Parker Follett was a quintessential utopian and a romantic—albeit a romantic writing about the practicalities of commerce. Her ideas are rooted in American optimism and egalitarianism, yet they also run counter to American individualism and belief in social engineering. She wrote before the dark days of fascism and communism, the hegemony of the military-industrial complex, and the confrontational politics of the labor, civil rights, and women's movements.

Hers is a philosophy of relationships stemming from a belief in human goodness and the cooperative spirit.

The very nature of her analysis makes it difficult to use, centering as it does around the idea that actions are interdependent, reflexive, and situational. She asked managers to use their judgment, recognize interdependence, use conflict constructively to elicit information, and find integrative solutions to problems. But she offered no specific techniques, no step-by-step approach, no strategies for success, no action plan.

Follett focused on that which makes us most human, but which is almost the most difficult to do and likely to bring the least short-term glory. As she herself put it, "integration leaves no thrill of victory" the way adversarial management does. And her ideas bump up against the politics of interest. In his commentary here, Nitin Nohria reminds us of Michel's "iron law of oligarchy" and the sobering reality that some situations are zero-sum. Similarly, Drucker argues that the human relations school, which pushed Follettian reasoning off the stage, preserved patriarchy and hierarchy in the guise of sensitivity to workers. When Follett wrote that "'cut-throat' competition is beginning to go out of fashion" and that despite competition among firms, "the cooperation between them is coming to occupy a larger and larger place," she was wrong. She might have been right in identifying the need: "What the world needs today is a cooperative mind." But she was wrong in assessing the likelihood that cooperation would overwhelm competition. At least in America. At least then.

And now? We should all stand on Follett's shoulders in order to see further into the possibilities for organizational perfectibility—even as we see the limits to a belief in human goodness. We should remember the enduring truths of behavior even as we witness the amazing transformations of social institutions in the global economy, from upheavals in countries and regimes to new challenges for companies and communities.

Perhaps every generation will need to rediscover Mary Parker Follett. I suspect that every few decades management prophets will arise who sound notes remarkably similar to Follett's. And every generation will have its own role models of visionary companies (just think of Ben & Jerry's as the 1990s equivalent of Lincoln Electric) and visionary thinkers.

Introduction
Mary Parker Follett: Prophet of Management

PETER F. DRUCKER

W<small>HEN</small> in 1941 I first became interested in management, I asked around about who the important people in the field were. Then I called on each and requested a list of books and articles to read. Not one of these experts as much as mentioned Mary Parker Follett. Only a decade later did I even hear her name. By then I had done a fair amount of work in the field as a writer and a consultant and in 1950 had actually become a professor of management. During those years I had gotten to know a good many of the people who were prominent in the field—then still a small and closely knit fraternity—and had worked with several of them. But not once, I am certain, did anyone speak of Mary Parker Follett or refer to her work. In 1951 I was working on a project that later became the "President's Course" of the American Management Association. Lyndall Urwick, the English management pioneer of the 1920s and 1930s, had just made his first post–World War II trip across the Atlantic. I showed him my draft, and he said: "What you say about dissent and conflict sounds like Mary Parker Follett."

"Mary *who*?" I said.

Yet during her lifetime—or at least until the 1929 Depression, four years before her death in 1933—Mary Parker Follett had been very visible, eminently successful, and highly influential as a lecturer and writer and consultant to business and government leaders on both sides of the Atlantic. Several of the people to whom I went for that early reading list had been active during the 1920s and 1930s in what was then called the "management movement." One

1

was Alvin Dodd, founder and long-time president of the American Management Association where, as I found out later, Follett had spoken several times. Another was Tom Spates, founder of the personnel profession and one of the pillars of the Bureau of Personnel Administration, before which Follett read her celebrated paper "Constructive Conflict" in 1925. Neither man, however, mentioned her name. Most puzzling, perhaps, is her absence from the reading list Harry Hopf gave me. A successful consultant and authority on managing insurance companies, Hopf had built a magnificent business and management library numbering several thousand volumes at his farm in Crotonville, New York—which after his death in 1949 became the nucleus of GE's famed Advanced Management Institute. Hopf gave me a list of six or seven pages and assured me that it contained everything "of the slightest importance" on management. A most catholic list, it introduced me to Taylor, Gantt, and the two Gilbreths—husband and wife; to Ian Hamilton and Lyndall Urwick; to Robert Owen, Walter Rathenau, Henry Fayol, Cyril Burt, and Hugo Muensterberg; to Elton Mayo and Chester Barnard. I owe to Hopf's list the realization that there was a discipline of management waiting to be born. But Mary Parker Follett's name was not on the list. Her books, of course, were in Hopf's library; but evidently he did not consider them "of the slightest importance."

Follett, however, had been the brightest star in the management firmament. And—to change the metaphor—she had struck every single chord in what now constitutes the "management symphony." Ten years later, not even her memory remained, at least not in her native America.[1] She had become a "nonperson."

WHY?

The expedient and politically correct answer today might seem to be, "Because she was a woman and had been discriminated against." It would be the wrong answer. America of the 1930s was full of female stars in every sphere of public life. In government and politics there were Eleanor Roosevelt and Frances Perkins, the first woman in a U.S. cabinet and tremendously powerful during the entire 12 years of FDR's administration. The country's two most prominent media people were women: Cissy Patterson, publisher of the *Washington Times-Herald,* and Iphigenie Ochs Sulzberger who ran the *New York Times.* Another woman, Dorothy Thompson, was the most brilliant, the most often quoted, and toward the end of the decade the most influential newspaper columnist. In academia a number of women were highly visible and constantly quoted college presidents: Virginia Gildersleeve of New York's Barnard, Aurelia Reinhardt of Mills College in California, and Constance Warren, the founder-president of "progressive" Sarah Lawrence. The serious theater had Lillian Hellman and Clare Boothe Luce. Even management had its female stars. These were the years during which Lillian Gilbreth became a celebrity as a writer, speaker, and consultant; during which Anna Rosenberg became the first woman in the top management of a major American corporation (at R.H. Macy, then the country's biggest department store) and the first "personnel vice president" anywhere. (Fifteen years later, during the Korean War, she became "boss" of the armed services as assistant secretary of defense for personnel.)

I still remember how surprised I was when I came to the United States as a young newspaperman in the 1930s and saw so many prominent, self-assured, powerful women in the public eye. I had grown up in the Vienna of the 1920s, where there were many professional women, but nothing like the galaxy of women to be seen in the forefront of most fields in America's public life.

These women saw themselves as leaders, as stars—not merely equal with the men, but superior to them. And they were accepted as such by their colleagues and by the public at large.

So there was no prejudice against the exceptional woman on the ground of her gender. By the same criteria, Follett was every bit as exceptional as any of the widely recognized women I have mentioned. Why did she become, instead, a nonperson?

The only explanation is that her ideas, concepts, and precepts were being *rejected* in the 1930s and 1940s. Hopf did not leave her off his reading list because of ignorance. He left her off because in 1941 he did not consider her work to be "of the slightest importance." What she had to say, the 1930s and 1940s simply did not hear and, equally important, did not *want* to hear. This holds for every one of the four central postulates of Follett's management work.

If Mary Parker Follett is known today at all, it is for her "Constructive Conflict." Follett begins her discussion of conflict (Chapter 2 of this volume) by saying: "As a conflict—difference—is here in this world, as we cannot avoid it, we should, I think, use it to work for us." This sounds innocuous enough. But what "use" does she propose? The first one is to use conflict to *understand*. Follett urges us never to ask who is right in a conflict—indeed, not even to ask *what* is right. The proper response, she tells us, is to assume that both sides are right. Rather, both sides are likely to give right answers but to different questions. The right use of conflict is therefore to ask: What must these people who differ with me and oppose me see as the right question if their position is a rational one and, indeed, a correct one? Then, the second step to make conflict—difference—"work for us" is to use the mutual understanding of each other's question to integrate both positions into a new and different answer that satisfies what each side considers right. The end result of conflict management—indeed, the only way to resolve a conflict—is not "victory," not "compromise." It is integration of interests.

In the 1930s and 1940s, this was unintelligible. *Politically* those decades were dominated by men and creed that knew the proper use of conflict was to conquer. They did not believe in conflict resolution; they believed in unconditional surrender. Their goal was not peace but war. And *society* was dominated—permeated, in fact—by a profound belief in class war, in which the very attempt to understand what was important to the other side was a sellout.

To give one example: In the late 1940s, Charles E. Wilson, the recently appointed CEO of General Motors (GM), wanted to introduce what we now call "quality circles" and a partnership between management and workers based on workers' responsibility for their own work and tasks—practices we now credit the Japanese with.[2] To find out what questions workers considered important, Wilson ran a companywide survey. The workers' response was overwhelming. But before GM could take any action, the United Auto Workers (UAW) protested to the National Labor Relations Board (NLRB) that even asking workers about their jobs was an "unfair labor practice." And it threatened to pull the GM workers out on strike. The survey implied the possibility of cooperation between company and workers, that there were areas in which both had the same interests—in other words, that there could be harmony. According to the UAW, this violated the axiom of conflict on which both the country's labor law and the union contract were based. I knew one of the NLRB members and went to Washington to talk with him about the issue. He was a Republican appointee and under daily attack from the union as "pro-management." But when I said something about both management and workers having "a common interest in the survival and prosperity of the company" (also one of Follett's arguments, although I did not know that at the time), my friend cut me short: "Any company that asserts such a common interest," he said, "is prima facie in violation of the law and guilty of a grossly unfair labor practice." He continued, "Labor relations have to be war; and their end result cannot be 'harmony'; it must be victory for one side and defeat for the other. The best you can hope for are rules of civilized warfare and armistice long enough for each side to bury its dead."

Equally incomprehensible in those years—at least for the great majority of executives, politicians, writers, and consultants and for public opinion in general—was Follett's second postulate, that management is not exclusive to business but the generic function of all organizations, even of government agencies. Government and business were seen as incompatible in the 1930s and 1940s. Those were the years in which "public administration" set up shop as a separate denomination with its own bishops and priests, its own schools, its own terminology, its own concerns. To Follett it was obvious—she said so many times—that business was a *social* institution. In the all-but-universal opinion of those years, however, business was nothing but an *economic* institution.

And what Follett meant by "management"—her third postulate—was equally strange to the management people of the 1930s and 1940s. To her, management was a *function*. To them, it was a *tool box*. Those decades saw a good deal of work on management, but it was work on procedures, techniques, methods, and practices. It was work on organizational rules such as the span of control, on specific behavior, on problems of personnel management such as compensation, and so forth. No one asked *what* they were doing, let alone *why* they were doing it. The question was always "*How* do we do it?"

Mary Parker Follett herself was a first-rate doer. What initially brought her to public attention was a virtuoso performance: the organization and management of vocational guidance centers in the Boston public schools in the early 1900s—the first such centers in the United States. And by all accounts, in her consulting work she always focused on action and demanded results. To her, management was clearly a discipline. The people who had started the "management movement" understood this, though perhaps only dimly. But they were not businesspeople. The first Management Congress was convened in Prague in 1922 by the American Herbert Hoover, then U.S. secretary of commerce after a distinguished career as a geologist and philanthropist (and soon to be president of the United States), and by Thomas Masaryk, president of the brand new Czechoslovak Republic and a distinguished historian. These men were far more concerned with what we now would call "industrial society" than with business, its efficiency, or its profits. By the 1930s—that is, by the time of the Great Depression—concern with management had shifted to specialties, efficiency, engineering, compensation, and training: the great concerns of the American Management Association, to judge by the topics of its meetings. And to people to whom management was a tool box to "fix" *immediate problems,* Follett did indeed make no sense.

Finally, what I call Mary Parker Follett's fourth postulate appeared to the 1930s and 1940s as not only irrelevant, but also counter to the zeitgeist, the "revealed truth" of those decades. Pauline Graham, editor of this volume and the guiding spirit behind the effort to ensure that Mary Parker Follett's legacy lives, has said that reinventing the citizen was Mary Parker Follett's primary and constant endeavor. This is surely the most penetrating insight into Follett and her work. But it also means that from the 1930s until very recently, Follett was "subversive." For beginning in 1929—by no coincidence, the year in which Follett's star began to set—the center of thought in politics and economics increasingly shifted to the question of how to make *government* more controlling, bigger, and more powerful. For 40 years all countries—the totalitarians in the vanguard, the others following—believed in the mega-state.[3] The one major American book on political theory written in the 1930s—and one that had tremendous impact—was Harold Lasswell's 1936 *Politics: Who Gets What, When, How.* But if politics was defined—as Lasswell defined it—as nothing but a fight for the spoils, there are only special interests and pressure groups. There are voters to be wooed and taxpayers to be milked. But citizens existed only as a rhetorical flourish.

In the United States those years, especially the 1930s, were years of intellectual ferment and innovative activity in higher education, for instance, but not in management. A Mary Parker Follett had to be *todgeschwiegen,* as the Germans say—had to become a nonperson. When we resumed serious work on management—under the impetus of World War II, the Marshall Plan, and the productivity teams—people such as Herbert Simon, Frederick Herzberg, and I worked without any knowledge of Follett, unable to nourish ourselves with her wisdom and build on her extraordinary insights.

Now we know that modern organizations have to be built on making conflict constructive—all the more so as the tensions and conflicts and differences are no longer primarily between capital and labor but within a knowledge organization. We know that management is the generic organ of all organizations, whether businesses or nonbusinesses, and that indeed major management challenges and opportunities are to be found not only in businesses but also in the military, local government, hospitals, and schools. We know that ours is a society of organizations and that each organization—and not only a business—is a *social* organization. We know that management has to be a discipline. And we know that just as the concern of cabinetmaking is the completed sideboard rather than hammer and pliers and screwdriver, the object and concern of management is the entire organization rather than tools and techniques. Finally, we know that restoring citizenship is the crucial challenge. If one lesson was taught by the collapse of the ultimate mega-state, totalitarian communism, it is that nothing can work unless it is based on a functioning civil society—that is, on citizens and citizenship. In other words, we know that Mary Parker Follett was not only right but superbly relevant, and her relevance persists today.

The selections brought together in this volume are only a small sample of her writings. But they clearly show that Follett had important things to say on many of the major topics in the management field—on leadership, for instance. Every one of her comments is fresh, pertinent, and insightful, but her true importance lies in her vision. She saw the society of organizations and she saw management as its generic function and specific organ well before either really existed. She did not attempt to be a "systematic philosopher." She would, I suspect, have considered it intellectual arrogance.

She was something far more important. She was the prophet of management.

Management and society in general should welcome her return.

NOTES

1. I have not made a thorough search of the American management literature of the 1940s. But a sampling confirms that the first mention of Follett in any American management book during and after World War II was in my *Practice of Management*, written in 1952–1953 and published in 1954 by Harper.
2. I have told this story in greater detail in the chapter, "The Professional: Alfred Sloan," in my book *Adventures of a Bystander* (first published in New York in 1979 by Harper & Row, and republished in 1991 and 1994 by Transaction).
3. For an explanation of the term, see my recent book, *Post Capitalist Society* (published in New York by HarperBusiness and in London by Butterworth-Heinemann, 1993).

Mary Parker Follett (1868–1933):
A Pioneering Life

PAULINE GRAHAM

O
NE DAY in 1965, while browsing at the Westminster Library in London, I experienced one of those miracles of discovery in which a neglected volume pulled by chance from a dusty shelf has the power to inspire a lifelong avocation.

The book, *Dynamic Administration: The Collected Papers of Mary Parker Follett,* was unknown to me. But the title caught my eye because at the time, after many years of running my own small accountancy practice, I had recently become general manager of a department store. I knew little about managing large numbers of employees but found to my surprise that I enjoyed leading people, developing ideas, and seeing change implemented.

My new activities, so different from my previous work, soon had me fascinated with fundamental management concerns such as leadership, conflict, and sources of power and authority. I wanted to understand these things both to satisfy my own curiosity and to be better at my job. When I broached such matters to my colleagues, they responded airily, "Your rights stem from your appointment, don't you worry." But neither the authority vested in me nor the store's good performance were sufficient to appease me, and the questions continued to nag. In what consequently became a dedicated search for answers and enlightenment, I had not found a management textbook, lecture, or seminar that spoke satisfactorily to the issues—until that fortuitous afternoon at the Westminster Library. In Follett, I realized I had discovered my mentor.

Dynamic Administration (first published in 1941) is a compilation of Follett's lectures on business organization and management, most of which she delivered between 1925 and 1933 at the annual conferences of the Bureau of Personnel Administration (BPA) in New York. In contrast to the single-issue focus of most management thinkers, Follett captured in twelve lectures the broad purview of business management as a total integrative function. She addresses, among other subjects, the issues of conflict, power, leadership, control, responsibility, consent, and participation and formulated principles to be applied to everyday situations in the workplace.

Her work is characterized by the cohesiveness and modernity of her thought, the immediacy and subtlety of her language, the breadth of her understanding, and the wisdom of her insights. Her concepts are as topical and relevant today as when she first articulated them in the mid-1920s.

After discovering Follett and becoming familiar with her, I could not understand her neglect and anonymity. Why had I not heard of her work in my various studies of business administration and management? Here was a figure of stature with much to offer practicing managers but someone whom I had encountered purely by chance. As I investigated further, I found that, in truth, Follett was not completely forgotten—she was given, in the pantheon of the great management thinkers, a few paragraphs. But in practice she remained largely unknown and unused. Clearly this was not good enough, and I decided that in due course, if no one else were to do it, it would fall on me to bring her back to the light of day. In the meantime I would spread the word about her teachings at every opportunity. When I mentioned her name to someone, I would gladly reply to the inevitable query, "Mary *who*?"

HER EARLY LIFE AND WORK

Mary Parker Follett was born in Quincy, Massachusetts, near Boston, in 1868, the older of two children (her sibling was a brother) in a family of long-established Quincy stock. She did not have a happy childhood. Her mother was a nervous invalid, and her father, whom she adored, died while she was in her teens. Already the domestic manager, Follett was forced by his death to take charge of the family's financial affairs. Although she later became estranged from her mother and severed her family ties, money on the mother's side would eventually make Follett financially independent.

She attended Thayer Academy in Braintree and the Society for the Collegiate Instruction of Women in Cambridge, an unaffiliated annex to Harvard University that gave women the opportunity to be taught by Harvard professors (incorporated as Radcliffe College in 1894 and now recognized as part of Harvard). After spending a year abroad at Newnham College in Cambridge, England, Follett graduated from Radcliffe College in 1898, *summa cum laude* in economics, government, law, and philosophy. Her formal education was to conclude with postgraduate work in Paris, but learning, whether formal or informal, remained a constant throughout Follett's life.

Plain in appearance, lacking in style, "a gaunt Bostonian spinster lady"[1] with a forbidding exterior, Follett nonetheless charmed almost everyone she met. Emotionally vulnerable, she appeared confident and self-assured. Intellectually an idealist, she grounded her idealism in strict factuality, making idealism and realism "meet in the actual."[2]

In 1896, while still a college student, she published a study titled *The Speaker of the House of Representatives,* in which she detailed the intricate workings of the legislative process and the methods used by effective speakers of the U.S. Congress to exert their power and influence. In this book Follett first exhibited the two-track approach that she would later apply to all her work: meticulous study of records and documents combined with personal contact with the individuals involved, in order to ascertain firsthand their thoughts, feelings, and actions. In researching her topic she interviewed former speakers—a novel undertaking for an undergraduate woman at the turn of the century. Reviewing the book for the *American Historical Review* in October 1896, Theodore Roosevelt (then president of the Board of Police Commissioners in New York and five years later president of the United States) declared it indispensable reading for any study of Congress.

When I speak about Follett, most people are astonished to find that it was a woman in the mid-1920s who set down the authoritative foundations of business organization and management, at a time when such activity was not even open to women. It is remarkable how much Follett knew and understood, how far ahead of her time she was, yet how readily she was accepted. And it is testimony to the personal power and charisma of Follett that, approaching 60 and without any experience in the business world, she could become a management thinker eagerly sought after by the business communities of both the United States and England.

Through her friends, interests, and connections, Follett knew everybody of distinction on the sparkling intellectual and social Boston/Harvard scene in the early twentieth century, a golden age of which she was an integral part. Fluent in German and French, she kept herself up-to-date with developments on both sides of the Atlantic in the physical and social sciences.

Her circle included the most forward-looking writers, philosophers, lawyers, and politicians, as well as the Boston aristocracy of the time. Follett's entrée into these rarefied surroundings was facilitated by the social standing and companionship of her longtime friend, Isobel Briggs, an Englishwoman some 20 years her senior. The two women lived together for 30 years; at their home at Otis House in Boston, Follett could almost daily be found working "in a fierce creative glow which left her exhausted, physically, nervously and mentally," as a friend once observed.[3]

Follett used her acquaintances to the fullest. If she wanted to learn about a subject, she would find from among her friends the authority on it, closet herself with that individual, and get to the heart of the matter. If no immediate friend were an authority, there would always be someone who knew the foremost expert and would be willing to bring them together.

Follett was a true democrat and respected all individuals regardless of their place in society. It is interesting to learn from Peter Drucker's contribution to this volume that, from the 1940s until recently, Follett was considered by many to be a subversive. When the Japanese first came across her work in the early 1950s, a number of writers took the view that she must be a Marxist because of her emphasis on the importance of the collectivity. But they soon learned better and started a Follett Association to study her in depth.

Follett was profoundly interested in the individual in society and how one could attain personal fulfillment while striving at the same time to create the well-ordered and just society. The answer, she concluded, lay in democratic governance, an abiding belief that was to inform all her activities and become the goal that inspired her for the rest of her life. She developed and remained true to this democratic ideal and practiced it throughout her career.

Follett's strength derived from her unique combination of skills, skills that flowed from her broad mastery of the social science field, her profound empathy with people, and her own practical experience in the ways of the world. In 1900, when she returned to Boston from her studies in Paris, some expected her to undertake a career in a quiet corner of academe. But this was not her style. She chose instead to become involved in the Roxbury Men's Club, in a rough section of Boston. She was undaunted and indomitable. On one occasion some young men locked themselves in the club's bathroom with a supply of liquor and refused to come out. Follett, alone with her friend Isobel Briggs, warned them that if they persisted she would get a ladder and climb in through the window, whereupon the young men sheepishly filed out.

With her cast of mind, it was perhaps inevitable that Follett would be an innovator. Very quickly she conceived the idea, unheard of at the time, of keeping school buildings open after school hours to serve as clubs for recreation and study. She insisted that to provide special buildings when the school buildings were already available "would have been bad management on our part."[4]

Recreation, she realized, was important, but work was even more so. Why not use the evening centers as placement bureaus as well? With her customary attention to detail, Follett instituted such bureaus and made them models for other cities to copy. They were incorporated into Boston's public school system in 1917 and, in a tribute to Follett's organizing ability, continued to be run for many years according to the original structures she had set up.

During those years in social work, Follett was a hands-on manager, initiating ideas and getting them accepted and implemented by others. When she found that something needed to be done, she applied herself first to a study of the subject and then made her recommendations. Nothing was too insignificant: she made a full study of the most economical way to bank furnace fires before bringing the matter up with the building's janitors.

Follett was to remain active in social work for 25 years. Throughout this period, local and national organizations continually appealed to her for advice and guidance. But while she was a practical day-to-day manager, Follett was also the keen observer and scholar. Through her work she was learning firsthand the dynamics of the group process—how people work together evolving, developing, and carrying out plans and tasks. She observed the creativity of the process and its potential for self-government. Her findings became the subject of her next book, *The New State: Group Organization the Solution of Popular Government*, published in 1918.

The new book was very different from *The Speaker of the House of Representatives*. In her earlier work, Follett had investigated the power game in the rough-and-tumble of American politics. In *The New State*, she advanced her own ideas about democratic government. This kind of governance, she declared, would not be achieved through rhetoric and the ritual transfer of formalized powers. Democratic authority would have to be created by the people themselves.

Broadly speaking, Follett was advocating the replacement of bureaucratic institutions by group networks in which the people themselves analyzed their problems and then produced and implemented their own solutions. This was true democracy, each individual taking part in the decision-making process and accepting personal responsibility for the result.

The New State made a great impact and confirmed Follett's reputation as an original and substantial political thinker. The book was reviewed in learned journals on both sides of the Atlantic. English statesman and philosopher Lord Haldane (later to become Follett's friend) wrote to her: "I am much impressed by the idealism and knowledge which the book breathes, and not less by the hopeful possibilities of the group or neighborhood method of bringing the State into reality in the individual which you are pressing on public attention."[5] Lord Haldane later wrote a long introduction to the third printing of *The New State,* published in London in September 1920.

The book made Follett a prominent figure internationally and brought invitations to Massachusetts to represent the public on arbitration boards, minimum wage boards, public tribunals, and other official bodies. These new positions enabled Follett to experience firsthand the politics of industrial relations. She saw how the parties to a dispute jockeyed for position, using all manner of strategems to gain the upper hand. Her interest now moved to business and industry and, always the scholar, she pondered and recorded her experience. Her next book, *Creative Experience,* published in 1924, was based on her exposure to these new fields.

FOLLETT'S MOVE INTO MANAGEMENT

Follett now attracted a completely different audience: businessmen who were fascinated by her novel views. She found the business world stimulating, vital, and exciting. Unlike politicians, economists, and academics, businesspeople were doers: if they thought an idea was worthwhile and likely to succeed, they would try it out to see if it actually worked.

A new career now opened up for Follett. She did not become a management consultant in the accepted sense of the term, but businesspeople increasingly asked for her help. She investigated specific problems in factories and organizations. She lectured on management subjects at business conferences, universities, and before other professional bodies, both in England and America.

The Bureau of Personnel Administration in New York, which held annual conferences for business executives and invited prestigious speakers for these occasions, set the seal of approval on Follett as a front-rank management thinker. Its director, Henry C. Metcalf, who had worked with Follett in the early 1900s and knew the range of her interests, asked her to lecture on "The Psychological Foundations of Business Administration" at the BPA's 1925 conference.

Nearly 60 years old then, Follett brought to the assignment a lifetime of study and experience, pursued and acquired for the express purpose of helping shape a fairer, more creative, and more productive society. Through her social work, she saw the wide gulf that separated the classes and the waste of human potential among the underprivileged. Instead of narrowing the gap, she thought, representative democracy had become a numbers game rather than a genuine union of individuals; true democracy depended on the tapping of the creative power inherent in every person. "We find the true man only through group organization. The potentialities of the individual remain potentialities until they are released by group life," she wrote in *The New State*.[6] "Thus," she added, "the essence of democracy is creating. The technique of democracy is group organization."[7]

The self-governing principle, she believed, facilitated the growth of individuals and of the groups to which they belonged; by directly interacting with one another to achieve their common goals, the members of a group fulfilled themselves through the process of the group's development. The principle applied to any group, whether large or small, in the workplace or the community, in the trade union or the professional association, in the church council or the music society.

In the New York lectures, Follett demonstrated how the ideas that contributed to a strong and healthy society could also contribute to a creative and successful business organization. "I want to show that the basis for understanding the problems of political science is the same as the basis for understanding business administration—it is the understanding of the nature of integrative unities."[8]

For Follett, a business was not merely an economic unit but a social agency that was a significant part of society. She placed the functions of business and management within the total social framework and emphasized their essential importance in making society fairer—her constant endeavor. The fact that she was an outsider who had never worked in a business enterprise proved to be one of her great strengths—as a political scientist with years of practical experience in social and public affairs, she brought to her business audience the wider vision and the broader knowledge.

The ensuing chapters cover most of Follett's concepts, tested against current thinking and present-day realities by some of our most distinguished contemporary management scholars. But a brief excursus at this stage on how she treats the issues of conflict and power may not be out of place to attune the reader to the originality of her thought and the acuity of her vision.

FOLLETT ON CONFLICT AND POWER

Conflict, Follett declares, is a fact of life. Instead of being hidden or ignored, it should be acknowledged and made to work for us. Instead of being viewed as warfare, it should be seen as the legitimate expression of differences. After all, conflict is difference—difference of opinion and of interest. Without conflict, without difference, there would be no progress. In all her writings Follett repeatedly emphasized the value of difference.

Developing her view of the collective idea in *The New State,* she explains that "the essential feature of a common thought is not that it is held in common but that it has been produced in common" through the integration of differences. "The core of the social process is not likeness," she observes, "but the harmonizing of difference through interpenetration."[9] On this point Follett cites Heraclitus: "Nature desires eagerly opposites and, out of them, it completes the harmony, not out of similars."[10]

In *Creative Experience* she makes the point that "fear of difference is fear of life itself. It is possible to conceive of conflict as not necessarily a wasteful outbreak of incompatibilities but a normal process by which socially valuable differences register themselves for the enrichment of all."[11] Celebrating difference, she is certain that "we do not want adjustment. We want the plus-values of the conflict."[12] She goes on to say that "we do not want to do away with difference, but to do away with muddle."[13]

Interestingly, Jon Katzenbach and Douglas Smith, in their widely acclaimed 1992 book, *The Wisdom of Teams,* emphasize the value of constructive conflict (inter alia openness, understanding, and respecting the others' viewpoints and interests) in creating the common purpose for all members of the team.

To make conflict productive, to turn it into an opportunity for change and progress, Follett advises against domination, manipulation, or compromise. "Just so far as people think that the basis of working together is compromise or concession, just so far they do not understand the first principles of working together. Such people think that when they have reached an appreciation of the necessity of compromise they have reached a high plane of social development. . . . But compromise is still on the same plane as fighting. War will continue—between capital and labor, between nation and nation—until we relinquish the ideas of compromise and concession."[14] Such approaches achieve only a brief respite; the conflict will go underground and will eventually resurface in a more virulent form. A better way is to find the integrative solution, the approach that solves a conflict by accommodating the real demands of the parties involved.

Follett indicates the method for finding the integrative solution: put your cards on the table and detail all aspects of your demand. Treat the conflict as a joint problem and work together to find its solution. Begin by making costless exchanges: what is essential for the other party may be unimportant for you. Always avoid an either-or situation, maintain an open mind, step outside the problem, be inventive. Little by little, as the joint field of vision is clarified, the true demands are uncovered and the moment comes when a solution emerges that meets your respective needs. Outside solutions—even sensible proposals introduced by well-meaning onlookers—will not succeed. The involved parties themselves, according to Follett, must find their own solution.

Speaking from personal experience, I can confirm that this method works much more often than one might think, although it cannot, of course, resolve the many facets of life that are irreconcilable. The integrative solution enables those involved to grow in mutual self-respect and to learn to work together, when cooperation may indeed be a challenge. Not every conflict is a mega-conflict, and every small conflict that can be resolved jointly today paves the way for dealing more effectively with the differences that will assuredly arise in the future.

A modest example from personal experience neatly illustrates the integrative solution. The central rule in the store I managed was that departments had to be listed alphabetically in the directories posted throughout the building. I wanted the listing to begin with the very popular "Young Fashions," while the Central Display manager insisted that, according to the rules, "Baby Linen" (a rather moribund department) had to come first. Remembering my Follett and curbing my temper, I suggested: "How about calling that depart-

ment *All Young Fashions?*" He was delighted. Alphabetical integrity
was maintained, a potentially explosive situation was defused, and
the basis for a cooperative relationship had been established.

"Find the integrative solution"—I spread that message far and
wide; there are quite a number of chief executives who carry with
them the injunction and the steps to implement it. Of course, I
explained and disseminated the method in my store. The results
were remarkable. Difficulties within sections and departments were
resolved internally by the staff instead of festering and erupting
into the dispute that I would have to step in to settle. Relationships
with customers became friendlier and more professional, substan-
tially reducing the number of their complaints. Somehow we found
we were getting better service from our central buyers and more
funding for capital expenditures. Above all, most people in the
branch became alert and inventive, wanting to take part in the
action. We had more time to think of better ways to serve our
customers, to help in the community, and to work toward our own
fulfillment.

Profitability, of course, went up; indeed, our branch became
the most profitable in the group. The other branch heads wanted
to know our secret. So, with Follett in hand, I took the training
sessions in their branches and passed the word on to their staff.
And so the circle widened.

Much later, research at my alma mater, the London School of
Economics (LSE) to which I returned for a year, showed me that
the field had widened globally. Conflict resolution had become a
topic studied in its own right in social psychology, international
relations, business and management, and other areas. Today, centers
and institutes of conflict resolution have sprouted throughout the
industrialized world and there is now a mini-industry on the subject,
with dozens of books, courses, conferences, seminars, and work-
shops. Conflict thinkers have also alighted upon "alternative dispute
resolution," a concept based on mutuality of interests. The method
is increasingly used in place of adversarial litigation in every area

where conflict arises—between spouses, neighbors, corporations, and contracting parties of all kinds.

As I studied the "latest" in conflict resolution at LSE, I thought of the wasted time and effort involved: as far back as 1925, Follett had already discovered the best ways to resolve conflict and I reflected on how we would do well to recall a central lesson of Follett that even now we have not fully absorbed: namely, that compromise is not only a useless expenditure of time and energy but also a demeaning activity that never results in permanent resolution of a dispute. If Follett had been the starting point, I reasoned, how much further along the subject might be today. Nonetheless it is gratifying to note that the Society of Professionals in Dispute Resolution in the United States, which ingathers those involved in mediation and arbitration in both the public and private sectors, established in 1991 the Mary Parker Follett Award and is applying Follett's teachings to its work, as are many other organizations and individuals.

On the issue of power, Follett urges us to reconsider the traditional "power-over" model because it is reductionist and self-defeating—increasingly severe measures must be imposed if domination is to be maintained, until eventually the cost of order becomes prohibitive. Although it is unlikely that power-over can be completely done away with, its use can be reduced. Follett suggests an alternative model, that of "power-with," also a natural and more productive approach than any system based solely on control: "If your business is so organized that you can influence a co-manager while he is influencing you; so organized that a worker has an opportunity of influencing you as you have of influencing him; if there is an interactive influence going on all the time, power-with may be built up."[15]

Power-with stems from the pooling of individual powers. Each member of a group has unique and sovereign power derived from the combination of knowledge, experience, and ability specific to him or her. Here, according to Follett, the job of the manager is to help the members of the group realize they have this power; unify these individual powers into the total power of the group; and make each individual responsible for shaping his or her contribution to fit the task as a whole. "Our contribution is of no value unless it is effectively related to the contributions of all the others concerned," Follett points out.[16]

Even in my retailing group—a model of industrial democracy with a constitution, branch councils, committees of communication, and ombudswomen—no one had heard anything like this. But the staff quickly saw that indeed each of us had a unique contribution to make to the common effort and that our work in the store was a joint endeavor. They developed pride and responsibility in their work and came to enjoy it.

Today, it is accepted that competition as a Darwinian exercise from which only the fittest will survive is an outdated and simplistic view—cooperation, based on the power-with concept, is seen increasingly as a more useful approach. Follett's wisdom is being recognized in the field of international business. Management practitioners and advisers are recommending that multinational corporations practice her concept of power-with as the more effective means of integrating their own international interests and harmonizing their relations with allied or joint-venture organizations.

CONNECTING AND INTEGRATING: THE BASES OF EFFECTIVE MANAGING

Thus Follett provides insights on leaders and followers, control, orders, authority, and many other issues. She goes beyond academic abstractions and received wisdom to dissect every sacred managerial and organizational tenet. Each concept is rigorously analyzed, tested against fact, and revealed in a new light as positive, practical, and radical. Then Follett integrates these concepts into a comprehensive and cohesive framework that provides parameters in which to operate successfully. In effect, she draws for managers a clear map of the various networks of relations surrounding every organization and shows how they can be better understood.

What is particularly attractive about Follett's ideas is that they mesh seamlessly with one another. The power-with concept, for example, is very much the principle that underlies the constructive resolution of conflict. Instead of power-over—exercising your power over the other party to get what you want—you employ power-with—working with the other—to satisfy mutual needs. Furthermore, her ideas are comprehensive. Whenever I read something sensible on business organization and management, I invariably catch myself saying, "But Follett was saying this 70 years ago, and saying it better."

I attribute her achievements to her ability to think broadly and deeply. Or, as she herself explained:

> We cannot departmentalize our thinking. . . . We cannot think of economic principles and ethical principles. . . . Underneath all our thinking, there are certain fundamental principles to be applied to all our problems.[17]

> I do not think we have psychological and ethical and economic problems. We have human problems with psychological, ethical, and economic aspects, and as many more as you like, legal often.[18]

Follett studied every occurrence, every situation, and every idea in its totality and context. She quoted the biological chemist who explains that "We have to study a whole as a whole, not only through an analysis of its constituents"[19] and the Gestalt psychologist for whom "the whole . . . is determined not only by its constituents but by their relation to one another."[20] It is that core principle of the dynamic of relations that Follett always took pains to explain:

I am emphasizing this matter of relation because, while it is customary now to speak of the "total situation," that phrase means to many people merely that we must be sure to get all the factors into our problem. . . . What I am emphasizing is not merely the totalness of the situation, but the nature of the totalness."[21]

Connecting crystallizes for me Follett's way of looking at the world. And this way reminds me of E. M. Forster's evocative phrase, "only connect," at the conclusion of his book *Howards End.* Thus the same truth can be vouchsafed to us by the visionary management thinker as well as the great novelist. Follett's way of looking at things does more than help resolve difficulties; it helps avoid them altogether. As a careful reading of a map prevents the taking of a wrong turn and enables one to travel with greater ease, so does the Follett vision keep one away from the cul-de-sac while indicating the most appropriate path to one's objective. It also sharpens one's sight and leads to the more discriminating judgment.

Follett, in effect, changes our field of vision. The way we view things determines our attitudes and our behavior. We are at all times creating our own future. By rearranging our way of seeing and putting what we see in the context of wider connections, Follett leads us to the more inclusive view and, ultimately, the wiser act. She helps us create our better future.

FOLLETT IN PERSPECTIVE

How does Follett's philosophy relate to the different schools of management that have emerged to date? Have her views become obsolete? Have they become superseded? Or has she still something relevant and novel to tell us?

Of course, management as a function integral to life has, perforce, been practiced throughout the ages. But it was not until the Industrial Revolution and the introduction of the factory system in England during the 1790s that management began to emerge as a separate and important discipline. And it was in the United States at the turn of the nineteenth century that management as a "science" came fully into its own.

The railroad magnates of the time had to create whole new organizations to build and operate their iron roads across the vast expanses of the American continent. The military model of authority provided the hierarchical chain of command, accounting procedures, and even the vocabulary for the management foundation of these large-scale organizations. But the military-style structures and systems were not entirely appropriate to the needs of factory production. And so the engineers came up with "scientific management," a movement codified by its founder Frederick W. Taylor in his 1911 book, *Principles and Methods of Scientific Management.*

As a member of the Taylor Society, Follett agreed that production had to be optimized. But she did not accept that this was best achieved by the strict division of labor, with each worker performing endlessly, under close supervision, the same repetitious task. She made the point that "We can never wholly separate the human from the mechanical side. . . . But you all see every day that the study of human relations in business and the study of operating are bound up together."[22]

The swing of the pendulum against the concept of workers as impersonal "hands" heralded the human relations school, whose members were often said to subscribe to the belief that managers followed the dictates of reason while workers adhered to those of sentiment. Accordingly, managers had to be trained in the skills necessary to satisfy the feeling-needs of the workers.

Follett did not agree with this dichotomy. In her view, managers and those they managed were of the same ilk, individuals governed by a mixture of reason, feeling, and character. People behaved as they did because of the reciprocal response that occurs in relationships. If workers were told not to think or were trained to be extensions of an assembly line, they would perform accordingly.

Follett was quite clear on this point—to get effective results, managers should not manipulate their subordinates but should train them in the use of responsible power. "Managers . . . should give the workers a chance to grow capacity or power for themselves."[23]

In the 1940s, the classification of superiors as thinkers and subordinates as feelers fell out of favor with some members of the human relations school. Group dynamics came into fashion. The proponents of this school saw the work group as the basic entity, leaders being unnecessary. Managers and managed would function as coworkers; various techniques such as brainstorming and sensitivity training could be called on as required to facilitate interactions between the two groups—leaders were superfluous.

Follett, for whom the group was of fundamental importance, studied and understood group dynamics well. Certainly she knew that leadership shifts from one person to another and is not exclusive to the manager. But leadership is still an essential constant. Whoever has the knowledge and experience in a specific case and shows the way is the leader for that occasion. Follett held that "The wish to govern one's own life is, of course, one of the most fundamental feelings in every human being"[24] and "One person should not give orders to another person."[25] She also held that it is the situation itself that determines what needs to be done. Each situation has its own order and its own law. This law can be discovered and the person—subordinate or manager—who discovers it and shows the way ahead is the leader in that situation. For Follett, leadership may be multiple and variable, now *A*, now *B*, depending on the specific situation. But in all cases it is indispensable.

In the 1950s, the management stylists came to the fore. In their view the manager had to adapt to subordinates and situation. Dozens of managerial personae—the grazer, the nurturer, and the hunter, to name just three—were identified and touted as best suited to handle specific tasks or situations. This emphasis on personality as a prerequisite for leadership had already been an evolving notion in Follett's time. Her reaction had been succinct: "Don't exploit your personality; learn your job."[26]

In the 1960s, interest turned from individuals to the organization itself. Theorists held that the organization had an ethological, cultural life of its own, quite independent of its task and the people who comprised it. Change, it was believed, could be accomplished only by changing the organization's culture. Follett would have agreed that the organization had a momentum of its own, but she could never envision an entity separate from its members. Parts and the whole, she believed, are bound together in dynamic interaction. The culture of an organization can be changed, but for an effective metamorphosis, the employees—the organization's life-blood—must themselves change or, at the very least, be influenced by a new leader.

With the 1970s came situational theory. The situationalists held that while each of the previous schools of thought had produced valuable insights, they had dealt only with isolated elements of a larger situation and therefore could not and did not produce an all-embracing theory. Situationalists urged that managers recognize and learn to handle the "total situation" and become "managers of situations." Connections between task, technology, and people were to be synthesized into a comprehensive "situation" to be managed as a whole. Follett would have agreed with their thinking. For her, the situation, unique and encompassing both internal and external factors, acquired an almost technical meaning. "We persons have relations with each other and we should find them in and through the whole situation."[27] There is a great deal of parallel thought between Follett and the situationalists.

The 1980s brought back general system theory to mainstream management thinking. This view holds that events and actions must be considered in their proper context and in their myriad connections, including their relationships with the natural environment of which they are a part. It posits that to save ourselves as well as nature we must renounce the belief that nature must be conquered and enslaved and accept that as individuals, enterprises, or industries, we belong to the same environmental ecosystem. Systemic thinking is the first step toward understanding system dynamics and appreciating that every action is the culmination of intermeshing causes and effects. Follett, of course, is the systemic thinker par excellence.

In today's world, independence is increasingly recognized as illusory and even ineffective as an organizing principle. Instead, interdependence is emerging at the forefront as the key to successful management, not only in the workplace but in every form of human endeavor. Democratic governance is the way to manage interdependence, as Follett pointed out in the 1920s. (As for diversity, the very stuff of true interdependence and democratic governance, we are now beginning to appreciate what Follett saw as invaluable decades ago.)

How Follett would have loved to see the modern recognition of her ideal of democratic governance, or the evolving, contemporary realization that the most effective way to organize people to achieve a goal is through the actions of teams of interdependent individuals. Involved in the assessment and execution of tasks, holding themselves responsible for their contribution as well as for the performance of the group as a whole—such teams are the embodiment of what Follett long espoused.

The concept of interdependence is of general application. It covers the whole field of knowledge. We are now realizing the interconnectedness of disciplines and gradually increasing emphasis on interdisciplinary activity. Follett well understood the underlying unity of knowledge. She meticulously studied the various subjects that could have a bearing on her interests. "I do wish," she once declared with evident feeling, "that when a principle has been worked out in ethics, it did not have to be discovered all over again in psychology, in economics, in government, in business, in biology, in sociology. It's such a waste of time."[28]

In 1926, Follett's companion, Isobel Briggs, died. Devastated by her loss, Follett later moved to London where she was to renew old acquaintances and make new friends. In 1933, after completing a series of lectures at the London School of Economics, Follett made a brief visit to Boston. While there, she had to go into hospital, and there she died in December 1933.

A brave, pioneering life ended; but her work, vital and insightful, lives on. Indeed, in practically every area when we begin to see the light, we find that Follett has already lit the pathway for us to follow. She remains startlingly modern and in many respects is still avant-garde. The assessment of Follett is unanimous: very much ahead of her time in the 1920s, she remains today, in Peter Drucker's telling phrase, the "prophet of management."

NOTES

1. Lyndall Urwick, letter of August 5, 1970 to Avrum I. Cohen, quoted in Cohen's unpublished thesis, "Mary Parker Follett: Spokesman for Democracy, Philosopher for Social Group Work, 1918–1933," Tulane University School of Social Work, 1971.
2. Mary Parker Follett, "Community Is a Process," *The Philosophical Review*, vol. XXVII, p. 587.
3. Unpublished memoir by Elizabeth Balch (1934). Cited by Pauline Graham in *Dynamic Managing—The Follett Way* (London: Professional Publishing and British Institute of Management, 1987), p. 7.
4. Report on School Houses as Social Centers by Mary Parker Follett, Chairman of School Houses Sub-Committee to Women's Municipal League of Boston (January 1909), cited by Graham in *Dynamic Managing*, p. 8.
5. Letter of January 12, 1920, from Lord Haldane to Mary Parker Follett, quoted in Cohen, "Mary Parker Follett," p. 169.
6. Mary Parker Follett, *The New State: Group Organization, the Solution of Popular Government* (London: Longmans, Green, 1920), p. 6.

7. Ibid., p. 7.
8. Mary Parker Follett, "The Psychology of Control," in *Dynamic Administration: The Collected Papers of Mary Parker Follett,* Elliot M. Fox and L. Urwick, eds. (London: Pitman, 1973), p. 155.
9. Follett, *The New State,* p. 34.
10. Ibid.
11. Mary Parker Follett, *Creative Experience* (New York: Peter Smith, 1971), p. 301.
12. Ibid., p. xiv.
13. Ibid., p. 6.
14. Follett, *The New State,* pp. 26–27.
15. Follett, *Dynamic Administration,* p. 76.
16. Ibid., p. 194.
17. Ibid., p. 148.
18. Ibid., p. 149.
19. Ibid.
20. Ibid., pp. 150–151.
21. Ibid., pp. 156–157.
22. Ibid., p. 95.
23. Ibid., p. 80.
24. Ibid., pp. 32–33.
25. Ibid., p. 30.
26. Ibid., p. 237.
27. Ibid., p. 31.
28. Cited by Professor C. Cabot, in "Mary Parker Follett: An Appreciation," *The Radcliffe Quarterly,* April 1934, pp. 81–82.

PART ONE

The Psychological Foundations of Business Organization

 O N E

 ⇌   ⇌

Relating: The Circular Response

T HE PRINCIPLE of integrating *interests* is not yet sufficiently recognized and acted on by jurists and economists, the principle of integrating *power* is not sufficiently acknowledged by political scientists. But while many political scientists and economists as well as statesmen and labor arbitrators have stuck to the theory of the balance of power, of the equilibrium of interests, yet life continually escapes them, for whenever we advance we slip from the bondage of equilibrium.

This view, which springs so insistently to the eye with every fresh study of social situations, is supported by our recent psychology which is giving us more than hints of a truth that may mean large changes for politics, economics and law. The heart of the truth about integration is the connection between the relating of two activities, their interactive influence, and the values thereby created. This chapter will be devoted to a consideration of that point, or rather to the contribution of psychology on this point; a separate chapter (IX) will take up, chiefly by illustration, what the study of social situations yields on the subject of integration as the creative principle.

Progressive experience, I say, depends on the relating. The ardent search for objectivity, the primary task of the fact worshippers,

---

Note: This chapter is reprinted from *Creative Experience* (New York: Longmans, Green, 1924), Chapters 3 and 4.

cannot be the whole task of life, for objectivity alone is not reality. The crux of philosophical controversy we have seen mirrored everywhere. As the subjective idealists have overemphasized the subject, and the realists, the object, so there are the historians who deny "economic determinism" and those who give it more than its place; there are the political scientists who talk of "the will of the people" and those who, in reaction to "empty will," give us the "objective situation" as always our ruler; there are the jurists who exaggerate abstract conceptions and those who see all truth in "social facts." In the arts, especially in painting, the swing of the pendulum between "subjectivity" and "objectivity" is most interestingly apparent. In psychology we have the introspectionists and the behaviorists.

I do not see how such opposing tendencies can be avoided while we see reality either in subject or in object; I do not see how we can run fast enough from one to the other to keep ourselves within the region of truth. But our latest psychology is taking a step beyond this and putting itself in line with the oldest philosophy. Holt,[1] more clearly perhaps than any other recent writer, has shown us that reality is in the relating, in the activity-between.[2] He shows us how in the "behavior-process" subject and object are equally important and that reality is in the relating of these, is in the endless evolving of these relatings. This has been the grain of gold of the profoundest thinkers from Aristotle to the present day. Of course the object is not created by the percipient; of course the subject is no more "a mere reflex arc" than it is an evangelical soul; nor are subject and object "products" of a vital force. For a century, roughly speaking, objective idealism has given us—its innermost truth—existence as unitary experience which upon analysis resolves itself into the two great generic differings which have been called subject and object. Now physiologists and psychologists in their treatment of response are approaching this view.

The present psychological treatment of response, by emphasizing "the total situation," a happy phrase showing the importance of the outer object or situation as constituent of the behavior process, is extraordinarily interesting to students of social research. Add to the total situation what might be called the evolving situation, as hinted in Holt's formula and clarified by him in other places, and you have an important contribution to the social sciences. This formula defines behavior as a function of environment and identifies thought (purpose, will) with that function. The use of the mathematical term function has many suggestive implications. For instance, this definition of behavior, taken with the rest of this writer's teaching, implies the possible reciprocal influence of subject and object, or to keep to the language of the mathematical analogy, implies that the variables of this formula *may* be interdependent, either being a function of the other.[3] He does, it is true, in one place speak of environment as if it were always an *in*dependent variable,[4] and that would make his formula inapplicable for what we see in most social situations; industrial conditions are influencing the behavior of trade unions while the behavior of trade unions is influencing industrial conditions. But while Holt uses the words "object" or "object of environment" continually, he often uses also "situation," "event," "process," and with these words it becomes more obvious that the "object" is being influenced by the "subject" while the "subject" is being influenced by the "object." Moreover, in the illustration he gives of the girl discriminating between different plays, he says that her choice influences "the sound moral development of the institution itself."[5] Here the theatre is not an independent but one of two interdependent variables. When we are employing this formula, therefore, we have to decide in the case in hand whether environment is an independent or one of two interdependent variables—it is in each case a question of observed fact.

The interweaving of the different factors of the evolving situation sometimes takes place so rapidly before our eyes as to make the process very plain. On a Wage Board, one year, we were up against an interesting objective situation: a drop in prices, indications of unemployment, and at the same time a demand for higher wages in that particular industry. In anticipation of the proposed heightened wage scale which our Board was to effect, some employers were turning off their less efficient workers. We had to ask each week the changes in that respect in the objective situation; those changes had been brought about by the trend of our deliberations, but also our deliberations were very much affected by these changes. We saw that it would be a disadvantage to the employees as well as to employers to have the minimum wage too high, since we had evidence in the actual situation, not mere threats, that that would mean a certain amount of unemployment.

This reciprocal influence, this evolving situation, fundamental for politics, economics and jurisprudence, is made clearer if for the words thought, purpose, will in a description of the behavior process, we substitute thinking, purposing, willing. It is not thought which Watson is writing about, but thinking, for surely Watson if anyone gives us thinking as a process. As long as we use the word thought there is a tendency to think that bodily mechanisms are the expression, the organs, of thought, whereas they *are* thought, or rather, they are thinking. Again, there is a tendency to conceive of thought as the thing we have left over when we have finished thinking, the thing which thinking produces. All static expressions should be avoided. Integrated organism (one psychologist speaks of "the completely integrated organism") is unfortunate, for the organism is the continuing activity of self-organizing, self-maintaining. We must be careful of the "eds" because they lead to "wholes," the wrong kind of wholes, the "influence of the whole on the parts," etc. Such expressions as "coördinated wholes" are seen in the writings of some of the behaviorists, but, unless explained, seem against the very truth which behaviorism is trying to stand for. An "-ed" becomes a stopping place to thought, and when man cannot think any further it is dangerous. God has been to many races and to many individuals the place where thinking stops, as mind is often "the sanctuary of ignorance."

To return to our consideration of the behavior process, Holt has made his formula clear by a description of the working of two laws: one from physiology, one from physics. First he has shown us the importance of the physiological law that when a muscle contracts,[6] the sense-organ in that muscle is stimulated so that there is an almost simultaneous afferent nerve impulse from the muscle back to the centre, and thus a circular reflex is established. Hence the contraction of the muscle is only in a certain sense "caused" by the stimulus; that very muscular activity is itself in part producing the stimulus which "causes" the muscular activity. Holt's estimate of the value of the circular reflex appeared in his Harvard lectures in 1917, perhaps earlier also, but as they have not been published I quote from Bok, although Bok's article came out at a later date. I quote at some length because I wish in a later chapter, in speaking of the political process, to recall the circular reflex as a law which observation shows us as operating on infra-personal, personal and social levels.

"The reflex arc is the path of the stimulations received in consequence of a function of the individual itself. . . ." "This view does not start from the function of the receptor, but just from the action of the effector, which sounds strange at first, since we are accustomed to look upon the action of the effector as a result only of irritation in the receptor. . . ." "On a visual stimulation the animal must react with a movement which alters the visual stimulations . . . in other words, so that the attitude very specifically changes with regard to the stimulation given. Thus the reflex-reaction must alter the perception of the reflex-stimulus: in other words, it must very specifically alter the relation of the animal towards that specific stimulus, it must 'respond' to that stimulus."[7]

This will throw much light on the interdependent variables of the formula given above when we come to use that formula for social psychology, whether one thinks of it only as an analogy or as the operation of the same law on different levels. We shall see that the activity of the individual is only in a certain sense caused by the stimulus of the situation because that activity is itself helping to produce the situation which causes the activity of the individual. In other words behavior is a relating not of "subject" and "object" as such, but of two activities. In talking of the behavior process we have to give up the expression act "on" (subject acts on object, object acts on subject);[8] in that process the central fact is the meeting and interpenetrating of activities. What physiology and psychology now teach us is that part of the *nature* of response is the change it makes in the activity which caused so-to-speak the response, that is, we shall never catch the stimulus stimulating or the response responding. The importance of this cannot be overestimated. Stimulus is not cause and response the effect. Some writers, while speaking otherwise accurately of the behavior process, yet use the word result—the result of the process—whereas there is no result *of* process but only a moment *in* process. Response is not merely the activity resulting from a certain stimulus and that response in turn influencing the activity; it is *because* it is response that it influences that activity, that is part of what response means. Cause and effect, subject and object, stimulus and response: these are now given new meanings. All the possibilities of connections in the neural pathways which we are now beginning to suspect, or rather to have evidence of through the work of Pavlov, Bechterew, etc., have new light thrown on them by this approach to response. On the social level, cause and effect are ways of describing certain moments in the situation when we look at those moments apart from the total process.

In the behavior process then we see the interlocking of stimulus and response, a self-sufficing process. Here there is no taint of the psychological fallacy which held the results of mere abstraction as primary *Dinge an sich*. We get completely away from the fallacy which dissected experience and took the dead products, subject and object, and made them the generating elements. The most valuable part of this teaching is that the reflex arc is the path of stimuli *received in consequence of* an activity of the individual. Thus experience is given us as self-creating coherence.

What we may now call circular response or circular behavior we see every day as we observe and analyze human relations, social situations.[9] We see it clearly in the European conferences because there it is evident that there is no static European situation; moreover, it is evident that we can never understand the European situation by watching stimulus and response as mere stimulus and response. We have another example in labor conflict which would be much simplified if employer's purpose and workmen's purpose would remain stationary while the situation developed, but they never do. We see the same thing in our own lives: as we perform a certain action our thought towards it changes and that changes our activity. Or we do something which requires courage and we become more courageous and do a braver thing. The relation between leaders and group is an excellent example of the reflex circle. All amicable discussion is another. The state and individual another. Or "the man and the hour." But we need not go further afield for the working of this law than the meeting of two individuals. You say, "When I talk with Mr. X he always stimulates me." Now it may not be true that Mr. X stimulates everyone; it may be that something in you has called forth something in him. That is why I said above that we must give up the expression "act on," object acts on subject, etc. Do we not see here, to quote Bok, "the path of the stimulations which are caused, actualized or altered by the future reflex-reaction?" Through circular response we are creating each other all the time. This seems too obvious to mention, and yet where is it taken account of sufficiently? Le Bon, one of the most penetrating of sociologists, tells us much of crowds, much of individuals, but does not reveal the process of a creative meeting of individuals.

To sum up this point: the most fundamental thought about all this is that reaction is always reaction to a relating. Bok finds it in the neuro-muscular system. Integrative psychology shows us organism reacting to environment plus organism. In human relations, as I have said, this is obvious: I never react to you but to you-plus-me; or to be more accurate, it is I-plus-you reacting to you-plus-me. "I" can never influence "you" because you have already influenced me; that is, in the very process of meeting, by the very process of meeting, we both become something different. It begins even before we meet, in the anticipation of meeting. We see this clearly in conferences. Does anyone wish to find the point where the change begins? He never will. Every movement we make is made up of a thousand reflex arcs and the organization of those arcs began before our birth. On physiological, psychological and social levels the law holds good: response is always to a relating. Accurately speaking the matter cannot be expressed even by the phrase used above, I-plus-you meeting you-plus-me. It is I plus the-interweaving-between-you-and-me meeting you plus the-interweaving-between-you-and-me, etc., etc. If we were doing it mathematically we should work it out to the nth power.[10]

This pregnant truth—that response is always to a relation, the relation between the response and that to which the response is being made—needs further consideration, for it is the basic truth for all the social sciences. Let us consider the implications of this statement, even although this will necessitate some repetition. First, my changing activity is a response to an activity which is also changing; and the changes in my activity are in part caused by the changes in the activity of that to which I am in relation and vice versa. My response is not to a crystallized product of the past, static for the moment of meeting; *while* I am behaving, the environment is changing because of my behaving, and my behavior is a response to the new situation which I, in part, have created. Thus we see involved the third point, namely, that the responding is not merely to another activity but to the relating between the self-activity and the other activity. The psychologists who are using the language of calculus have opened up whole reaches of thought for us, for the principles of relation as given by differential calculus help us to a clear understanding of this fundamental principle of life. Let us take an illustration—we can take one from our simplest, everyday experience—and see what help mathematical thought gives us. Think of the boy going to school. He is not responding to school merely, but also to his own response to school. That is, the going to school may so stimulate him that he works much better than at home with his mother; his activity is a function of the activity that is set up between him and school. And the school too is affected by the activity-between; through either his or his parents' demand upon it, it may improve its methods. And so the interweaving goes on: the more the school alters the boy, the more chance is there of the boy altering the school. This is a situation which suggests the calculus, for if the child's going to school so stimulates him that he works harder, his performance is continuously changed by that very performance. Hence the functional relation between the two cannot be expressed in terms merely of the boy and the school, there must always be included the activity-between.

Thus the relating involves an increment that can be measured only by compound interest. In compound interest part of the activity of the growing is the adding of the growing. This is the same with all organic growth. Simple response, if there were such a thing, would be like simple interest—if there were such a thing. There is no such thing as simple interest in the organic world; the law of organic growth is the law of compound interest. Organic growth is by geometrical progression. This is the law of social relations. France and Germany have surely not been "influencing" each other by simple, but by compound interest. We have always the increment of the increment.

Before considering social phenomena from this point of view, let us note two points that we shall have to keep in mind: first, the objective situation as constituent part of the behavior process; secondly, that internal conditioning is of equal importance with external conditioning. Both these points are very important for social research. Often, for instance, we see the head of an industrial plant trying to solve a situation by studying his men rather than by considering men and situation, and the reciprocal effect of one on the other. In regard to the second point, as the psychologist notes the neuro-muscular interplay, using every possible instrumentation to make it apparent, as he takes into consideration the factors contained in the mechanisms which are maintaining the functions he is studying, which are modifying these functions, so the sociologist must note as carefully, must see as an integral part of the causal process, internal as well as external conditioning. Of course we shall remember that what is internal in the mechanism has also come from integration. When the organism experiences certain lacks, there arises a disturbed nervous system which causes the animal to make movements to supply these lacks from its environment. These responses to external environment caused by general motor restlessness integrate with the internal stimuli and the general motor restlessness becomes specific conduct. Thus "behavior" emerges, always from the activity-plus. In one of his lectures Holt put it this way, "If driven by metabolism, we have a disturbed nervous system, that system will so act toward environment as to put environment in that state which will make it send to the nervous system what it needs."[11] In this sentence the efficacy of the inter-relating becomes still more apparent. Much of our older psychology failed to note sufficiently the interlacing of external stimulus and the conditions of neural, muscular and glandular response. Only recently I was surprised to see the question asked by a psychologist: "Is behavior internally or externally conditioned?" The factors of intra and extra-organic stimulation are not only equally important but are bound up together. They must be considered simultaneously. We have now a wholly dynamic psychology. The neuro-muscular mechanisms of the behaviorists tend in the hands of some writers (only in some) to become as static as the old "mental states." Behavior "pattern" is a figure of speech and not altogether a good one. We shall have, if we are not careful, as much trouble with the "patterns" of the behaviorists as the behaviorists have felt they had with the "minds" of the older psychologists.

The matter of internal and external conditioning has an exact parallel in the social sciences. No one can understand the labor movement, the farmer movement, international situations, unless he is watching the integrating of internal stimuli, the lacks felt, with the responses to environment caused by these lacks. Moreover, the so-called stored-stimuli are exactly as important for sociologist as for psychologist; the sociologist has to consider in each case how far the person or persons are acting from present stimuli and how far from action patterns already existing. Let us take an illustration which involves all the points so far given:

The workman responds to

1. Employer: wages, share in profits or management, conditions of factory, etc.
2. General conditions: cost of living, etc.
3. His own desires, aspirations, standards of living, etc.
4. The relation between his responding and the above.

The important things to notice here are: first, that the workman is responding to something in himself as well as to something outside; for instance, we have now to add to the factors which made the internal conditioning of the workmen of 1914, the restlessness caused in many by the varied life and experiences (including even foreign travel) afforded by the war, the change in his desires caused by the lavish expenditure of war profits which he sees about him, etc., etc. Secondly, he is responding to the relating between his responding and the environment. Finally, all the factors involved are varying factors and must be studied in their varying relations. By the use of the language of calculus in the definition of behavior which we are considering, we are brought at once to the heart of every situation: the relating of things that are varying, which makes the relating vary. The Checker Taxi Company announced this week a cut in rates because of an increased volume of business; it thus makes volume of business the independent variable. Mr. Ford, on the other hand, when he reduced the price of his cars *in order to* increase volume of business, made the rate the independent variable. But both did the same thing: they measured a varying thing in relation to a varying thing, taking into account that these were affecting each other simultaneously.

We must therefore in the social sciences develop methods for watching varying activities in their relatings to other varying activities. We cannot watch the strikers and *then* the mill-owners. We cannot watch France and *then* Germany. We all know that the action of the mill-owners is changing daily the action of the strikers, that the action of the strikers is affecting daily that of the mill-owners; but beyond this is the more subtle point I am trying to emphasize here, that the activity between mill-owners and strikers is changing the activity of mill-owners, of strikers. We have to study not only a changing France in relation to a changing Germany, but also a changing France whose changes have been partly caused by the relation between its variations and Germany's variations. That is, France is not responding to Germany, but to the relation between France and Germany. To return to the language of our formula: the behavior of France is not a function of the behavior of Germany, but of the interweaving between France and Germany. The interweaving which is changing both factors and creating constantly new situations should be the study of the student of the social sciences. Trade unionism is not today a response to capitalism; it is a response to the relation between itself and capitalism. It is of the utmost importance to bear this constantly in mind. The concept of responsibility takes on entirely new meaning with the introduction of the notion of circular response into the social sciences. The farmers are not responding to the middlemen or to middlemen plus economic conditions or even to middlemen plus economic conditions plus their own desires, but to the relation between themselves and the whole total environment, or rather the relating becomes another element of total environment.

Much light is now thrown on the subject of Chapter I, the relation of "facts" to the social process. We cannot study the "psychology" of the workman, the "psychology" of the employer, and then the "facts" of the situation, as so often seems to be the process of investigation. We must study the workman and the employer in their relation to the facts—and then the facts themselves become as active as any other part of the "total situation." We can never understand the total situation without taking into account the evolving situation. And when a situation changes we have not a new variation under the old fact, but a new fact.

A professor of philosophy told me that it made him dizzy to talk with me because, he says, he wishes always to compare varying things with something stationary. But this philosopher could not go to Europe most economically in his summer vacations unless someone were watching for him the relation of speed to fuel consumption and from this determining rates of change that are themselves functions involving variables. Suppose a school-boy should say to his instructor in calculus: "You are making my head swim; I cannot compare unless you give me something stationary to compare with." The only thing his instructor could reply would be: "You will have then to leave this universe; in this one we so often have variations in relation to other variations that we are obliged to learn to think in the terms of those conditions." That is, if in calculus we measure a changing activity by an activity which is also changing, if there is involved rate of change, and also rate of change of rate of change, this is only the same as in all life. But psychology sometimes abstracts from life. For instance, a behaviorist tells us that if a man disregards the red flag at a railroad crossing and crosses in front of the train, he will be fined or imprisoned, and the red flag will thus acquire that much more "meaning" for him. If he suffers from loss of limb or kills the occupants of his car, the red flag acquires still more "meaning" for him. True as an abstraction, true on the supposition that this is all that happens. What is forgotten in this illustration is that the railroad company is not slumbering meanwhile, and the second time the man may not meet red-flag-plus-meaning, but gates, at the railroad crossing.

Take again the classical illustration of the child and the candle. It is a capital illustration supposing the candle to be stationary, in other words, to be a nucleus for "meaning," but it is not always. The child burns its hand. The mother may say, "We must put electricity into the nursery," or, "We must have no uncovered flames in the nursery." This possibility is not ignored by those psychologists who use this illustration, for it is the same kind of thing that is indicated when they speak of the mother holding the child's hand away from the flame instead of teaching him something about it. I am not, therefore, quarrelling with the illustration, but only pointing out that the process of education would be easier for all of us if red flags and candles merely rolled themselves into bigger balls of "meaning"; we should in that case learn how to behave toward first one object and then another until our education was completed. And this is, indeed, a large part of education, particularly in infancy and youth, but it becomes a smaller and smaller part as we get older. We usually cannot apply what we learn from one experience to the next because the next will be different. Moreover, it is usually we ourselves who have made the next experience different. It is the child's burning himself, perhaps, which makes him find something different the next time he puts his hand out. And when we remember all that the child has to learn about flame—to discriminate between flame bare and flame enclosed, between flame enclosed with a conducting and a non-conducting substance, to distinguish between the lighting, heating and burning qualities of flame—we see how complex the matter becomes. But however you enlarge the equation with more brackets, etc., the conditioning equation expressing the relation of the variables remains the same. That is why I think the formula I have cited so useful for the social sciences if we understand and accept what is implicit in it, namely, that behavior is not a function of environment but a function of the relating of behavior and environment.

This seems to me the most illuminating thought that has been given us of recent years for the study of social phenomena. Holt's formula does not give it to us explicitly, but his treatment of circular response does, his emphasis on the significance of the *organization* of reflex arcs and of the functional reference of behavior, the some- thing "new" of his "critical" moments of evolution, his insistence on the fact that behavior is not a function of immediate stimulus, and his use of the functional theory of causation. The last two points will be taken up in the next chapter. We now see behavior not as a function of environment, but as a function of the relation between self and environment. The activity is a function of itself interweaving with the activity of which it is a function. In the illustration given above of the cut in rates by the Checker Taxi Company, the rate was not really a function of volume of business, but, since the rate increased the volume of business, the rate was a function of the relation, the interlacing relation, between rates and volume of business. We must be sure that our formula will fit an evolving situation.

It will perhaps be thought that I am rather forcing the use of mathematical language in this chapter, but I am using this language deliberately for several reasons. First, in order to unfold the implica- tions in the words function and variables used in the definition of behavior which I have been employing; secondly, because I find the language of calculus so stimulating to my own thought on this subject that I hope others will too; in the third place, because the word function is used so widely, and often carelessly, nowadays, that I think we had better look into its origin and make sure that we use it accurately.

We have now, to repeat in summary, three fundamental princi- ples to guide us in our study of social situations: (1) that my response is not to a rigid, static environment, but to a changing environment; (2) to an environment which is changing because of the activity between it and me; (3) that function may be continuously modified by itself, that is, the activity of the boy going to school may change the activity of the boy going to school. Or it might be put thus: that response is always to a relating, that things that are varying must be compared with things that are varying, that the law of geometrical progression is the law of organic growth, that functional relating has always a plus value. The social sciences must learn to deal with that plus, to reckon literally with it. A dynamic psychology gives us instead of equivalents, plusvalents. It is those which we must look for in every situation. These are the "novelties" in the psychologist's "critical" moments of evolution. It is impossible to overemphasize this point; it means a new approach to the social sciences. In the farmer-middleman controversy, find the plusvalent. In the France-Germany situation, find the plusvalent. Let every statesman and diplomat, every legislator and judge find the plusvalent; it is the only approach possible to politics or industry or international relations or our own smallest everyday problems. *Progressive* experience on every level means the creating of plusvalents.

In the physical sciences, we have some interesting, although not wholly exact, parallels of the plus value of the relating. In chemistry we find a chemical substance X decomposing into another Y at a rate proportional to the amount of X undecomposed; at the same time by a reverse reaction Y is decomposing into X at a rate proportional to the amount of Y present. X is continuously influencing Y at the same time that Y is continuously influencing X.

In engineering we have what is called "regeneration." A radio receiving set takes in only a small amount of energy from the electromagnetic waves that reach it, but this is made to control the output of a source of considerable energy located in the set. In some sets a part of the latter energy is carried back to the former, so that the former is now intensified and effects an increased output; and the process repeats itself, building up the power of the set perhaps a thousandfold. This "regenerative" action occurs in many physical and chemical processes and is used by engineers in devising mechanical apparatus, electrical and other.

A dynamic physics studies activity rather than mass; it defines things in terms of activity, not in terms of mass. Present-day physics tells us that the rate of change of the activity may not be proportional to the mass of what is active but to the activity of the mass. We had not a dynamic physics until this was seen. It used to be said that in organic growth the increment of the organism in a given time is proportional to the magnitude of the organism itself. Now, looking at the "organism" as an activity, we should have to use some word which would include magnitude and intensity of the activity.

To conclude this chapter: the most significant thing in recent thinking is, I think, the correspondence of thought in different fields and on different levels. Philosophy has long taught us the unity of experience. You can tear it to pieces if you will and find subject and object, stimulus and response, or—you can refuse to; you can claim the right to see it as a rational interplay of forces, as the functioning of a self-creating coherence. Consciousness is the living interplay of a self-generating activity. Or, consciousness is the living interplay of myriads of self-generating activities which all generate themselves as a moment of the interplay. The most fundamental idea of philosophy is, I think, the recognition that there is no *Denkform* in which as mould all thought is cast, but rather a constant mode of self-generating as thought, a perpetual law of unifying to which the free activity submits itself, law and freedom each the entelechy of the other. Study of social situations reveals the working of this principle. In psychology and physiology, also, we find certain conclusions which lead us to think that experience on every level may be found to be an interrelating in which the activity of the relating alters the terms of the relating and also the relating itself. Politics, industry and law need the impetus of this thought. Our older social philosophy gave us the pernicious theories of the balance of power between nations, of adjustment between capital and labor. It gave us always equivalents; our more recent thinking shows us how to create plusvalents. This will be developed further in the chapter on Experience as Creating.[12]

Because the word function is being increasingly used to express relation, there are certain warnings necessary. First, we should not use the word function to excuse us from studying each situation; this I have seen done several times recently. A phrase may be a legitimate short-cut in exposition, but it is inexcusable to let it be a short-cut in investigation. Secondly, we must not confuse function as relation and function as quantity. For us function is not a quantity left over when the activity of relating is completed; function is the activity of relating, it is the operation, not what results. A function is always functioning; our interest in it is on that very account. In the third place, the independent variable is independent only within a certain equation and our equations are constantly changing. We must not confuse a variable which is constant from moment to moment in the same statement, and varies only from statement to statement, with one that varies in the same statement. This is very important to remember in social psychology. The constant of one situation may not be, probably will not be, the constant of the next situation. In studying any one situation we look on this quantity as constant while the mutual effects of varying quantities are studied; two facts or individuals, let us say two activities, adapt themselves to each other in a certain way for any given situation; change the situation and they will probably adapt themselves in a different way.

Take the economic "law of supply and demand." According to that law price is a constant function of demand: as demand increases, price increases; as demand decreases price decreases. But this law is true only on a certain assumption: that supply is fixed, that there is a certain amount of the commodity in existence which stays fixed. This is an assumption which speculators are always trying to make true, but in ordinary, legitimate, economic operations it is seldom a possible assumption *except for one situation*. Probably demand is increasing the volume of business which, in most cases—in the case of manufactured articles the materials for which can be got in practically unlimited quantities—lowers the cost of production. As a matter of fact, therefore, increased demand means, other things being equal, eventually decreased prices. Thus the function assumed for one situation cannot be carried over into another. Price is a developing situation; it depends on an interweaving; it is a function not of an independent variable alone but of the relation between it and the independent variable. Thus to say that demand raises price is wrong except in regard to a given situation. To put this into mathematical language (which seems to respond more readily than any other to our present thinking on this subject), the error would be to take a variable constant for an absolute constant. Given the amount of commodities at any minute and taking demand as an independent variable, the price will be the function of that, but from situation to situation the supply changes. The economist makes no mistake here; I am giving this as an illustration of the *kind* of error in thinking sometimes made by those who use the word function nowadays rather carelessly. In the use of the word function, the thing to be kept constantly in mind is the developing situation.

EXPERIENCE IN THE LIGHT OF RECENT PSYCHOLOGY: INTEGRATIVE BEHAVIOR

I said above that Holt has shown the dynamic nature of his thought most clearly by his use of the reflex circle and the functional theory of causation. This theory, that "every physical law is in the last analysis the statement of a constant function between one process or thing and some other process or thing," Holt makes one of the basic principles of his psychology. The "bead" theory of causation which once prevailed in physics, and "which tried to describe causal process in terms of successive 'states,' the 'state' of a body at one moment being the *cause* of its 'state' and position at the next,"[13] is as fatal for psychology, he tells us, as for physics. It is equally fatal for sociology. It is the theory by which statesmen and diplomats so often try to solve national and world problems and fail. Behavior on neither level is governed by immediate stimulus. Both psychologist and sociologist note that as the number of integral reflexes involved in behavior increases, the immediate stimulus recedes further and further from view as the significant factor.[14] The stimulus becomes the total situation of which the total behavior is a function. As the psychologist finds that what the bee is *really* doing is laying up honey in its home, that it is only incidental that it sips from this flower or that, so in studying social relations we find that a situation of which behavior is a constant function is usually very complex. We must observe every case of behavior as a whole; this must never be forgotten in the study of social situations. The next chapter will be taken up with the *Gestalt* concept, which is a concept of wholes, and which some psychologists think will have more influence on all our thinking than any single concept has for long exercised. In Chapter VI behavior as response to a complex stimulus will be again considered in connection with the importance of total environment in the conception of adjustment.

This appreciation of "total behavior" brings us back again to our formula: the will or purpose of a man or group is to be found in that activity which is a constant function, or a combination of such functions, of some aspect of his environment. I said in the last chapter that this formula, with its implied definition of behavior as a function of the interweaving between the activity of organism and activity of environment, gives us a new approach to the social sciences. In saying that, I do not ignore the many signs we already see of this approach. Mr. Earl Howard, labor manager for Hart, Schaffner & Marx, told me that the first question he always asks himself in regard to any complaint or request of the workman is, "What in the conditions of this plant or industry, or in general living conditions, has caused this attitude on the part of the workman?" This is very different from the manufacturer who told me that when a workman came to him with a complaint, he always set someone to study the psychology of that man. We can hardly estimate the difference Mr. Howard's method would make in industrial relations. The similarity between this method and that advocated by our present psychology seems to me significant. Mr. Howard studies variations in their relation to other variations; also he takes into account all the elements of "the total situation." The rule for politics or industry, for trade unions or manufacturers' associations, should be exactly Holt's rule for man: "study his movements until we have discovered . . . that object, situation, process (or perhaps merely that relation) of which his behavior is a *constant function*."[15] The American workman today is responding neither to high post-war prices nor to his accumulated rancor against capital; he is reacting to a situation of which these and other factors form component parts.

It must be remembered, however, that when I speak of a "new" approach to the social sciences, I am thinking of conscious approach; success in human relations has always meant if not the conscious, at any rate the unconscious, use of this principle of present psychological thought, but today we have an increasing amount of deliberate social analysis and conscious use of certain fundamental principles.

It now seems clear that we must look for purpose within the process itself. We see experience as an interplay of forces, as the activity of relating leading through fresh relatings to a new activity, not from purpose to deed and deed to purpose with a fatal gap between, as if life moved like the jerks of mechanical toys with only an external wire-puller to account for the jerks, or a too mysterious psychic energy. What we possess always creates the possibilities of fresh satisfactions. The need comes as need only when the possible satisfaction of need is already there. There is no gap in the process. The automobile does not satisfy wants only, it creates wants; this is the meaning of our formula for sociology. The automobile was not invented to solve the farmers' problems.

The purpose in front will always mislead us. Psychology now gives us end as moment *in* process.[16]

Sociologists, too, look for purpose in "so far" integrated behavior. We are urged by whips, not rewards. Our aims are in the motor-mechanisms of our neuro-muscular apparatus. No magic wand will change these, it is a process. Many psychologists use the expression "striving towards some goal," but we can see in our own lives that the urge is always the lack; the goal changes as we try one means after another of meeting that lack. With the workman the urge is inadequate conditions for normal living. The goal changes from year to year as he conceives, for the bettering of those conditions, one method after another: shorter hours, higher wages, share in profits, share in control, nationalization of industry, etc. The relation of preconceived end to growing end must be carefully watched, with all that contributes to the change, with all that happens because of the change. You cannot coördinate purpose without developing purpose, it is part of the same process. Some people want to give the workmen a share in carrying out the purpose of the plant and do not see that that involves a share in creating the purpose of the plant. A noted teacher of ethics tells us, "A citizen is one who helps to realize the purpose for which this nation exists." The citizen must also help to *make* the purpose.

It could be put this way. Purpose is always the appearing of the power of unifying, the ranging of multiplicity into that which is both means and ends, the One holding Many.

I have given examples in an earlier chapter of the difference between preconceived and actual purpose. We can find those differences for ourselves every day in what we see and what we read. There are no static purposes for us to lay our hands on; put salt on the tail of the European purpose today—if you can. We make two mistakes in regard to purpose when we are considering social process: we try to substitute an intellectualistic purpose for that involved in the situation, or, when the purpose appears from out the activity, we think, by some strange mental legerdemain, that

that was the purpose which had been actuating us all along. But our dealings with our fellowmen should not be so different from those with our natural environment. Last summer I noticed a strange plant in our pasture. I did not know what it was, I had no picture in my mind of what flower or fruit it would bear, but I freed it. That is, I dug around it and opened the soil that the rain might fall on its roots, I cleared out the thistles with which it was entangled so that it might have room to spread, I cut down the undergrowth of small maples near so that it could get the sun. In other words, I simply freed it. Every friendship which is not treated in this way will surely suffer; no human relation should serve an anticipatory purpose. Every relation should be a freeing relation with the "purpose" evolving. This is the truth underneath the admonition that we should not pray for specific things.

But the great mistake people often make is to say, when the flower and the fruit appear, "This [the particular flower or fruit] was what I was working for." We must be ever on our guard against post facto purposes. We have all had experience of the modifications which take place in a policy when we begin to carry it out. When legislation establishes what is called a general policy, and a commission is appointed to form specific regulations and provisions to see that that policy is carried out, it often happens that the commission finds a different purpose developing from that on which the legislation was founded, and has then to try to get the law changed in such a way as to embody the new or the actual purpose. Activity always does more than embody purpose, it evolves purpose. With the general acceptance of this fact, part of our political and legal science will have to be rewritten. All history which jumps from one dramatic moment to another falsifies the situation; history must be viewed as continuously evolving relations, just as the steam in the boiler, no matter how rapidly it increases, yet always increases gradually.

We must remember, moreover, in any analysis of ends, that what we call ends are often means. Take the formation of a stock company for the building of a railroad. Of all those who buy stock perhaps no one is interested in the "purpose" of that company: the opening of a new route of communication. Some wish an investment for their money, others wish to speculate, others to control the direction of the traffic, others to influence the selection of the route in order that real estate values in which they are interested shall be increased.[17]

The matter of purpose, interests, needs, requires much more empirical study, and certainly a volume to itself; I can give here only the briefest indications of the way recent psychology has illumined one of the most important conceptions of the social sciences.

I said above that we are to look for purpose in the so-far integrated behavior of the organism. I shall recall this later in the chapters on law and politics. Political leaders cannot persuade people to adopt purposes, the legal order cannot assign purposes; they are found in the so-far integrated behavior of people. Moreover, when we see end as involved in the process, not in contentless will, we see that we cannot "choose" our ends as some would have us "choose" a cause to be loyal to. Life is richer than this: we have now a far greater responsibility, a nobler ethics, not less but a larger freedom. Choice is not given up but is put further back in the process. When we do not understand this, it may mean disaster for us, for as we cannot make arbitrary choices, so we cannot postpone choice; we cannot make up later for the lost moment, that is, not directly. Choice has a place in the process, we must learn exactly where the place is and act on that knowledge. If we try to make a choice with our "minds" when another already exists in our neuro-muscular apparatus, we only come up against a dead-wall of impossibility. Or rather we have to attack our problem differently; we have to set to work to change our motor mechanisms.

Through our observation of human relations, through the teachings of psychology, we learn then that from our concrete activities spring both the power and the guide for those activities. Experience is the dynamo station; here are generated will and purpose. Further, and of the utmost importance, here too arise the standards with which to judge that same will and purpose. Men used to say that they relied on their wives' intuitions, but wives today are more apt to be out viewing facts for themselves than staying at home intuiting. I think that for some time we have been a little astray in regard to the relation of standards to the social process. We have, for instance, long thought of ourselves as a nation of idealists who have wonderful ideas and struggle to carry them out. But take the average New England town: it is sunk in the apathy of accepted routine; someone comes along and proposes that it shall do something. The citizens, being Americans, have the genius for doing; they *do* and then they have the ideas involved in the doing. Someone told a certain New England village that it ought to have a social welfare department; the inhabitants did not know what it was or what it was for, but they organized it and did it well too, and then they told themselves and the neighboring towns what their purpose *had been* (notice tense) and one would have thought that all their lives they had been longing for a social service department.

Our ideals are involved in our activities. Take for instance all the talk of "getting together" which has filled our press and public halls for the last fifteen or twenty years. It has been assumed that our lives were growing too isolated and that we ought to correct this. Not at all. After we had begun to live together, crowded in cities and factories and mines, after our whole organism had got set and attuned to living together, then we heard that we must cease (!) our separate lives and "get together." But we never heard of this duty of getting together until it was a *fait accompli,* then behold it became an aspiration—after the event! Herd instinct? Christian brotherhood? No, it is the inevitable tendency to make an ideal of the fact. Here we are, our whole industry and business system based on credit, on faith and coöperation, and then we cry out, heads in sand, "Let us take example from the little loving ants and bees and bring association and coöperation into our daily lives." But they are *in* our daily lives all the time and that is the reason we are thinking of them. Coöperation in the business world did not come about by emulating the bees and the beavers, as some of the biologists exhort us to do. One by one the integrations are made, as environment changes, and the behavior patterns constructed.

We do not adapt our activities to ends in front or to principles behind.

I am not implying that I wish this were different. To get our ideals and our culture from our daily life means that they have a vital energy which can be used refluently on that life. Many of us are ashamed of our "mechanical age" and deck it out with trimmings which are like the buttons of dresses which don't button, put there for ornament only; but we must realize that our daily living may itself become an art, that in commerce we may find culture, in industry idealism, in our business system beauty, in mechanics morals—the ethics of the lathe are of a pretty fundamental kind. People tell us that "when the spirit of art spreads far enough down we shall redeem the sordidness of our present civilization," but grown-up people cannot tie apples on the trees and then pick them. Only when the spirit of art rises from the roots of our mechanical age will it "redeem our civilization." The divorce of our so-called spiritual life from our daily activities is a fatal dualism. We are not to ignore our industry, commerce, etc., and seek spiritual development elsewhere; on the other hand we shall never find it in these, but only by an eternal influence and refluence. If we point with satisfaction to our material progress, it is only because of its evidence of a virility, a robustness, which is capable of fruitful interweavings. There is energy flowing from it which, uniting with other energies, will create new men and new environment.

In many of the arguments for shorter working hours this is forgotten, and we have a kind of time-theory of salvation: keep the debasing influences of industry to certain hours of the day, employ the others in some educational way, and if the race is keenly enough run the spiritualizing influences will win out. But we cannot split ourselves up like this, the eight-hour influences will continue into the leisure period; it is the eight-hour influences themselves that we must reckon with.

Yet we see many signs that we are not unappreciative of the relation of all our doing to all our thinking. Why are we getting engineers as presidents of colleges? Why is the very word becoming one to conjure with, "social engineering," etc.? It is because we have made up our minds that we want the doer-thinkers.

To sum up this chapter: one of the chief contributions to sociology of the psychology I am trying to indicate is the *continuing* activity of the specific-response relation, the relatings and then the evolving of these relatings. The essence of this psychology is that the "release" and the integrating are one process: this is as important for ethics as for physiology or psychology; for sociology its value is inestimable.

When some of the behaviorists tell us that "knowledge lives in the muscles" they seem to leave out the deeper truth of the continuing activity. I am objecting here merely to the word "knowledge." I think it better when practicable to keep to verbs; the value of nouns is chiefly for post mortems. It is just here that Holt gives us, in *Response and Cognition*,[18] a fundamental part of his teaching: the activity of knowing including the knower and the known. After all what *Response and Cognition* does is not so much to explain knowledge as to abolish it—to abolish it in favor of knowing, of an activity, of a process which involves knower and known but which never looks from the windows of either. The knower knows (an active verb) the known; reality is in the knowing.

The profound truth we have now recognized we could express differently by saying that you can define the actors only in terms of the process. Modern playwrights are beginning to see this. And we ourselves are beginning to appreciate more and more plays and novels written by those who have this understanding. The old-fashioned hero dominated the situation and came out alone to bow before the curtain, and we did not care very much *what* he had conquered, we were "thrilled" by the act of conquest. And we certainly did not analyze the difference between conquest and defeat, a subtle matter indeed and often hidden far beneath the surface. But nowadays we do not think of the hero alone or with his feet upon the fallen foe—in fact we may have to look among the prostrate foes for the hero—we see him in the multitudinous relations of life, we see him in his significance to some of the meanings of his age.

I think we can now go back to our formula and its definition of behavior as a function of environment, and bring to it a larger understanding. I should like, for social psychology, to express it as follows: Thinking (willing, purposing) is *specific* relating of the interdependent variables, individual and situation, each thereby creating itself anew, relating themselves anew, and thus giving us the evolving situation.

The important points to bear in mind are:

1. Behavior is both internally and externally conditioned.
2. Behavior is a function of the interweaving between activity of organism and activity of environment, that is, response is to a relating.
3. By this interlocking activity individual and situation each is creating itself anew.
4. Thus relating themselves anew.
5. Thus giving us the evolving situation.

These two chapters are obviously not a wholesale endorsement of what has been called behaviorism,[19] for the behaviorists as belated mechanists leave much to be desired. But Holt's thought seems to me to go further and to be more discriminating. It is pregnant and important for the social sciences because it makes us think of our problems in terms of process and not of "pictures." The self-sustaining process which this writer gives us is the fundamental law of human activity. And this psychology is both a challenge and a reward: it carries in one hand the compass for the journey, and in the other the only gift we can ever hope for for all our pains, the opportunity for greater pains, for harder things. We give ourselves to our task and our task not only becomes larger but at the same time it becomes deeper and higher. The reward for all activity is greater activity.

The full acceptance of life as process gets us further and further away from the old controversies. The thought I have been trying to indicate is neither conventional idealism nor realism. It is neither mechanism nor vitalism: we see mechanism as true within its own barriers; we see the *élan vital* (still a thing-in-itself) as a somewhat crude foreshadowing of a profound truth. It is now possible to rid ourselves of the limitations of these more partial points of view; we have now given to us new modes of thinking, new ways of acting.

NOTES

1. Edwin B. Holt: *The Freudian Wish, The Place of Illusory Experience in a Realistic World* (one of the studies in *The New Realism*), *The Concept of Consciousness*. I have also had the privilege of reading some of Dr. Holt's unpublished lectures as taken down by students. There are undoubtedly many things in this book with which Dr. Holt would not agree, some inferences which he might think mistaken, but I have given what for me are the implications of his thought.
2. In *The New Realism*, p. 366, he defines reality as "some very comprehensive system of terms in relation." He expresses this more actively later, although nowhere explicitly as a definition of reality. In fact the word reality is now very little used; it does not fit in with our present mode of thinking.
3. Perhaps an illustration, although it may be only roughly accurate, would make this clearer. Take the European situation and a gold mine in America. The European situation and the amount of gold taken out of the mine are two interdependent variables either one of which may be taken as a function of the other. The European situation will vary according to the amount of gold taken out, that is, it "depends" on it, and it is equally true the other way around, for the total amount of gold taken out will depend somewhat on the European situation. Increase the birth-rate in Europe and more gold will be taken out at Nome. If, however, we should be speaking not of the actual amount of gold taken from the mine, but of the percentage per ton of

gold in quartz in a mine, the matter is quite different. The European situation is affected by the variation in this percentage, but the percentage varies quite independently of the European situation; increase the birth-rate in Europe and you do not increase the percentage per ton. We have no longer two interdependent variables; the percentage of gold per ton is an independent variable of which the European situation is a function.

4. *The Freudian Wish*, p. 95.

5. *Op cit.*, p. 124.

6. A sense organ has been stimulated, the energy of stimulation has been transformed into nervous energy, this nervous energy has passed along an afferent nerve to the central nervous system and has passed through this and out by an efferent or motor nerve to a muscle where the energy is again transformed and the muscle contracts.

7. S. T. Bok, *The Reflex-Circle,* in *Psychiatrische en Neurologische Bladen,* Amsterdam, *Juli-Augustus,* 1917. See also James, *Principles of Psychology,* II, 582, and Baldwin's *Mental Development in the Child and the Race,* 2nd ed., pp. 133, 263 ff., 374 ff.

8. This has important consequences for psychology, for as long as we thought of matter as something "acted on" we inevitably thought of "sensory experimentation," etc., in a certain way. A truly dynamic psychology, by giving us both environment and ourselves as activity, has implications which have not begun to be unfolded yet.

9. I believe physiologists have not decided yet how far the sensory side of circular response is necessary to its continued functioning even although necessary to its formation, and if I were trying to establish any exact parallel between the physiological circular reflex and circular response as seen by the students of social research, such questions would be important for us, but I hope it is understood that no such exact parallel is intended.

10. I mean by this that if we could formulate the process mathematically, we should obtain a differential equation or a set of differential equations to be solved by integration.

11. See also Kempf. "Whenever the autonomic . . . apparatus is disturbed . . . it compels the projicient sensori-motor apparatus to so adjust the receptors in the environment as to acquire stimuli having the capacity to produce adequate postural readjustments in the autonomic apparatus." Edward J. Kempf, *The Autonomic Functions and the Personality,* p. 1.

12. It has been pointed out to me that the term plus-value does not express my idea since the very thing I am opposed to is the plus-relation, the one-by-one connection rather than the integration. But I am certainly opposed to the word super, which has been suggested in its place, for the "something new" of integration is not "over" or "more than" or "greater than" the parts, as often erroneously claimed for "wholes." I think plus-value *is* what I mean,

for I am not referring to a plus-plus relation of the parts, but expressing the fact that integration gives an additional value, one more value, but not necessarily a greater or super value. See pp. 98–102 for further consideration of this point which is perhaps the most important in the whole range of discussion on human relations.

13. *Op. cit.,* p. 157.
14. ". . . the development from reflex action to highly organized behavior is one in which the correlation between stimulus and organism becomes less and less direct, while that between the organism and the object of response becomes more and more prominent." *Op. cit.,* p. 169.
15. *Op. cit.,* p. 163.
16. "It is not true that we do something in order to attain a dead and static 'end'; we do something as the necessary but subordinate moment in the *doing* of something more comprehensive. The true comparison then is not between deed or means and thought or end, but between part deed and whole deed." "The doctrine of the wish shows us that life is not lived *for ends.* Life is a process. . . . Its motion is forward; yet its motive power comes not from in front (from 'ends') but from behind, from the wishes which are in ourselves." *Op. cit.,* pp. 93–94, 132.
17. See Jhering, *Law as Means to an End,* p. 32.
18. Supplement to *The Freudian Wish.*
19. Although I wish to acknowledge fully my indebtedness to Watson.

Constructive Conflict

THE SUBJECT I have been
given for these lectures is *The
Psychological Foundations of Business Administration,* but as it is
obvious that we cannot in four papers consider all the contributions
which contemporary psychology is making to business administration—to the methods of hiring, promoting and discharging, to the
consideration of incentives, the relation of output to motive, to
group organization, etc.—I have chosen certain subjects which seem
to me to go to the heart of personnel relations in industry. I wish
to consider in this paper the most fruitful way of dealing with
conflict. At the outset I should like to ask you to agree for the
moment to think of conflict as neither good nor bad; to consider
it without ethical pre-judgment; to think of it not as warfare, but
as the appearance of difference, difference of opinions, of interests.
For that is what conflict means—difference. We shall not consider
merely the differences between employer and employee, but those
between managers, between the directors at the Board meetings,
or wherever difference appears.

As conflict—difference—is here in the world, as we cannot
avoid it, we should, I think, use it. Instead of condemning it, we

Note: This chapter is reprinted from Elliot M. Fox and L. Urwick, eds., *Dynamic
Administration: The Collected Papers of Mary Parker Follett* (London: Pitman,
1973), pp. 1–20. This paper was first presented before a Bureau of Personnel
Administration conference group in January 1925.

should set it to work for us. Why not? What does the mechanical engineer do with friction? Of course his chief job is to eliminate friction, but it is true that he also capitalizes friction. The transmission of power by belts depends on friction between the belt and the pulley. The friction between the driving wheel of the locomotive and the track is necessary to haul the train. All polishing is done by friction. The music of the violin we get by friction. We left the savage state when we discovered fire by friction. We talk of the friction of mind on mind as a good thing. So in business, too, we have to know when to try to eliminate friction and when to try to capitalize it, when to see what work we can make it do. That is what I wish to consider here, whether we can set conflict to work and make it *do* something for us.[1]

METHODS OF DEALING WITH CONFLICT

There are three main ways of dealing with conflict: domination, compromise and integration. Domination, obviously, is a victory of one side over the other. This is the easiest way of dealing with conflict, the easiest for the moment but not usually successful in the long run, as we can see from what has happened since the War.

The second way of dealing with conflict, that of compromise, we understand well, for it is the way we settle most of our controversies; each side gives up a little in order to have peace, or, to speak more accurately, in order that the activity which has been interrupted by the conflict may go on. Compromise is the basis of trade union tactics.[2] In collective bargaining, the trade unionist asks for more than he expects to get, allows for what is going to be lopped off in the conference. Thus we often do not know what he really thinks he should have, and this ignorance is a great barrier to dealing with conflict fruitfully. At the time of a certain wage controversy in Massachusetts, the lowest paid girls in the industry were getting about $8.00 or $9.00 a week. The demand made by two of the representatives of the girls was for $22.40 (for a minimum wage, note), obviously too great an increase for anyone seriously to think of getting at one time. Thus the employers were as far as ever from knowing what the girls really thought they ought to have.

But I certainly ought not to imply that compromise is peculiarly a trade union method. It is the accepted, the approved, way of ending controversy. Yet no one really wants to compromise, because that means a giving up of something. Is there then any other method of ending conflict? There is a way beginning now to be recognized at least, and even occasionally followed: when two desires are *integrated*, that means that a solution has been found in which both desires have found a place, that neither side has had to sacrifice anything. Let us take some very simple illustration. In the Harvard Library one day, in one of the smaller rooms, someone wanted the window open, I wanted it shut. We opened the window in the next room, where no one was sitting. This was not a compromise because there was no curtailing of desire; we both got what we really wanted. For I did not want a closed room, I simply did not want the north wind to blow directly on me; likewise the other occupant did not want that particular window open, he merely wanted more air in the room.

I have already given this illustration in print. I repeat it here because this instance, from its lack of any complications, shows my point at once I think. Let us take another illustration. A Dairymen's Co-operative League almost went to pieces last year on the question of precedence in unloading cans at a creamery platform. The men who came down the hill (the creamery was on a down grade) thought they should have precedence; the men who came up the hill thought they should unload first. The thinking of both sides in the controversy was thus confined within the walls of these two possibilities, and this prevented their even trying to find a way of settling the dispute which would avoid these alternatives. The solution was obviously to change the position of the platform so that both up-hillers and down-hillers could unload at the same time. But this solution was not found until they had asked the advice of a more or less professional integrator. When, however, it was pointed out to them, they were quite ready to accept it. Integration involves invention, and the clever thing is to recognize this, and not to let one's thinking stay within the boundaries of two alternatives which are mutually exclusive.[3]

Take another case. There is sometimes a question whether the meetings of works committees should be held in the plant or outside: the argument for meeting inside is the obvious advantage of being near one's work; the argument against, the fear of company influence. I know one factory that made what I consider an integration by having the meetings of the works committee held in the separate club building of the employees situated within the factory grounds. Here the men felt much freer than in any other part of the plant.

A friend gave me this example. He was called on jury service in a murder trial. The District Attorney asked him whether he had any objection to capital punishment. He replied, "Yes, definitely so." The "conflict" was then on, for the judge thought this opinion incapacitated him for service in a murder trial. My friend summed up the incident to me in these words: "After the judge had subjected me to a kind of cross-examination, I was put into the jury box, but neither the judge nor myself was left as victor; the experience had changed us both. We found the solution instead of vindicating the pre-judgment of either of us; the solution being that it is possible to render a verdict in accordance with evidence so that you need not evade your duties as a citizen whatever your opinion of capital punishment."

By far the most interesting examples of integration which have come to my attention recently were four sent to the London *Times* by Gilbert Murray, four integrations which he had found in the Report of the Dawes Committee.[4]

It is often difficult to decide whether a decision is a true integration or something of a compromise, and there is a flaw I think in one of the four cited by Gilbert Murray. But signs of even partial integration, signs even that people want integration rather than domination or compromise, are encouraging.

Some people tell me that they like what I have written on integration, but say that I am talking of what ought to be instead of what is. But indeed I am not; I am talking neither of what is, to any great extent, nor of what ought to be merely, but of what perhaps may be. This we can discover only by experiment. That is all I am urging, that we try experiments in methods of resolving differences; differences on the Board of Directors, with fellow managers or heads of departments, with employees, or in other relations. If we do this, we may take a different attitude toward conflict.

The key-word of psychology today is desire. If we wish to speak of conflict in the language of contemporary psychology, we might call it a moment in the interacting of desires. Thus we take from it any connotation of good or bad. Thus we shall not be afraid of conflict, but shall recognize that there is a destructive way of dealing with such moments and a constructive way. Conflict as the moment of the appearing and focusing of difference may be a sign of health, a prophecy of progress. If the Dairymen's League had not fought over the question of precedence, the improved method of unloading would not have been thought of. The conflict in this case was constructive. And this was because, instead of compromising, they sought a way of integrating. Compromise does not create, it deals with what already exists; integration creates something new, in this case a different way of unloading. And because this not only settled the controversy but was actually better technique, saved time for both the farmers and the creamery, I call this: setting friction to work, making it *do* something.

Thus we see that while conflict as continued unintegrated difference is pathological, difference itself is not pathological. The fights in the Democratic convention were a hopeful sign for the Democratic party. What I think we should do in business organization is to try to find the machinery best suited for the normal appearing and uniting of diversity so that the difference does not stay too long crystallized, so that the pathological stage shall not be reached.

One advantage of integration over compromise I have not yet mentioned. If we get only compromise, the conflict will come up again and again in some other form, for in compromise we give up part of our desire, and because we shall not be content to rest there, sometime we shall try to get the whole of our desire. Watch industrial controversy, watch international controversy, and see how often this occurs. Only integration really stabilizes. But by stabilization I do not mean anything stationary. Nothing ever stays put. I mean only that that particular conflict is settled and the next occurs on a higher level.

Psychology has given us the phrase "progressive integratings"; we need also the phrase progressive differings. We can often measure our progress by watching the nature of our conflicts. Social progress is in this respect like individual progress; we become spiritually more and more developed as our conflicts rise to higher levels. If a man should tell you that his chief daily conflict within himself is—Shall I steal or not steal?—you would know what to think of his stage of development. As someone has said, "A man is known by the dilemmas he keeps." In the same way, one test of your business organization is not how many conflicts you have, for conflicts are the essence of life, but *what* are your conflicts? And how do you deal with them? It is to be hoped that we shall not always have strikes, but it is equally to be hoped that we shall always have conflict, the kind which leads to invention, to the emergence of new values.

Having suggested integration as perhaps the way by which we can deal most fruitfully with conflict, with difference, we should now consider the method by which integration can be obtained. But before we do that I want to say definitely that I do not think integration is possible in all cases. When two men want to marry the same woman, there can be no integration; when two sons both want the old family home, there can usually be no integration. And there are many such cases, some of little, some of great seriousness. I do not say that there is no tragedy in life. All that I say is that if we were alive to its advantages, we could often integrate instead of compromising. I have a friend who annoys me in this way. She makes a statement. I say, "I don't agree with that because . . ." and I intend to give my reasons, but before I have a chance she says, "Well, let's not fight about it." But I had no intention of fighting.

BASES OF INTEGRATION

If, then, we do not think that differing necessarily means fighting, even when two desires both claim right of way, if we think that integration is more profitable than conquering or compromising, the first step toward this consummation is *to bring the differences into the open*. We cannot hope to integrate our differences unless we know what they are. I will give some illustrations of the opposite method—evading or suppressing the issue.

I know a factory where, after the War, the employees asked for a 5 percent increase in wages, but it was not clear to either side whether this meant a 5 percent raise over present wages or over pre-War wages. Moreover, it was seen that neither side wished to know! The employees naturally preferred to think the former, the managers the latter. It was some time before both sides were willing to face the exact issue; each, unconsciously, hoped to win by keeping the whole problem hazy.

One of the longest discussions I ever heard on a minimum wage board was in regard to the question of fares to and from work: first, whether this item should be included at all with board, lodging, etc., in a cost-of-living budget, that is, whether transportation to and from the plant should be a cost on production. When finally it was decided to leave the item in and allow 60 cents a week for it, instead of the $1.20 which the 10-cent Boston car fare would necessitate if this item were to be allowed for in full, it seemed to me a clear case of evasion or suppression. That is, the employers were not willing to face at that moment the question whether wages should include transportation. I sat on that board as a representative of the public, and I suggested more than once during the discussion that we should find out whether most of the girls in that particular industry did live near the plant or at a distance too great for walking. Also I suggested that we should find out whether, if they lived near the plant, the cost of board and lodging in that neighbourhood was so high that it would more than offset car fares. But the employers in this instance were not ready to face the issue, and therefore the clearly evasive decision of 60 cents was made.

Another interesting case of suppression occurred in a committee of which I was a member. The question was a disagreement concerning the pay of two stenographers who were working for us. Those who urged the higher amount persisted in speaking of the stenographers' day as an eight-hour day because the hours were from nine to five, although with the hour out for lunch that obviously makes a seven-hour day.

Wherever you have the fight-set, you are in danger of obscurities, conscious or unconscious. As long as trade unionism is a defensive movement, as long as employers' associations are defensive movements, we shall have obscurities. As long as internationalism is what it is, evasion will go on. Of course not to *appear* to evade is part of good diplomacy, for you don't want the other side to think you are trying to "get by" on anything. But we shall continue to evade or suppress as long as our real aim is not agreement, but domination. Lord Shaw, chairman of the Coal Commission, put it as one of the essentials in arbitration that both sides should genuinely desire agreement. Here we get a very direct lesson from psychology.

The psychiatrist tells his patient that he cannot help him unless he is honest in wanting his conflict to end. The "uncovering" which every book on psychology has rubbed into us from some years now as a process of the utmost importance for solving the conflicts which the individual has within himself is equally important for the relations between individuals, or between groups, classes, races, nations. In business, the employer, in dealing either with his associates or his employees, has to get underneath all the camouflage, has to find the real demand as against the demand put forward, distinguish declared motive from real motive, alleged cause from real cause, and to remember that sometimes the underlying motive is deliberately concealed and that sometimes it exists unconsciously.

The first rule, then, for obtaining integration is to put your cards on the table, face the real issue, uncover the conflict, bring the whole thing into the open.

One of the most important reasons for bringing the desires of each side to a place where they can be clearly examined and valued is that evaluation often leads to *revaluation*. We progress by a revaluation of desire, but usually we do not stop to examine a desire until another is disputing right of way with it. Watch the evolution of your desires from childhood, through youth, etc. The baby has many infantile desires which are not compatible with his wish for approbation; therefore he revalues his desires. We see this all through our life. We want to do so-and-so, but we do not estimate how much this really means to us until it comes into conflict with another desire. Revaluation is the flower of comparison.

This conception of the revaluation of desire is necessary to keep in the foreground of our thinking in dealing with conflict, for neither side ever "gives in" really, it is hopeless to expect it, but there often comes a moment when there is a simultaneous revaluation of interests on both sides and unity precipitates itself. This, I think, happened in Europe at the London Conference last summer, or rather it happened before that and led to the Conference. Integration is often more a spontaneous flowing together of desire than one might think from what I have said; the revaluing of interests on both sides may lead the interests to fit into each other, so that all find some place in the final solution.

The bearing of all this on business administration is, I hope, obvious. A business should be so organized (this is one of the tests for us to apply to our organization) that full opportunity is given in any conflict, in any coming together of different desires, for the whole field of desire to be viewed. Our employees should be able to see, as we should be able ourselves to see, the whole field of desire. The *field of desire* is an important psychological and sociological conception; many conflicts could, I believe, be prevented from ending disastrously by getting the desires of each side into one field of vision where they could be viewed together and compared. We all believe to a certain extent in Freud's "sublimation," but I believe still more that various desires get oriented toward one another and take on different values in the process of orientation.

It will be understood, of course, that all this applies to ourselves as well as to the other side; we have to uncover our sub-articulate egoisms, and then, when we see them in relation to other facts and desires, we may estimate them differently. We often think it is a question of eliminating motives when it is only a question of subordinating them. We often, for instance, treat personal motives as more ignoble than we need. There is nothing necessarily discreditable in the politician "standing by" his friends. The only ethical question is how much that motive is weighing against others. The unethical thing is to persuade yourself that it is not weighing at all.

I have time barely to mention a very important point: the connection between the *realignment of groups* and a revaluation of interests. I have found this important in watching the realignments of political parties. We must in any conflict between groups watch every realignment to see how far it changes the confronting desires, for this means how far it changes the conflict.

I began this section by saying that the first step in integration is to bring the differences into the open. If the first step is to put clearly before ourselves what there is to integrate, there is something very important for us to note—namely, that the highest lights in a situation are not always those which are most indicative of the real issues involved. Many situations are decidedly complex, involve numerous and varied activities, overlapping activities. There is too great a tendency (perhaps encouraged by popular journalism) to deal with the dramatic moments, forgetting that these are not always the most significant moments. We should not follow literary analogies here. You may have a good curtain with, to quote Kipling, the lovers loving and the parents signing cheques. Yet, after all, this may not be the controlling moment in the lives of these people. To *find the significant rather than the dramatic features* of industrial controversy, of a disagreement in regard to policy on board of directors or between managers, is essential to integrative business policies.

Such search is part of what seems to me the second step in integration. If the first step is to uncover the real conflict, the next is to take the demands of both sides and break them up into their constituent parts.[5] Contemporary psychology shows how fatal it is to try to deal with conglomerates. I know a boy who wanted a college education. His father died and he had to go to work at once to support his mother. Had he then to give up his desire? No, for on analysis he found that what he wanted was not a college education, but an education, and there were still ways of his getting that. You remember the southern girl who said, "Why, I always thought damned Yankee was one word until I came north."

This method of *breaking up wholes* is the way you deal with business problems; it is the method which precedes business decisions. Take the case of inaugurating a system of approval shipment. A. W. Shaw, in his *Approach to Business Problems,* shows the sub-problems involved here:

1. What will be the effect on collections and on the cost of shipment?

2. What is to be the credit policy?

3. Will the stock in transit or in the hands of customers reduce the number of turnovers per year?

4. Will the risk of damage to returned goods be great enough to jeopardize the regular profit?

5. Will the increase in sales more than offset any added cost in the administrative department?

6. Also psychological factors, as customers' curiosity and caution.

I have given this illustration at length because it seems to me that this is the method which should be applied to controversy. I wish indeed that every controversy might be considered a problem.

You will notice that to break up a problem into its various parts involves the *examination of symbols,* involves, that is, the careful scrutiny of the language used to see what it really means. A friend of mine wanted to go to Europe, but also she did not want to spend the money it would cost. Was there any integration? Yes, she found one. In order to understand it, let us use the method I am advocating; let us ask, what did "going to Europe" symbolize to her? In order to do that, we have to break up this whole, "going to Europe." What does "going to Europe" stand for to different people? A sea voyage, seeing beautiful places, meeting new people, a rest or change from daily duties, and a dozen other things. Now, this woman had taught for a few years after leaving college and then had gone away and led a somewhat secluded life for a good many years. "Going to Europe" was to her a symbol, not of snow mountains, or cathedrals, or pictures, but of meeting people—that was what she wanted. When she was asked to teach in a summer school of young men and women where she would meet a rather interesting staff of teachers and a rather interesting group of students, she immediately accepted. This was her integration. This was not a substitution for her wish, it was her *real* wish fulfilled.

I have given other illustrations of symbols in Chapter IX of my book, *Creative Experience.* There was an interesting one in the Loeb-Leopold case. I think there should have been taken into consideration in that case what life imprisonment symbolized. As there was no question of freeing the boys, the decision was to be made between death and life imprisonment. Therefore, when the latter sentence was given, that was a symbol, it seemed to me, of victory for the boys, especially since everyone thought that their detention would last only a few years. In many cases, on the other hand, life imprisonment is a symbol of defeat. I do not think that this was taken into account sufficiently in considering the effect of the sentence on the country.

It is, of course, unavoidable to use symbols; all language is symbolic; but we should be always on our guard as to what is symbolized. For instance, the marketing cooperatives say that they want their members to keep their pledges. That statement is a symbol for what they *really* want, which is to get enough of the commodity to control the market. Every day we use many more not-understood symbols, many more whole-words, unanalysed words, than we ought to. Much of what is written of the "consumer" is inaccurate because consumer is used as a whole-word, whereas it is quite obvious that the consumer of large wealth has different desires and motives from the consumer of small means.

We have been considering the breaking up of the whole-demand. On the other hand, one often has to do just the opposite; find the whole-demand, the real demand, which is being obscured by miscellaneous minor claims or by ineffective presentation. The man with a genius for leadership is the one who can make articulate the whole-demand, unless it is a matter of tactics deliberately to conceal it. I shall not stop to give instances of this, as I wish to have time for some consideration of a point which seems to me very important for business, both in dealings with employees and with competing firms, and that is the anticipation of demands, of difference, of conflict.

Mr. Earl Howard, labour manager for Hart, Schaffner and Marx, said to me once, "It isn't enough merely to study the actual reactions of your employees; you must anticipate their reactions, beat them to it." That—to beat them to it—is exactly what each firm does try to do with its competing firms, but I do not think many managers study and anticipate the reactions of their employees as carefully as they do those of competing firms. It would be just as useful.

You could probably give me many illustrations of the *anticipation of response*. We could find innumerable examples in our households. A man liked motoring, his wife walking; he anticipated what her response might be to a suggestion that they motor on Sunday afternoon by tiring her out playing tennis in the morning.

The middlemen are deliberately anticipating response on the part of the farmers. In their struggle with the marketing co-operatives, they are basing their calculations of the future on the assumption that the particularistic tendency of the farmer is such that he cannot be held in line permanently, that he has been carried off his feet by victory and promises; moreover, that the use of legal power in enforcing contracts will in the end defeat the movement, that the farmer will surely rebel against this sort of coercion.

The anticipation of conflict, it should be noted, does not mean necessarily the avoidance of conflict, but playing the game differently. That is, you integrate the different interests without making all the moves. A friend of mine says that my theory of integration is like a game of chess. I think it is something like that. The tyro has to find his solution by making his actual moves, by the crude method of changing the places of his chessmen. A good chess player does not need to do this, he sees the possibilities without playing them out. The business man in dealing with competitive firms is like the good chess player. As the real conflict between two good chess players is a conflict of possibilities that would be realized if they played them out, so in business you do not have to make all the moves to make your integrations; you deal with antecedents, premonitory symptoms, etc. You do not avoid doing certain things, you have done them without doing them.

But assuming that in our business we do watch response and anticipate response, that still is not going far enough. It is not enough to ask to what our employee or our business confrère or business competitor is responding, nor even to what he is likely to respond. We have to prepare the way for response, we have to try to build up in him a certain attitude. Of course every good salesman does this, but its necessity is not so fully recognized in other departments, and we shall therefore consider this question further in a later paper.

Yet even *preparation for response* is only a small part of the matter; we shall have to go deeper than that. There is *circular* as well as *linear* response, and the exposition of that is I think the most interesting contribution of contemporary psychology to the social sciences.[6] A good example of circular response is a game of tennis. A serves. The way B returns the ball depends partly on the way it was served to him. A's next play will depend on his own original serve plus the return of B, and so on and so on. We see this in discussion. We see this in most activity between one and another. Mischievous or idle boys say, "Let's start something"; we must remember that whenever we act we have always "started something," behaviour precipitates behaviour in others. Every employer should remember this. One of the managers in a factory expressed it to me thus: "I am in command of a situation until I behave; when I act I have lost control of the situation." This does not mean that we should not act! It is, however, something to which it is very important that we give full consideration.

Circular response seems a simple matter, quite obvious, something we must all accept. Yet every day we try to evade it, every day we act and hope to avoid the inescapable response. As someone has said in another connection, "We feed Cerberus raw meat and hope that when we lie between his paws, he will turn out to be a vegetarian."

The conception of circular behaviour throws much light on conflict, for I now realize that I can never fight you, I am always fighting you plus me. I have put it this way: that response is always to a relation. I respond, not only to you, but to the relation between you and me. Employees do not respond only to their employers, but to the relation between themselves and their employer. Trade unionism is responding, not only to capitalism, but to the relation between itself and capitalism. The Dawes plan, the London Conference, were obviously moments in circular behaviour. Circular behaviour as the basis of integration gives us the key to constructive conflict.

OBSTACLES TO INTEGRATION

Finally, let us consider the chief *obstacles to integration*. It requires a high order of intelligence, keen perception and discrimination, more than all, a brilliant inventiveness; it is easier for the trade union to fight than to suggest a better way of running the factory. You remember that the Socialist Party in Italy had a majority before Mussolini came in. But they would not take responsibility; they preferred to stay fighting, to attack what others were doing rather than to do themselves. They do not, I think, compare favourably with the English Labour Party.

Another obstacle to integration is that our way of life has habituated many of us to enjoy domination. Integration seems to many a tamer affair; it leaves no "thrills" of conquest. I knew a dispute within a trade union where, by the skillful action of the chairman, a true integration was discovered and accepted, but instead of the satisfaction one might have expected from such a happy result, the evening seemed to end rather dully, flatly; there was no climax, there was no side left swelling its chest, no one had conquered, no one had "won out." It is even true that to some people defeat, as well as conquest, is more interesting than integration. That is, the person with decided fight habits feels more at home, happier, in the fight movement. Moreover, it leaves the door open for further fighting, with the possibility of conquest the next time.

Another obstacle to integration is that the matter in dispute is often theorized over instead of being taken up as a proposed activity. I think this important in business administration. Intellectual agreement does not alone bring full integration. I know one factory which deliberately provides for this by the many activities of its many sub-committees, some of which seem rather trivial unless one sees just how these activities are a contribution to that functional unity which we shall consider in a later paper.

I have been interested to watch how often disagreement disappears when theorizing ends and the question is of some definite activity to be undertaken. At a trade union conference, someone brought up the question of waste: how could the workmen help to eliminate waste? But it was found that most of the union men did not think it the job of the workmen to eliminate waste; that belonged to the management. Moreover, they did not think it to their interest to eliminate waste; wages were fixed by the union, by collective bargaining; everything saved went to swell profits; no more went into their pockets. It was seen, however, that there was another side, and the argument went on, but without coming to any agreement. Finally, however, by some manœuvering on the part of the chairman, it was acknowledged that there were certain forms of waste which the unions could be got to take cognizance of. A machinist, a plumber and a carpenter undertook to take up with their unions the question of how far they could agree to take some responsibility for these particular types of waste. I hope the fact then emerged, when it was considered as a practical issue, that for some forms of waste the management is responsible, for some forms the employees, and for some forms the union.

A serious obstacle to integration which every business man should consider is the language used. We have noted the necessity of making preparation in the other man, and in ourselves too, for the attitude most favourable to reconciliation. A trade unionist said to me, "Our representatives didn't manage it right. If instead of a 15 percent increase they had asked for an adjustment of wages, the management would have been more willing to listen to us; it would have put them in a different frame of mind." I don't quite see why we are not more careful about our language in business, for in most delicate situations we quite consciously choose that which will not arouse antagonism. You say to your wife at breakfast, "Let's reconsider that decision we came to last night." You do not say, "I wish to give you my criticism of the decision you made last night."

I cannot refrain from mentioning a personal experience. I went into the Edison Electric Light Company and said to a young woman at a counter, "Where shall I go to speak about my bill?" "Room D for complaints," she replied. "But I don't wish to make a complaint," I said. "I thought there was a mistake in your bill." "I think there is," I said, "but I don't wish to complain about it; it was a very natural mistake." The girl looked nonplussed, and as she was obviously speechless a man came out from behind a desk and said: "You would prefer to ask for an adjustment, wouldn't you?" and we had a chat about it.

I think that the "grievance committees" which exist in most factories are a mistake. I do not like the "trouble specialists" of the Ford plant. I wish it were not so often stated that shop or department committees were formed to "settle disputes." If you will get lists of these so-called "disputes," you will find that often they have not so much of the fight element in them as this word implies. But much of the language expressing the relation between capital and labour is that of a fight: "traditional enemies," the "weapon of the union," etc.

I have left untouched one of the chief obstacles to integration— namely, the undue influence of leaders—the manipulation of the unscrupulous on the one hand and the suggestibility of the crowd on the other. Moreover, even when the power of suggestion is not used deliberately, it exists in all meetings between people; the whole emotional field of human intercourse has to be taken fully into account in dealing with methods of reconciliation. I am deliberately omitting the consideration of this, not because I do not feel its importance as keenly as anyone, but because in these few papers we cannot cover everything.

Finally, perhaps the greatest of all obstacles to integration is our lack of training for it. In our college debates we try always to beat the other side. In the circular announcing the courses to be given at the Bryn Mawr Summer School for Workers, I find: "English Composition and Public Speaking; to develop the art of oral and written expression." I think that in addition to this there should be classes in discussion which should aim to teach the "art" of cooperative thinking, and I was disappointed that there was no such course in the programme of a school for workers. Managers need it just as much. I have found, in the case of the wage boards which I have been on, that many employers (I ought in fairness to say not the majority) came to these joint conferences of employers and employees with little notion of conferring, but to push through, to force through, plans *previously* arrived at, based on *preconceived* ideas of what employees are like. It seems as if the methods of genuine conference have yet to be learned. Even if there were not the barriers of an unenlightened self-interest, of prejudice, rigidity, dogmatism, routine, there would still be required training and practice for us to master the technique of integration. A friend of mine said to me, "Open-mindedness is the whole thing, isn't it?" No, it isn't; it needs just as great a respect for your own view as for that of others, and a firm upholding of it until you are convinced. Mushy people are no more good at this than stubborn people.

As an indirect summing up of this discussion, I should like to emphasize our responsibility for integration. We saw in our consideration of circular response that my behaviour helps create the situation to which I am responding. That implies (what we have daily to take into account) that my behaviour is helping to *develop* the situation to which I am responding. The standard of living goes up not only while, but partly because, it is being studied. This conception of the developing situation is of the utmost importance for business administration. It makes it impossible to construct a map of the future, yet all our maxims of foresight hold good; every business should reconcile these two statements. We should work always with the evolving situation, and note what part our own activities have in that evolving situation.

This is the most important word, not only for business relations, but for all human relations: not to adapt ourselves to a situation—we are all more necessary to the world than that; neither to mould a situation to *our* liking—we are all, or rather each, of too little importance to the world for that; but to take account of that reciprocal adjustment, that interactive behaviour between the situation and ourselves which means a change in both the situation and ourselves. One test of business administration should be: is the organization such that both employers and employees, or co-managers, co-directors, are stimulated to a reciprocal activity which will give more than mere adjustment, more than an equilibrium? Our outlook is narrowed, our activity is restricted, our chances of business success largely diminished when our thinking is constrained within the limits of what has been called an either-or situation. We should never allow ourselves to be bullied by an "either-or." There is often the possibility of something better than either of two given alternatives. Every one of us interested in any form of constructive work is looking for the plus values of our activity. In a later paper, on *Business as an Integrative Unity,* we shall consider how we can find in business administration those plus values which alone mean progress, progress for the individual and for whatever business or service we have undertaken for ourselves and for our community.

NOTES

1. *Cf. Creative Experience,* p. 300: "What people often mean by getting rid of conflict is getting rid of diversity, and it is of the utmost importance that these should not be considered the same. We may wish to abolish conflict, but we cannot get rid of diversity. We must face life as it is and understand that diversity is its most essential feature. . . . Fear of difference is dread of life itself. It is possible to conceive conflict as not necessarily a wasteful outbreak of incompatibilities, but a *normal* process by which socially valuable differences register themselves for the enrichment of all concerned."

2. *Cf. The New State,* Chapter XIV, for a discussion of the relations of capital and labour. "The weakness of arbitration and conciliation boards, with their

'impartial' member, is that they tend to mere compromise even when they are not openly negotiations between two warring parties" (p. 115).

3. For a fuller exposition of the principle of integration as the foundation of Mary Follett's thought on the subject of group psychology, see *Creative Experience*, Chapter IX, "Experience as Creating." *Cf.* p. 156: "Integration, the most suggestive word of contemporary psychology, is, I believe, the active principle of human intercourse scientifically lived."

4. In a Letter to the Editor in *The Times*, June 6th, 1924, Professor Gilbert Murray writes to draw attention to the influence of previous decisions and methods of the League of Nations on the members of the Dawes Committee. He quotes four matters on which French and British opinion was widely divergent, but where agreement was reached by the mutual adoption of League solutions in previous comparable problems. These instances are illustrations of the method of "integration" that Mary Follett was so keen to expound. (The matters in dispute were: the currency of German reparations payments; the fixation of total German liability; the necessity of external control, or wisdom of trusting completely to German good faith; the relation of German capacity to pay to the problem of fixing the final total liability.)

5. *Cf. Creative Experience*, pp. 167–8: "Again, labour and capital can never be reconciled as long as labour persists in thinking that there is a capitalist point of view and capitalists that there is a labour point of view. There is not. These are imaginary wholes which must be broken up before capital and labour can co-operate."

6. *Cf. Creative Experience*, Chapter III, "Experience in the Light of Recent Psychology: Circular Response" [Chapter 1 of this volume].

COMMENTARY

Follett: Constructive Conflict

John Child

I FIRST came across the work of Mary Parker Follett in 1963 when, as a doctoral student, I was tracing the development of British thinking on management.[1] Although Follett was virtually forgotten by that time, it was apparent that some decades earlier she had enjoyed a significant presence in the British management movement through the lectures she gave at Oxford and the London School of Economics, and through the subsequent efforts of Lyndall Urwick and Henry Metcalf to have these published. The more I read her lectures and papers, the more I was taken with the clarity, force, and practical relevance of her ideas. The result was that she had pride of place in the very first course of lectures I gave in 1967 as a young research fellow at Aston University. Since that happy introduction 30 years ago, Follett has influenced almost every facet of my teaching and research.

It became quite evident to me that Follett was considerably more sensitive to the realities of relationships in industry than were her contemporary American writers on management. It is instructive in this respect to compare her with Elton Mayo, whose approach was seen at the time to be complementary to Follett's, yet soon came to eclipse it. Why this was so is part of the Follett enigma, and I think it may have been due to two main factors. First, Mayo's advocacy of the so-called human relations approach secured much greater publicity, partly because it claimed the backing of the famous Hawthorne experiments at Western Electric Company and partly because of Mayo's powerful institutional position at the Harvard Business School. Second, Mayo's approach appealed directly to managers, conveying as it did a welcome and straightforward message. It ascribed a privileged rationality to managers that legitimated their authority and was naturally attractive to members of the management movement working on their behalf. So when British management writers (including Urwick) looked to synthesize the ideas of the two thinkers into a common managerial philosophy, they adopted a vision of paternalistic, top-down management that came primarily from Mayo and his colleagues and that was, in fact, intrinsically alien to Follett's basic premises.

There was, for example, a very significant divergence between Follett's concept of constructive conflict, which is the subject of this chapter, and Mayo's deep abhorrence of conflict in any form.

Follett believed that people at all levels in an enterprise could come rationally to accept the "law of the situation" and that therefore, through discussion, a mutually acceptable and innovative integrative solution could be found to many conflicts. She anticipated that integration could be achieved through participation in decision making, on the basis of the functional knowledge that each party to an issue could offer. Mayo and his colleagues, by contrast, assumed that ordinary employees were largely governed by a "logic of sentiment," which was of a different order from managers' rational appraisal of the situation in terms of costs and efficiency. Conflict with management was thus an aberration that threatened the effectiveness of organizations. Although my internal Ph.D. examiner accused me of having shown inadequate respect in my thesis to Mayo's arguments, I still maintain that they appeared naive, and even disingenuous, when set beside those that Follett advanced. It did not add to the quality of British management thinking that the human relations school obscured Follett's recommendations, which derived from a more profound social, political, and psychological understanding of relationships.

In any event, it is Follett who has stood the test of time. With the benefit of hindsight, we can see how her ideas and insights anticipated by some 40 years several mainstreams of contemporary conventional management wisdom. Her approach to participative problem solving, based on the concepts of constructive conflict and power-with, anticipated both the work of Likert and McGregor on participative leadership, and the principles of effective teamwork expounded more recently by Tom Peters and others. The lectures she gave at the London School of Economics in 1933 on coordination and the process of control in many respects foreshadow the analysis of integration and differentiation advanced by Lawrence and Lorsch. Perhaps most fundamental of all, the "law of the situation," which was for Follett the benchmark against which organizational decisions should be made, and against which integrative solutions to conflicts could be found, directly anticipates modern contingency analysis—still the most useful perspective on offer to practicing managers.

Follett was concerned to find "the most fruitful way of dealing with conflict."[2] Her great insight was to recognize that conflict was not necessarily pathological and a manifestation of failure. It was, rather, the "appearance of difference."[3] Difference was unavoidable in the world, and since it reflected a variety of opinions and interests, it could be used creatively. Follett identified three "main ways" of dealing with conflict. Domination by one party over the other(s) offered a quick solution, but one that was unstable because it bred resentment and unconstructive because it suppressed nondominant perspectives that had the potential to add value. Compromise, the second mode, was likely to leave all parties dissatisfied and to result in a suboptimum solution. The third method of conflict resolution, and the one Follett advocated, was integration. This entailed the search for an innovative solution, "in which both [or all] desires have found a place."[4] The most fruitful way of dealing with conflict, in Follett's view, was the one that would leave the parties satisfied and at the same time promote organizational learning. She warned that it would be naive to assume that integration is always possible, but claimed, nevertheless, that it is often feasible and worth the attempt.

What links Follett's analysis to modern thinking and justifies the description of her whole approach as one of *dynamic* administration (as Metcalf and Urwick chose to call it) is the insight that "Integration involves invention, and the clever thing is to recognize this, and not to let one's thinking stay within the boundaries of two alternatives which are mutually exclusive."[5] She also recognized that the *process* of conflict has to be understood in order for the phenomenon to be dealt with constructively. The concept of circular behavior indicates that in a conflict situation people react not just to others, but also to the relationships pertaining between them.

In addition, the parties involved in conflict may well realign and reevaluate their interests during the process.

Only a reading of the lecture itself will adequately convey the richness of Follett's analysis and its essential practicality. Quite remarkable is the way that the whole tenor of her argument, stressing the possibilities for a fluid and positive reconstruction of structured positions, anticipates Giddens's concept of structuration, which has been so influential in modern sociology. Rephrasing this in Follettian terms expresses one of the most powerful and hopeful insights into our social life, namely, that we have the power through open debate and discussion to examine and reconstitute the assumptions and structures within which we are confined. This, for me, has been the real message of constructive conflict.

There are two areas of management, both of major contemporary importance, into which Follett's analysis of constructive conflict has given me new insights. The first concerns the introduction and implementation of information technology in the workplace. The second is the management of international business ventures.

The introduction of powerful new integrated systems of information technology opens up the possibility of radical changes in the organization of work, hence it exposes the conflicting interests and perspectives of different occupational groups that might at other times remain relatively subdued. Ray Loveridge and I concluded from an examination of how IT had been introduced in European services that the process is one of "contested learning."[6] Learning to use IT is necessarily contested because (1) the technology offers considerable choice in how it is used, (2) these choices can have considerable costs and benefits for the employment, career advancement, and intrinsic job interest of different groups, and (3) IT is sufficiently new for no one professional group to have established hegemony over it as the unchallenged experts on its use.

Our investigation into 35 different cases of IT introduction, in European banking, health care, and retailing businesses, led to the conclusion that in most of them the full potential of the new technology was not being realized. The reasons for this lay in the fact that decisions on IT implementation were often being reached either on the basis of domination by a coalition of top management and IT support specialists, or through an inadequate compromise arising from the issue becoming enmeshed within a traditional industrial-relations bargaining framework. The most innovative uses of IT were found in Sweden, where a much more participative and problem-solving approach was generally adopted, albeit in somewhat ponderous form. Our overall conclusion appears, on reflection, to constitute a total vindication of Follett's insights on the constructive handling of conflict:

> The rapid development of IT will not be achieved without the establishment of more open and informed discourse between those at the level of strategic decision-making and those at the level of direct operations where these decisions are implemented. The greatest single barrier to effective learning in this most vital of developments for our future lies in the organizational inhibitions that prevent the free interchange of views from all who have something to offer.[7]

I turn now to internationals, the second area in which Follett's analysis of constructive conflict has given me new insights. The number of international business alliances and joint ventures has exploded since the mid-1980s, as has the value of the foreign direct investment on which they are founded. Many of them have the potential to contribute in a vital manner to the advancement of developing countries through the technology, knowledge, and standards they transfer. They are, however, a notoriously difficult form of organization to manage, especially when they are structured as joint ventures between partners whose interests, approaches to management, and national cultures often differ. The constructive resolution of conflict is essential to their success, both for the immediate task of putting together a viable operation and for promoting effective learning between joint staffs and managements over the longer term.

Studies that colleagues and I have made of international joint ventures between foreign investors and local companies in China and Hungary have identified different ways in which mutual accommodation can be reached. These appear to have different implications for their longer-term development. We have found that Follett's categorization of conflict-resolution modes provides the best available starting point for distinguishing between these approaches and for drawing out their consequences for organizational learning.[8]

Domination by investing foreign joint-venture partners is frequently found in two main forms. The first we have called "forced learning," in which the foreign partners attempt unilaterally to force through changes in management and working practices. They usually try to do this through extensive resocialization of local staff via training programs and the introduction of new incentive systems. Although the term "forced" refers to the way in which the process of change is brought about, not necessarily how it is perceived by those on the receiving end, it often meets with reluctance on the part of host-country personnel. It may give rise to behavioral changes, but not new understanding (cognitive change) or personal acceptance. The second form of domination is manifest in "imitation." Here there may be little resistance to foreign methods, but these are copied and followed without much apparent new understanding, or (in that sense) much personal engagement, on the part of host-country staff. For example, in several Hungarian joint ventures the previous dependence of managers on higher government authorities was transferred to a new dependence on foreign "expert" partners, in which their instructions were followed but without much apparent new understanding. As a result, the Hungarians were unable to contribute to the integration of foreign thinking with their knowledge of the local situation in a way that would have led to a more innovative approach.

A form of compromise that side-steps the challenge of integration is what we have called "segmentation." Here one partner manages certain activities of the venture according to its preferred approach, while the other partner does so in other areas. This approach may serve to avoid certain conflicts between the two sets of managers and staff, but it clearly affords very limited opportunities for learning between them.

Integration was the declared aspiration of a number of foreign joint venture partners, but it was actually found in only a few cases. One Sino-American venture had, by and large, adopted Follett's principles without being aware of their origin. It devoted much time to consensus-building discussions, which allowed Chinese staff to contribute actively to the formulation of policy. This effort to align everyone's objectives in a common direction through participatory group discussion removed some of the reluctance of the Chinese personnel to assume responsibility for decisions because the process led them to understand and commit to policy. They also became aware that they enjoyed support from their foreign colleagues for actions they took in line with agreed-on objectives. This joint venture was able to achieve both cultural synergy and a close alignment between the partners' objectives in the manner Follett recommended.

As Follett pointed out, domination by those who claim superior knowledge, be they IT specialists or the exponents of a long-established management tradition, will often produce fast results—the quick fix or big bang. Integration, however, offers far better prospects for a long-term solution that enjoys the understanding and support of all groups concerned and promotes the kind of learning experience that may well continue to reproduce and sustain itself. Follett's guidelines on the constructive handling of conflict still afford some of the best advice in the whole literature on management today.

NOTES

1. John Child, *British Management Thought* (London: Allen & Unwin, 1969).
2. Henry C. Metcalf, and L. Urwick, eds., *Dynamic Administration: The Collected Papers of Mary Parker Follett* (London: Pitman, 1941), p. 30. [In this volume, the reference appears on p. 67.]
3. Ibid. [In this volume, p. 67.]
4. Ibid., p. 32. [In this volume, p. 69.]
5. Ibid., p. 33. [In this volume, p. 70.]
6. John Child and Ray Loveridge, *Information Technology in European Services* (Oxford: Blackwell, 1990).
7. Ibid., p. 382.
8. John Child and Livia Markoczy, "Host-Country Managerial Behaviour and Learning in Chinese and Hungarian Joint Ventures," *Journal of Management Studies*, vol. 30, pp. 611–631.

THREE

Power

I ASKED a number of workmen in two factories, both of which had some form of employee representation, "If a question came up where you had to decide between loyalty to your union and loyalty to the works, which would you choose?" The answer was always, "The union." Then I asked for their reasons, and here is the summary: (1) "I have taken an oath to the union; (2) the union is a permanent relation, the factory is not; (3) the unions have power back of them, the works council has not." Oath, permanency, power, but the greatest of these, I felt, was power.[1]

Power, or control, is a word which we find on almost every page of English labour literature, and frequently enough in our own. One of the leaders of the Sheffield Shop Stewards movement said: "We organize for power," the baldest and most succinct statement I have seen.

One of the most urgent problems of business today is the relation of bargaining to value, and bargaining rests on power. He seems to get the best of the bargaining who has the greatest power. But is bargaining the only determinant of value, whether of goods, labour, or what not? What of scientific management? Does not

Note: This chapter is reprinted from Elliot M. Fox and L. Urwick, eds., *Dynamic Administration: The Collected Papers of Mary Parker Follett* (London: Pitman, 1973), pp. 66–87. This paper was first presented before a Bureau of Personnel Administration conference group in January 1925.

every business man find one of his most pressing problems to be: how to integrate bargaining and scientific methods? As far as I have seen, scientific methods do not, cannot perhaps, set exact values; at present they merely set the limits of the bargaining process. Within those limits bargaining still goes on.

In discussing this question of power, we shall first give some general consideration to the subject and then to labour's demand for power.

THE "URGE" TO POWER

No word is used more carelessly by us all than the word "power." I know no conception which needs today more careful analysis. We have not even decided whether power is a "good" word or a "bad" word. Is the wish for power the desire of grasping and unscrupulous men, is it the "instinctive" urge of our lower natures; or is power a noble, the noblest, aim? Or is it neither of these? What is power? Is it influence, is it leadership, is it force? Why do we all like power? Because we wish to use it to satisfy our desires, or do we just like the feeling in itself? In the case of the men you meet every day in business, either your business associates or your workmen, do you find them trying to satisfy an "urge" to power; or do you find them merely trying to get what they want and seeking power in order to secure their ends? We are often told that there are many men who, after they have accumulated enough wealth to satisfy every want, keep on accumulating from mere love of power. Do you think this is so or do you think that there are still unsatisfied desires which motivate their activity?

Among the psychologists there is much difference of opinion on this subject. Some tell us that the urge to power is instinctive, is inherent in all human beings; others deny this and say that power is desired merely as means to an end. Dr. Floyd H. Allport, in his *Social Psychology*,[2] tends toward the former point of view. Dealing with social control, he tells us that there is a universal tendency to produce reactions in others, a tendency which probably originated in the habit developed in infancy and early childhood of controlling parents and nurses in order to secure satisfaction of the bodily needs. As we grow up and become more self-sufficient, the old habit persists in an inclination to control merely for the sake of controlling; not now, you see, means to end. I do not know whether this is so or not, for I do not think we have sufficient proof yet to establish its validity, but it is certainly interesting. Dr. Allport points out that the drive for the control of others (he has committed himself to a good deal by using the word "drive") often does not go to the extent of trying to determine their reactions, but simply to make them react. We could all give instances of this. My guide in the Adirondacks, if we came on a deer out of the hunting season, as we paddled up some lonely creek, would startle me, after an instant's silence, with a sudden yell. He could not shoot, but he could shout and make the deer run, make it *do* something.

We often see between two people the wish, not necessarily to get submissive reactions, but to get any reactions at all. A man will deliberately rustle his newspaper so that his wife will react in some way. She may not look up and smile either; she may frown, or she may irritably ask him to stop making a noise, but he gets some satisfaction even from that. (Perhaps I ought in fairness to add that the only time I have seen this done, it was the wife who rattled the newspaper.)

There are jurists also who talk of a "natural urge" to power, who tell us that the wish to keep a balance of power is such an urge. They say, for instance, that when you feel gratitude, it is the "urge" to regain an equilibrium which has been destroyed by the favour you have had conferred upon you. We can call it by a fine name, elevate it to a virtue, but what it really means is, we are told, that if I am under obligation to you for some favour conferred, I feel an unpleasant sense of your power, and so I return the favour in some way in order to restore the equilibrium between us which has been disturbed. This seemed to me a very strange idea the first time I came across it, but that very day I asked a man, staying in Boston to give a month's lectures at the Harvard Business School, what he thought of the idea, and instead of saying, as I expected, that it was absurd, he replied: "Of course it's so; here I am spending a month with [a well-known man in Boston] and I shall feel that I am in his power until I can think of some way of paying it back."

Some ethical teachers tell us that the whole subject resolves itself into the question: What do you want power for? This is not a wholly bad question for those interested in business administration. Take the alarm over absentee ownership voiced by a number of people. A good thing, too, that it should be; yet when we hear of the effort of some management to free itself from the domination of absentee-owned capital, we immediately think, What is their motive?

Bertrand Russell has had a good deal to say lately about the *motive* for power. He is very pessimistic over the development of science, for he says that the benefits go to the power-holders, and that the purposes of the power-holders are in the main evil.

But whether power is "good" or "bad," whether it is sought as means to end or as end in itself, most people are much of the time trying to get power. In conversation people try to impress others with their ideas, their feelings or their personal experiences. Some writers call this the egoistic impulse, but that seems too general; on further analysis we should probably find that it comes from the desire for ascendancy. For instance, the psychologists tell us that we like telling a good story because it makes us the centre of interest. Perhaps, in addition to this, it is because for that moment we are controlling others, for an instant we have others completely under our sway. And we must remember that this desire for ascendancy which we see in some form in almost every conversation, is by no means always, nor perhaps usually, because we wish to use at the moment the power gained; we like to bank our power, and keep a good balance on hand to use in large lumps as occasions arise when such use would be of distinct benefit to us.

I think the best way of understanding power would be to make some study of it in our daily lives—in our homes, in our business, or wherever we are—to observe when it appears and why and what the results are. I am always hoping in a group of this kind to find some one or two who will be sufficiently interested to do this with me, watch to see what gives one person influence over another: social position, professional standing, the special knowledge of the expert, wide experience, mere wealth, age, sex, certain personal characteristics, even physical strength. If any of you will do this I want to suggest that in such study you take provisionally the following definitions of power, control, authority, and see what you think of them. Power might be defined as simply the ability to make things happen, to be a causal agent, to initiate change.[3] Perhaps the "urge to power" is merely the satisfaction of being alive. Of course there are many different kinds and degrees of satisfaction. The boy throwing stones at a bird gives us an example of a very elementary kind; his "urge" is to make the bird do something—fly away. As a fuller kind of satisfaction we might note that of the violinist. It has always seemed to me that the violinist must get one of the greatest satisfactions of being alive; all of him is enlisted, he surely feels power. Probably the leader of an orchestra feels more. And this comes nearer the kind of power the head of a business feels.

Control might be defined as power exercised as means toward a specific end; authority, as vested control. And we should remember in this study that power and strength are not always synonymous; it is sometimes through our weakness that we get control of a situation. In the London Conference last summer Germany's greatest power was her economic impotence. That is, her bargaining power was the result of the economic condition to which she had been reduced by the demands made upon her by the Allies. We all know that the invalid in a household has, and sometimes exercises quite ruthlessly, power over the well and strong members of the family.

We should notice, too, in this observation of power which I am urging, all the different uses of the word. I saw the other day "the power of Wall Street" spoken of as an ominous thing. Is the power of Wall Street a good thing, a bad thing, or neither? A man said to me once: "I like deer shooting because it gives me a sense of power." Robert Wolf's method of beating one's own record, which he has used so successfully, is in part an appeal to the sense of power. As I have just mentioned Wall Street, we might perhaps to some advantage compare the power of Wall Street with the power aimed at by Mr. Wolf for his workers. I have found this observation of the way the word power is used an interesting study. I am making a list of all the different definitions I come across, by novelists or artists or wherever, and I find this all helping me in my observation of power in everyday life. I think it would help also in business administration, make us more alert and more discriminating; make us wiser in our decision when an employee asks for more "power," when he claims that something belongs to his province which we had taken for granted was in ours. We may decide for him or against him, I am not saying that this foretells what our decision will be, but if we have given some attention to this subject, we shall feel surer that our decision is just; we shall also be able to save time when examining his claims by this preliminary consideration of the subject, by knowing a little where we stand in general before we have to take up a particular situation.

A very interesting thing to observe, which I must not omit to mention, is the connection between rivalry and power. I wish you would watch yourselves and competing firms and see if you can draw any line between rivalry and "urge to power." The psychologists see a difference here. One tells us that in contests of strength of handgrip between two boys in laboratory experiments, it was found that the rivalry attitude gave way almost immediately to an attitude on the part of the stronger to *conquer* his opponent. This is significant for business competition.

We have innumerable opportunities for the study of power; we might to great advantage, I think, study the farmers' present striving for power. Are they seeking merely higher and more uniform prices; or do they wish to gain power over, or equal to, other groups?

I think one certain gain would come from a study of power: we should learn to distinguish between different kinds of power. For instance, there is the man who beats his rivals by getting, by hook or crook, special privileges in regard to freight rates. That gives him power. But the man who beats his rivals through better business administration, by producing better goods at equal price to the consumer, or the same goods at less price, has power too. We have here obviously two different kinds of power.

POWER-WITH VERSUS POWER-OVER

We have been considering what we must watch if we wish to study the question of power. Let us see if we can get a little nearer the core of this question. So far as my observation has gone, it seems to me that whereas power usually means power-over, the power of some person or group over some other person or group, it is possible to develop the conception of power-with, a jointly developed power, a co-active, not a coercive power.[4] In store or factory I do not think the management should have power *over* the workmen, or the workmen over the management. It is right for the employers to resist any effort of the unions to get power-over. In discussing *Business as an Integrative Unity* we considered the difference between the "independent" power which the English labour unions are seeking (I use their expression) and joint power. Every demand for power should be analysed to see if the object is "independent" power or joint power. That should be one of the tests of any plan of employee representation—is it developing joint power?

If anyone thinks that the distinction between power-over and power-with is a fanciful or personal distinction, I am pleased to be able to say that these two prepositions are used to mark a distinction in law; you have rights over a slave, you have rights with a servant.

Of course at present, as I have said, most of us are trying to get power-over. Much of what is called "applied psychology" has this for its aim. The salesmanship classes teach this (although I tried to show in discussing "The Giving of Orders" that a sounder psychology could do better than this); the men being told how to conduct business interviews are being taught this. The so-called psychology of advertising is not concerned with giving information but with gaining power. Many of the trade unionists in the labour education movement wish education for power, that is, increased power in the fight with capital. The head of a Central Labour Union said to me: "I'm for the Trade Union College; we lose out because we send a $1,500 man to meet a $10,000 man; the trade unionists have got to educate themselves." I must in justice, however, add that I know unionists who are trying to develop power in the unions in the sense of increased ability to join with management in a co-operating efficiency, a co-operating responsibility, and this is a happy sign.[5]

And I certainly need not go to either capital or labour to find examples of power-over. Reformers, propagandists, many of our "best" people are willing to coerce others in order to attain an end which *they* think good. I have seen it stated, in what was supposed to be a progressive article, that workmen should be led, not driven. Well, leading is often power-over. The demagogue, the ward boss, the labour leader, the crowd orator, all lead, all try to "persuade"—a very innocent sounding word until you examine it. A workman, however, said to me: "In this factory they don't just try to persuade us, they try to convince us"—a very discriminating statement on the part of this man and a tribute to the management of that factory.

This is something we have to watch for in our study of power, in a conference between two or three business men, a consultation of doctors or wherever, namely, how far persuasion is taking the form of power-over. Some very keen observation and subtle discrimination are needed here, for you will see many ways by which this is sought: reason, suggestion, emotion, ascendancy of personality, etc. And since industry today is tending toward the conference method, toward committee government, this is an important study. One of the tests of conference or committee should be: are we developing genuine power or is someone trying unduly to influence the others? A workman in a plant where there is employee representation said to me: "I don't want to be led and I don't want to be patronized, and I watch all the time to see if I am." Notice particularly the first phrase, "I don't want to be led."

But we are now getting near a subject which I decided not to include in these talks because it has been treated so fully and so adequately by others—by Le Bon, by Martin, by Allport—and that is what crowd psychology tells us of power; it is obvious that the getting of power might be considered largely as a matter of creating conditions favourable to suggestibility. Much of the crowd literature assumes that ninety percent of our life is lived under the laws of suggestion and imitation, which means power-over. Granted as large a percent as you please, I still think we may recognize that there is such a thing as power-with.

The insidiousness of power-over is very well illustrated by Gandhi. Surely his method of non-co-operation was a use of power, the only power he and his followers had: the nonpayment of taxes, the boycotting of English merchandise, refusal of honours and titles, of civil and military posts, refusal to attend schools, etc. Gandhi made declaration of "war to the end." Well, war is war. I cannot see that Gandhi's *method* is so different from that of any strike. In his *Letter to all the English of India* of October 27th, 1920, he said: "I wish to conquer you by my sufferings." Was not this a rationalization in effect? It was literally true, but while to Gandhi this had a high, spiritual sound, what was it really but a wish to gain power, to gain power through suffering? We find nowhere in Gandhi's life, letters or speeches any wish to discover a meeting ground for his party and the English. He says he believes in "the power of the humble," thus using the very word power. Was it their humility which gave Gandhi's party the measure of success which they had, or was it their unanimity, their earnestness and sincerity, their passion of conviction?

We see here how closely power is connected with the fight image when Gandhi calls his struggle a "war of the spirit." In order to make conflict constructive, I think we should try to abolish the war image as rapidly as possible. When the tobacco co-operatives of Greensboro, N.C., were invited to their second annual picnic at the Guilford Battle Ground, they were urged to come to "the spot where our fathers fell in deadly combat with the enemies of political freedom," and hear "the living heroes of today in mortal combat with the subtle, intriguing enemy of farm economic freedom." This is not the spirit of Gandhi, but the same fighting appeal is made in both cases.

This is a rather long introduction to our subject. And these preliminary considerations have been of the most general character. My aim has been, not exhaustive analysis, but to arouse in you a wish to be more analytical toward your own experience in regard to the matter of one person having what is commonly called power over another person, or one group over another group, one nation over another nation.

But even with all that I have left out we have time now to consider only two points, and those very briefly: how to reduce power-over, and labour's demand for power. One way of reducing power-over is through integration, which we considered in our first evening together. The integrating of desires precludes the necessity of gaining power in order to satisfy desire. Do you remember the instance I gave of the conflict in the Dairymen's League in regard to precedence at the creamery platform, a conflict which became so serious that it almost broke up the League? If either side had won in the fight, there would have been power-over, but by finding a solution by which the desires of both sides were satisfied, by integrating the desires of the two sides, power-over was prevented.

I hope it will be seen that what I have called legitimate power is produced by that circular behaviour described in our first talk. This is, I think, almost the heart of the whole matter and deserves more attention than this mere passing notice. Circular behaviour is the basis of integration. If your business is so organized that you can influence a co-manager while he is influencing you, so organized that a workman has an opportunity of influencing you as you have of influencing him; if there is an interactive influence going on all the time between you, power-with may be built up. Throughout history we see that control brings disastrous consequences whenever it outruns integration. Is not that the trouble in India? Russia has to use arbitrary authority because she has not yet learned to integrate. And was it not perhaps the greatest weakness in Woodrow Wilson that he thought control could outrun integration?

We can get still nearer the core of our problem in this matter of reducing power-over by recalling what we spoke of in our second paper, when we were considering the question of giving orders, as the law of the situation. If both sides obey the law of the situation, no *person* has power over another. The present-day respect for facts, for scientific methods, is the first step in this method of seeking the law of the situation, and already we see that it has influenced the whole tone of industrial controversy. Take the case of bargaining between employers and employees. As wages are coming more and more to be fixed by cost-of-living charts, by time-studies, by open books on cost of production, bargaining is more and more eliminated or, I should say, subordinated. It might be put thus: bargaining becomes limited by the boundaries set by scientific methods of business administration; it is only possible within the area thus marked out.

It is the same in international controversy. The pitting of power against power goes on, yet the reports of the expert are today taken into account to such an extent as appreciably to limit the bargaining process. Every commission, industrial or international, has its staff of economists, statisticians, accountants, engineers, experts of all kinds. The Dawes Plan has been spoken of as a triumph of the bankers. Is it not rather a triumph of facts against empty assumptions? The Dawes Plan first of all disposes of certain fictions. Nowhere do we see more clearly than in the case of reparations the value of facts against assumptions; as time went on it came more and more clearly to be seen that it was not a question of "sympathy" for France or for Germany, but of the facts of the situation. Facts, by reducing the area of irreconcilable controversy, reduce power-over.

As clearly as we see that the consideration of facts reduces power-over, do we see that the withholding of facts is often used as a means to gain power-over. The chief weapon of the speculators is to keep facts from the public. Open prices have been fought for years because so many business men have been afraid they would mean a loss of power. The co-operatives have arraigned big business for its secretive methods, yet I know at least one marketing co-operative which refuses to publish warehouse receipts, or to give information as to solvency, to publish prices until the end of the year, to give overhead cost or number of members, because they fear that such information will give power into the hands of the middlemen.

Do we not see now that while there are many ways of gaining an external, an arbitrary power—through brute strength, through manipulation, through diplomacy—genuine power is always that which inheres in the situation? Our first search should always be to discover the law of the situation. For instance, the middlemen are preventing the farmer from having the power which belongs to his situation; it is hoped that the marketing co-operatives will give him that power. Yet, as I have indicated above, we have not got rid of power-over in the co-operatives. I do not think we shall ever get rid of power-over; I do think we should try to reduce it.

To sum up our consideration of power-over. Power-over can be reduced: (1) through integration, (2) through recognizing that all should submit to what I have called the law of the situation, and (3) through making our business more and more of a functional unity. In a functional unity each has his function—and that should correspond as exactly as possible with his capacity—and then he should have the authority and the responsibility which go with that function.

LABOUR'S DEMAND FOR POWER

Perhaps it will throw some light on the subject of power if we consider labour's demand for power. While the employer's attitude on this question of workers' share in management has radically changed of late years; while the employer no longer says, or not often, "These men have the damned impudence to want to run my business," still he has not sufficiently analysed the workers' demand for power. Let us ask ourselves some questions in regard to the workers' wish for what they call share in control.

1. Is this the instinctive urge to power?

2. Is it, on the other hand, a means—to higher wages, shorter hours, better working conditions?

3. Is it the "instinct" of workmanship, and therefore a means to an end? That is, does the workman, suffering sometimes under inefficient management, wish enough share in management to enable him to do his work as he thinks best? The glass-bottle makers in England will not work under a man who is not trained as a glass-bottle hand. It seems obvious that we should encourage all the "power" which tends to increase pride in craft skill.

4. Is it because so many "instincts" are thwarted by modern machine industry; do all these instincts cry out together for "power"?

5. Is there more in the old claim than has yet been recognized, that the worker wants to be treated as a man, not as a "hand"?

6. How far is it an expression of an inferiority complex?

7. Is it to improve status?

8. How far is it a reaction against officialism or the abuses of officialism?

9. Does the worker want to accumulate power to use in the struggle between capital and labour?

10. Is the worker trying to get power without responsibility, those two which can never be divorced? I have seen it stated: "Labour wants wages, hours and security without financial responsibility but with power enough to command respect." How naïve. Many of us would like power without responsibility! Is that possible, or is it the old story of eating and having your cake?

11. Is it that the most fundamental thing in man is his "urge" to self-expression and self-determination, combined with his ever seeking the larger, the more complete? Are these twin impulses at the heart of his being perhaps the chief reason for the workers' demand for power?

You can probably think of other reasons, I have put these eleven down quickly. Further with respect to this point, let us consider especially those two expressions which we hear daily, the delegation of power and the balance of power.

In the literature on employee representation, we read much of the delegation of power. Myers[6] tells us that the power of the Works Committee is "delegated," that the board of directors or the stockholders have the ultimate authority. The Nunn, Bush and Weldon Shoe Co. say that they have "delegated" to their employees the power of fixing wages and hours of work and the right to discharge. I read again, "Authority must be distributed from its source, and filters down through delegation to all parts of business organization." Power must be distributed from its source? Very well, but what is the source? A workman in a factory I was visiting said to me, "Who do you think is the boss here?" It seemed, he said, difficult to discover him. "Is it the Manager of the Works," he asked, "or is it the President? But these are responsible to the Directors. Is it then the Directors? But they are responsible to the people. Is it then the people?" I tried to find out what he meant by the people, but he was rather vague about that. This interested me, however, because I had not thought I should find the old question of sovereignty, which I had struggled with in political and legal science, cropping up in modern industrial organization in such direct manner. The only legitimate boss, sovereignty, is, I believe, the interweaving experience of all those who are performing some functional part of the activity under consideration.[7]

I do not think that power can be delegated because I believe that genuine power is capacity. To confer power on the workers may be an empty gesture. The main problem of the workers is by no means how much control they can wrest from capital or management, often as we hear that stated; that would be a merely nominal authority and would slip quickly from their grasp. Their problem is how much power they can themselves grow. The matter of workers' control which is so often thought of as a matter of how much the managers will be willing to give up, is really as much a matter for the workers, how much they will be able to assume; where the managers come in is that they should give the workers a chance to grow capacity or power for themselves.

There are many ways in which power develops naturally if there is no hindrance. Let me give this as an illustration. We often think of the development of large-scale industry as limiting the individual's opportunity for managing. In some ways this is not true. Take, for instance, what is called "the instinct for workmanship." Formerly, in the time of individual production, this "instinct" was expressed in the individual's own work. Now that individual production has given way to group production, this "instinct" cannot be expressed unless the individual workman has something to say about group organization and the technique of group production. This seems to me a natural development of genuine power.

It is true indeed that the workmen cannot have anything to say about the technique of group production, about group organization, without the co-operation or even the initiative of management; but there is something here which is not covered by the word "delegation."

INTEREST, RESPONSIBILITY, POWER— AN INDISSOLUBLE PARTNERSHIP

One thing should be borne in mind beyond anything else in the consideration of this subject, and that is that you should never give authority faster than you can develop methods for the worker taking responsibility for that authority. We may find also that we should not give workers authority without some corresponding stake in the business. In a certain store which has a form of profit-sharing, the employees voted one December not to open the store on the day after Christmas, after taking into account the number of people likely to come out on that day against the expenses of operation. But in the case of another holiday when the same question came up, thinking that this time there would be no appreciable effect on the numbers of people shopping, they voted to open. They had the "power" in both cases, and if that "power" had been divorced from a stake in the business they would probably have voted in both cases to close the store. Interest, responsibility, power—perhaps here is an indissoluble partnership. Of course in a case like this the responsibility may have been enough without the stake in the business.

We have an unfortunate precedent in the use of such phrases as the delegation of power, etc. Many writers on government say that the power of the State should be *divided* among various groups;

many tell us that power should be *transferred* from one group to another; many that it should be *conferred* on the smaller nations. Hence it has been natural for many economists who write of something they call "industrial democracy" to tell us that the power now held by owners and managers should be *shared* by the workmen. These expressions, while containing indeed a partial truth, nevertheless at the same time *hide* an important truth, namely, that power is self-developing capacity. This fact is hidden by that expression which has become a pet phrase of the guild socialists, "encroaching control." Divided or conferred authority is non-psychological authority; "encroaching control" is not a genuine control. Power is not a pre-existing thing which can be handed out to someone, or wrenched from someone. We have seen again and again the failure of "power" conferred. You could give me dozens of cases. The division of power is not the thing to be considered, but that method of organization which will generate power. The moral right to an authority which has not been psychologically developed, which is not an expression of capacity, is an empty ethics. This applies to management as well as to workers. We have always to study in a plant how far the authority of the management is real, how far it comes from fulfilling function, from knowledge and ability, and how far it is a nominal or an arbitrary authority.

The difficulty of the political scientists quoted in the above paragraph is that they are confusing power and authority. To confer authority where capacity has not been developed is fatal to both government and business. Those political scientists who use the words power, control and authority as synonymous, are confusing our thinking.

If you want the best philosophical as well as the best psychological principle by which to test the legitimacy of "power" (by which you probably mean authority), you will ask whether it is integral to the process or outside the process, that is, whether, as we have said, it grows out of the actual circumstances, whether it is inherent in the situation. You cannot confer power, because power is the blossoming of experience. I think a non-understanding of this is the limitation of an article on "Authority" by Ludwig Stein which came out in the September *Atlantic* and was a good deal talked about by business men. Professor Stein says: "That the Bolsheviki had to substitute for the dictatorship from above one from below is a classical example for the sociology of authority." And again, later on: "The fact that old authorities are overthrown only to permit new ones to be created in their stead irresistibly forces the conclusion that authority represents a social-psychological necessity." It does not force me to that conclusion, but to the conclusion that we shall always be seeking an external, and arbitrary authority until we learn to direct our efforts toward seeking—the law of the situation.

There is something in regard to an authority which is not the recognized law of the situation which we should not fail to note in passing, and that is, that an arbitrary authority may rouse very disagreeable reactions. These not only make things difficult for you, but actually reduce your power. Charles Francis Adams used to say: "Increase powers and you decrease power." And only the other day I heard it said that commissions with mandatory powers have less power than those with advisory powers because they put people's backs up. All this is worth consideration.

And we must not omit to mention that most common of fallacies, that when we join with others, we deliberately give up a part of our "power," as it is called, in order to get certain privileges which will issue from the union. When a grower signs a co-operative contract, he is supposed to give up a certain amount of "power." Does he? His marketing capacity is certainly increased by his joining with others. The delusion of the "independent" farmer is now exposed to all. Take again the notion of the sacrifice of sovereignty, that each nation must sacrifice a part of its sovereignty for the sake of the benefits which will come from a League of Nations. This is the rationalization of the sentimentalist. No nation intends to sacrifice anything; when a nation sees that it is to its interest to become a part of the League of Nations it will do so. Sovereignties must be joined, not sacrificed. We find this fallacy expressed in regard to business administration by those writers who tell us that the manufacturer ought to surrender a part of his power in order to gain a spirit of contentment in the factory.

As a summing up of this question of conferring or sharing power, I should say that if we have any power, any genuine power, let us hold on to it, let us not give it away. We could not anyway if we wanted to. We can confer authority; but power or capacity, no man can give or take. The manager cannot share *his* power with division superintendent or foreman or workmen, but he can give them opportunities for developing *their* power. Functions may have to be redistributed; something the manager does now had better perhaps be left to a division superintendent, to a foreman, even to a workman; but that is a different matter; let us not confuse the two things. Indeed, one of the aims of that very redistribution of function should be how it can serve to evolve more power—more power to turn the wheels. More power, not division of power, should always be our aim; more power for the best possible furtherance of that activity, whatever it may be, to which we are giving our life.

So much for the delegation of power; and now let us consider balance of power. It almost seems as if our conclusions in the preceding paper in regard to joint power did away automatically with the conception of balance of power; yet no conception is more widely held. A labour leader said a few years ago: "We must give up each trying to wrest power from the other side"; so far a very good idea, but he added, "and find an absolute balance of power." He had no notion of a unit of power. I do not think the balance of power will get labour much further than a domination of power.

Myers[8] evidently believes in the balance of power between workers and executives, as do many others. So does Professor Commons, who, in speaking of the desired equilibrium between capital and

labour, says: "If one is suppressed the other becomes dictator."
Certainly, but it seems to me that there is a way out of the difficulty
other than the one indicated by Professor Commons.

Many people make co-ordination and balance synonymous,
which seems to me a mistake. The guild socialists do this. Their
co-ordinating congress, they tell us, is an arbitrator or court of
appeal to keep the balance of power between co-ordinate autono-
mies. This is surely poor philosophy and the religion of the fearful;
they are so afraid of power that they say: "Let us all have equal
power." I think the aim of co-ordination should be the building up
of a functional total. I think we may learn that a jointly developing
power means the possibility of creating new values, a wholly different process from the sterile one of balancing. Not to rearrange
existing values, but to bring more into existence is the high mission
of enlightened human intercourse.

COLLECTIVE BARGAINING AS THE DETERMINANT OF VALUE

I began this paper by asking: "What is the determinant of value?"—
surely the most important consideration for business administration
whether we are speaking of value of services or what not. Most labour
men tell us that value is, or should be, determined by collective bargaining. Many business men say that value should be determined by
scientific methods which will do away with collective bargaining. But
trade unionists do not want to do away with, or even to narrow the
field of, collective bargaining; they want to bargain over everything.
They have bargained over wages and hours; now many of them say
that they should have the opportunity of bargaining over changes in
the technique of industry, since these involve changes in the working
conditions. If you tell them that industrial technique is a purely scientific matter, then they reply: "It is never the question alone of the
advantage of a new method; but of who is going to get the advantage?
If the worker is to get his share that must be bargained for."

This is true as far as it goes. Bargaining is at present necessary, and the result of bargaining rests on the relative strength of the two sides. If we are studying any particular industrial controversy, one of the first steps is to seek the sources of power of the moment. We ask, "What are the general conditions which give to capital or labour the greater economic power of the moment?" Unemployment gives power to the employer; also lack of education among the workmen; also the fact that the employees are not in a position to wait. On the other hand, the power of the workers is reinforced by the strength of the unions back of them, and their strength has increased with the number of unions and the numbers in them.

It is true, therefore, as things are now, that everything should be done to reduce the inequalities in the bargaining power of labour and capital, but I think at the same time we should see beyond that, that our ultimate aim should be different. I do not think this the final secret of solving the problems of business administration. Professor Commons says: "Unless the labourer can speak as a representative of associated labourers, he cannot speak with equal power." While I believe in encouraging employee associations, while I think it a grave weakness of some systems of employee representation that there is not adequate connection between Works Councils and the whole body of workers, still my reason for my very strong advocacy of employee association is not chiefly to bring about equal power, but because this helps us to approach functional unity. I should want to make a "side," not for a fair fight, not for fighting at all, but in order that it should enrich the whole. If I were a manufacturer I should want to consolidate my workers, not in order to give them greater strength in a fight, but in order that they should, by conscious unity, be a stronger part of my plant and thus strengthen my whole organization. I think we should never forget, what we spoke of at greater length in the preceding paper, that there are two kinds of "sides." There is all the difference in the world between controversial sides and integrative or contributing sides. I am interested only in the latter. I differ therefore from those people who say that the greatest fairness to the worker is to give him equal power in the bargaining process. My whole business philosophy is different from this. I think we owe both the worker and ourselves more than that.

I trust that the difference between this "equal power," so much talked of, and the power-with we have been considering, is evident. Equal power means the stage set for a fair fight, power-with is a jointly developing power, the aim, a unifying which, while allowing for infinite differing, does away with fighting. When the Sheffield Shop Stewards said, "We organize for power," did they mean power-over, equal power, or power-with? The history of the Shop Stewards' movement in England is sufficient answer to this question.

Yet I do not want to be misunderstood on the matter of collective bargaining. It is of course necessary at present; without it both wages and working conditions would fall below even minimum standards.[9] And, of course, if we do have bargaining we should give the two sides equal advantage as far as possible. I am trying to say merely that I think it is wise to decide, before we begin on any reorganization of our business, whether we believe in collective bargaining as an *ultimate* aim, or whether we accept it for the moment and surround it with the fairest conditions we are able to, at the same time trying to make our reorganization plan look toward a functional unity, which if it does not abolish collective bargaining (it may not) still will give to it a different meaning from that which it has at present. The best point about collective bargaining is that it rests on conference and agreement (there are methods of adjustment, as arbitration, which do not), but I believe in conference, not as an episode of war, but as one of the necessary activities in the process I have called a functional unifying. Would not the unqualified acceptance of collective bargaining as now generally understood commit us to the view that industry must remain at the mercy of shifts in "power" from employer to workman, from workman to employer? And is there any hope for a steady and wholesome progress with that condition of things?

But I am aware that we have begun on what ought to be another talk, and must therefore end rather abruptly. Should collective bargaining, we asked, be the determinant of value? Not for ever, I think; certainly not in the narrower meaning of that term. It seems to me that value is an interweaving, and that the clever business administrator must know both the strands and the pattern they make.

NOTES

1. *Cf. Creative Experience,* Chapter X, "Power: the Condition of its Validity," and *The New State,* Chapter XXIX, "Political Pluralism and Sovereignty."
2. Houghton-Mifflin Company, Boston, 1924.
3. This is not my own final definition of power, which I shall give at another time, but it is good I think so far as it goes, and therefore can be used legitimately without involving ourselves at present in a definition which might have fuller connotation, but which might not be so simple to handle and apply in our daily jobs.
4. *Cf. Creative Experience,* p. xii: "Our task is not to learn where to place power; it is how to develop power. . . . Genuine power can only be grown, it will slip from every arbitrary hand that grasps it; for genuine power is not coercive control, but coactive control. Coercive power is the curse of the universe; coactive power, the enrichment and advancement of every human soul."
5. *Cf. Creative Experience,* p. 184: "Some trade unionists are beginning to see the finer function of combination, combination in order to develop power in themselves rather than power over others."
6. James Myers, *Representative Government in Industry* (New York: Doubleday-Doran, 1924).
7. *Cf. The New State,* p. 271: "Real authority inheres in a genuine whole. The individual is sovereign over himself as far as he unifies the heterogeneous elements of his nature. Two people are sovereign over themselves as far as they are capable of creating one out of two. A group is sovereign over itself as far as it is capable of creating one out of several or many. A state is sovereign only as it has the power of creating one in which all are. Sovereignty is the power engendered by a complete interdependence become conscious of itself."
8. *Op. cit.*
9. Moreover, I should not include in an objectionable kind of collective bargaining all of the present "agreements" between capital and labour, some of which are arrived at by a different process than that of bargaining alone.

FOUR

The Giving of Orders

I HAVE taken for these five talks[1] the subject of Control. It is a word on everyone's lips today, for conscious as we are of muddle and failure, we ask, how shall we pass from chaos to control? Some tell us that the State should take control of banking, the railways, the mines. Others tell us that we should have a National Planning Board to take control of industry. The Soviets have taken control of Russia. Mussolini has taken control of Italy. Yet do we always quite know what we mean by the word control? I propose in these five talks to consider the conception of control in business organisation and business management. I hope we shall be able to get behind both academic abstractions and traditional conceptions and try for a thoroughly realistic treatment of authority, power, leadership, control. We can do this only by looking at the actual practice in business plants—factories, banks, shops, stores. Here we find these words acquiring new meaning. Certain changes have been going on in business practice which are destined, I believe, to alter all our thinking fundamentally. I think this is a contribution which business is going to make to the world, and not only to

Note: This chapter is reprinted from L. Urwick, ed., *Freedom & Co-ordination: Lectures in Business Organisation by Mary Parker Follett* (London: Management Publications Trust, Ltd., 1949), pp. 16–33. This paper, as well as those to be found in Chapters 5, 6, 7, and 8, was first delivered in January 1933 to the newly formed Department of Business Administration at the London School of Economics.

the business world but eventually to government and international relations.

I want therefore to consider in these talks what conception of control, of authority, is emerging from present business practice. I shall speak first of one way in which authority is exercised, the giving of orders. I think we shall find underlying our present practice in order-giving certain principles which may help us to understand authority. Next we shall consider more carefully that subject. We shall ask, What is the basis of authority? Why have some authority over others? Why have they and what is the thing they have, what is authority really? My third lecture will be leadership, on what is essential to leadership. And I do not mean leadership in the highest places only, but what is essential to the leadership of the under executive or of the foreman. My fourth lecture will be on co-ordination, on how to join all the diffused authority, the scattered leadership, we find in the complex organisation of modern industry. And then on my fifth and last evening, I shall speak of control more particularly, shall consider the process by which we gain control of a situation. On that evening, I shall give what I consider the four fundamental principles of organisation, for the object of organisation is control.

I said that tonight I wanted to talk about the giving of orders. There is a very marked and an extraordinarily interesting change taking place in our thinking on this subject. Arbitrary orders are beginning to go out of fashion. One man told me that the word order had not been used in his factory for twenty years. I was much interested last October in the report of an interview with Herr Emil Ludwig when he was here for the production of his play *Versailles*. He had high praise for his London producer and said, "We work ten hours a day. . . . I have never seen anything like it. And yet he rules without giving orders. He exercises authority without claiming authority."

Mr. Filene tells us: "My brother and I do not issue orders. My father never ordered things done, he thought no one got anywhere with such power unless he had his organisation with him." Another business man writes of "those superintendents and foremen who think of their job as consisting solely in that simple but archaic practice of ordering." This man, you see, calls ordering an archaic practice.

We find the same thing in the army. A general in the American army tells us that there is a very different idea in regard to orders appearing in military training. He says that when he was at West Point all that he was taught was to look stern when he gave orders, and if he was not obeyed to send the delinquent to the guardhouse. Not a minute of the four years of military training was given to the management of men although that was going to be the principal job of everyone there. He took his first command and not only he wasn't popular, but he wasn't accomplishing what he wanted to do. Then he was sent to teach in the military department of a college. There he found he was really up against the problem of how to handle men, for there was no guardhouse there to which to send refractory students. He tells us that that experience taught him how to handle men without forcing them, and he went back to the regular army knowing that he had learned how to control without giving orders. There are many in the army now, he says, who have learned this lesson.

But of course this word is still used in the army and also in industry. In the more progressively managed businesses, however, it does not today mean an arbitrary command. If anyone doubts this, I should say to him, look at business as it is being conducted today in many plants and watch where the orders come from. What is their origin? Heaven does not privately convey them to the top executive; they arise out of the work itself and many subordinates may have contributed to them. Consider the analysis of executive jobs which is being made in some plants. This can be done in two ways. You can have an expert do it or you can do it as they did in a certain large bank. There they had each man make an analysis of his own work. Out of that analysis rules for his job were formulated. But whether the analysis is made by the man on the job or by an expert, in both cases the rules of the job come from a careful, analytic study of the work itself.

In some factories the same method is used for operating jobs. The job is studied, a conclusion is reached as to the most effective way of performing it, and then that way is standardised until a better way is found. Hence the expression used in many factories today is not orders but standard practice. Men do not "obey orders" but "follow standard practice." In such plants the worker sometimes takes part in the preliminary studies made to determine standard practice. Or if new methods are devised by the research and planning departments, still in many instances they are not finally adopted without a shop try-out, and the workers usually have a chance in this shop try-out to make objections. If they do not make objections, they have practically assented to the new methods. In plants where there are shop-committees, explicit approval is obtained from the shop-committees.

I think we may say, therefore, that when the right order is found by research, the orders given by the foreman are coming to be considered not as anything arbitrary on his part, but as information in regard to standard practice, as training in method. Moreover, what is called the work-order is given in some factories by the despatch clerk and not by the foreman. This makes it clear to all that it is part of the whole plan of the factory and not anything arbitrary on the part of the foreman. And an important consequence of this is that the foreman is now released for more constructive work. There is a very marked change in this respect from even a few years ago. Executive intelligence is not today expended in issuing commands, but is released for the solving of new problems, the planning of further developments.

But in all this I am talking of the more progressively managed industries. Many are not conducted in this way. The head of a large engineering firm said to me, "I tell my people what to do and they have to do it, and that's all there is to that." And another general manager told me, "I'm the boss in this place and I stand no interference from subordinates." As, therefore, we still find arbitrary methods in many places, let us consider their disadvantages. We may say that the first disadvantage is that we lose what we might learn from the man actually on the job if we do not invite his co-operation in deciding what the rules of the task shall be. An upper executive said to me, "I want the criticism of my men; I can learn a lot from the man on the job."

The second disadvantage is one which anyone who knows anything at all about industry is fully aware of, namely, the friction between workers and foremen. I said to one girl at a big factory, "What do you think would be the best improvement that could be made in a factory?" She replied instantly, "To get rid of foremen." This was amusing, but it shows, I fear, the usual attitude. Yet it is being found in those plants where orders are part of the general plan, are standard practice, that there is much less friction between workers and foremen.

This is easily understood. The arbitrary command ignores one of the most fundamental facts of human nature, namely, the wish to govern one's own life. "I don't like being bossed," a man in a factory told me. Another workmen said to me, "I'm willing to obey but I won't be commanded." I think that a very interesting remark. Probably more industrial trouble has been caused by the manner in which orders have been given than in any other way. In The Report on Strikes and Lockouts, a British Government publication of a few years ago, the cause of a number of strikes is given as "illegal harassing conduct of the foremen," "alleged tyrannical conduct of an under-official," "the alleged overbearing conduct of officials." Again, the metal and woodworking trades in a British aircraft factory declared that any treatment of men without regard to their feelings of self-respect would be answered by a stoppage of work.

But even if instructions are properly framed, are not given in an overbearing manner, there are many people who react violently against anything that they feel is a command. It is often the command that is resented, not the thing commanded. I think it is told in the life of some famous man that when he was a boy and his mother said, "Go and get a pail of water, John," he always replied "I won't" before taking up the pail and fetching the water. This is significant: he resented the command, but he went and got the water, not I believe because he had to, but because he recognised the demand of the situation. That he knew he had to obey, that he was willing to obey.

I have given two disadvantages of issuing arbitrary directions, namely, that we lose possible contributions from those directed and that such directions are apt to cause friction between workers and foremen. There is a third very serious disadvantage. No one has a greater asset for his business than a man's pride in his work. If a worker is asked to do something in a way which he thinks is not the best way, he will often lose all interest in the result, he will be sure beforehand that his work is going to turn out badly. I have read that it is characteristic of the British workman to feel "I know my job and won't be told how." This attitude might be met by a joint study of the particular situation, it being understood that the worker out of his experience has as much to contribute to that study as anyone else. Or if a better way of doing some particular job has been found by the research department, the worker should be persuaded that this really is a better way, not merely told to do it in that way. It is one of the things we should be most careful about—never to interfere with the workers' pride in his work.

Again and again we disregard the fact that workers are usually as eager to attain a certain standard, as wishful that their performance shall be maintained at a high level, as their employers. We often tend to think that the executive wishes to maintain standard, wishes to reach a certain quality of production, and that the worker has to be goaded in some way to this. Again and again we forget that the worker is often, usually I think, equally interested, that his greatest pleasure in his work comes from the satisfaction of worthwhile accomplishment, of having done the best of which he was capable.

A fourth disadvantage of the arbitrary command is that it decreases the sense of responsibility, and whatever does that just so far lowers the chance of business success. It has been noticed by some heads of departments who have encouraged criticisms and suggestions from their subordinates that instead of getting more kicks and general unpleasantness, they get less, because now the man who kicks is expected to suggest something better.

The arbitrary foreman may indeed get hoist with his own petard. I knew a case where a workman reacting against such a foreman deliberately carried out a wrong direction instead of taking it back to the foreman and asking about it, and thus wasted a large amount of material in order that his foreman should be blamed for the waste. Thus the man who demands a blind obedience may have it react on himself. When the accomplishment of a department is the result of a feeling of joint responsibility on the part of all concerned, that accomplishment is likely to be of a higher grade.

But while people should not be asked to follow directions blindly, at the same time a subordinate should not have the attitude of carping, of finding fault, of thinking things from above wrong. The attitude most desirable for receiving orders is intelligent scrutiny, willingness to suggest changes, courtesy in the manner of suggesting, and at the same time no prejudice in regard to what is prescribed, but the assumption that the way prescribed is probably the best unless one can show some convincing reason to the contrary.

If arbitrary command, the exaction of blind obedience, breaks initiative, discourages self-reliance, lowers self-respect, how shall we avoid these disasters? Chiefly in four ways I think. First, by depersonalising orders. I have already referred to that when I said that in the more progressively managed businesses orders were being changed to "standard practice," to "rules of the job," to merely a way of doing the work which is accepted as the best way. But then we are speaking only of routine work, of repetitive work. And a fresh direction may have to be given at any moment. What principle should guide us here? How can we avoid too great bossism in the giving of orders and the inevitable resentment which will follow?

I think the solution is exactly the same for the special order as for the general order, namely, to depersonalise the matter, to unite those concerned in a study of the situation, to see what the situation demands, to discover the law of the situation and obey that. That is, it should not be a case of one person giving commands to another person. Whenever it is obvious that the order arises from the situation, the question of someone commanding and someone obeying does not come up. Both accept what the situation demands. Our chief problem then is not how to get people to obey orders, but how to devise methods by which we can best discover what the order shall be. When that is found the employee could issue direction to the employer as well as employer to employee. This often happens quite easily and naturally: my stenographer or my cook points out the law of the situation to me, and I, if I recognise it as such, accept it even although it may reverse some previous direction I have given.

An order then should always be given not as a personal matter, not because the man giving it wants the thing done, but because it is the demand of the situation. And an order of this kind carries weight because it is the demand of the situation. I found something in a novel which recognises and expresses this point. The hero of the novel, Richard Hague, was a large-scale farmer in England. And he was a very successful farmer. The author, after telling how Hague got the most out of all his materials down to the very spark with which he lighted a fire, went on to say: "And it was the same with people. He got use out of them, though not through . . . being personally exigent in any way. It was always the force of circumstances that seemed to make the demand, not himself. He merely made it clear to them what it was that needed doing. . . . So little did it seem an affair personal to him that the sheep needed driving off the corn, or a message carried into the hayfield, that he hardly intervened. He might just call somebody's attention to what was needed, but it was the corn, the cattle, the world that required the service, not he." And later the author tells us: "He evidently considered that the task itself made some claim on anybody who happened to come across it, made itself the most interesting and most necessary thing in the world, so that no one could resist it."

If orders were depersonalized I am sure we should get rid of much of the complaint by workers of tyrannical treatment, but there is another difficulty at the opposite extreme from this, and that is when not enough orders are given. The immediate superior is often so close to the worker that he does not like to give orders at all. If you go into any large shop here in London, you usually find the head of a department sitting at a desk among the salesmen or saleswomen. This person is only a little removed in the scale of authority from those under him or her; moreover, they are working together all day and it is not pleasant to get on bad terms with those with whom you are so closely associated. We often therefore find too great leniency here. Instead of an overbearing authority, we find that dangerous *laissez-faire* which comes from a fear of exercising authority. Of course we should exercise authority, but always the authority of the situation.

I overheard the following conversation in a large shop. The head of the women's cloak department called out, "You're No. 36, Molly, aren't you? There's someone on the telephone complaining about something you promised yesterday." "Well, I like that," said Molly, "some of these people would complain in Heaven." I don't know what took place after that, but I think probably, from what I saw, that that was all that happened, except that of course the lady who had not received her cloak had to be appeased. I think probably that head of department did not like to reprimand the saleswoman and so did nothing. And of course she ought not to have reprimanded her. But that was not the only alternative. I think the solution for too little authority being exercised is exactly the same as for too much. I think that situation should have been investigated, not in order to blame anyone but in order to improve store technique. Perhaps the fault was with the saleswoman, perhaps it was in the dressmaking department where the cloak was being altered, perhaps it was in the delivery department, or perhaps, very likely, it was in the organisation of the shop which did not provide for that relation between departments which would ensure the best results. A study of that incident in the cloak department need not have resulted in blame, but such study would certainly have given the people concerned better control of such situations in the future.

And that is always our problem, not how to get control of people, but how all together we can get control of a situation.

To find the law of the situation rather than to issue arbitrary commands, I have called depersonalising orders. I think it is really a matter of re-personalising. We, persons, have relations with each other, but we should find them in and through the whole situation. We cannot have any sound relations with each other as long as we take them out of the setting which gave them their meaning and value. The divorcing of persons and situation does a great deal of harm. While, therefore, I have said that orders should be depersonalised, a deeper philosophy shows us personal relations within the whole setting of that thing of which they are a part. Within that setting we find the so-called order.

And please remember that in all this I am not merely theorising and telling you what I think ought to be done, I am telling you some of the ways which I have found in practice in business of avoiding arbitrary commands. If the most important is the depersonalising of orders (it is convenient to keep to that word), next in importance certainly comes training. The general manager of a clothing factory said to me, "Times are changing; we don't order people any more, we train them." They have in this factory what is called a Vestibule School where a girl is trained for her job; she is not expected to pick it up as she goes along through orders given by the foreman. This has made a great difference in the feeling between the girls and the foremen in that factory, and in the cheerfulness of the girls and in their interest in their work.

Such preliminary training is, to be sure, given in many places. Here in London many of the shops have classes in salesmanship. In these classes many things are taught, many hints given, which without such classes would have to be given as "orders" from the head of the department. In such shops, when a saleswoman is selling a dress, for instance, she is not thinking of orders, she is simply doing her job as she has been trained to do it. And there is a great difference between thinking of what you are doing as the technique of your job or as following commands.

But I am speaking now of preliminary training. Much training also has to be done by foremen and heads of departments as the work goes on—training in regard to new methods, further teaching where instructions have not been fully understood. Censure is becoming old-fashioned in the best-managed plants. When mistakes are made, it is assumed that it is a case for more instruction. We hear little of blame, reprimand, the old weapon of authority. And this point of educating instead of blaming seems to me very important. For nothing stultifies one more than being blamed. Moreover, if the question is, who is to blame?, perhaps each will want to place the blame on someone else, or, on the other hand, someone may try to shield his fellow-worker. In either case the attempt is to hide the error and if this is done the error cannot be corrected.

If the first rule for giving orders is to depersonalise the order, for order-giver and order-receiver together to find the law of the situation, and if the second rule is to replace orders as far as possible by teaching the technique of a job, a third rule might be to give reasons with the order. Some firms make it a rule to do this and I think that the firms who follow this rule find a distinct advantage therein. I know it takes time to give reasons, but I believe it saves time in the end in work done more cheerfully, more intelligently and more alertly.

I do not of course mean that an order should be discussed every time it is given, only that reasons should be given for new orders. And not always then. For many orders are time-saving devices. A superior officer often tells a subordinate officer to do something on the assumption that if he could be given all the reasons for it he would agree, I say only that when possible, reasons should be given with new orders.

An advantage of not exacting blind obedience, of discussing your instructions with your subordinates, is that if there is any resentment, any come-back, you get it out into the open, and when it is in the open you can deal with it. It is the underground come-back that does the harm, both because you cannot deal with it unless you know about it and also because its underground nature increases its intensity.

One fact which helps to show the advantage of giving your reasons with instructions is that factory after factory has had trouble with instructions posted on bulletin boards. Many general managers will tell you that posted orders don't work.

I know a lady who posted over the sink in her kitchen the proper sequence of dish-washing. Her cook did not say what she felt about it, but a few days later she put her own feelings into the mouth of someone else by saying, "Mrs. Smith's cook came to see me yesterday and she said she wouldn't have that in her kitchen."

This instance throws some light, also, on what I have said of the advantage of the rules of the job being the outcome of joint study. If this lady had said to her cook and maids, "Let us think out the proper sequence of dish-washing and then stick to it," all might have been well perhaps. There would have been nothing to resent if they had had a share in making the rules.

If we can run our business more efficiently by substituting for arbitrary commands a joint study of the situation, by more training of the worker, and by giving reasons for directions, it is also true that it will be of inestimable help to take measures that all shall know the purpose or purposes of factory, shop or bank, the purpose back of all directions. I am sure that if this were done directions would be more cheerfully and more carefully obeyed. Over and over again this is ignored, but I believe it is going to be one of the largest factors in our future industrial success.

One of the best speeches I ever heard was in York at the Rowntree Cocoa Works. When a number of new girls are taken into the Works, Mr. Seebohm Rowntree gives a talk to them. He tells them how one little girl being careless in dipping chocolates may cause the young man who takes a box of chocolates to his best girl on Saturday evening to say that he will not buy Rowntree's chocolates next time. And then he shows the girls how this affects far more than Rowntree profits, how it will make less employment in York for girls and boys and men and women. And so on and so on. He goes on from such simple illustrations to show them their place in the industry of England. I do not believe that the girls who hear one of these talks can ever look at the "orders" given them in quite the same way as they would if they had not been shown what lies back of the orders. This firm has found a way of making its employees share in a common purpose, of making them feel a joint responsibility, of making them feel co-partners in a common enterprise.

I have given four rules for the giving of orders. We might sum these all up by saying that the one who gives an order should try to bring those ordered into the situation. They should not be kept outside. They should be brought into the same picture. That is not very clear but I will illustrate. A friend of mine told me that he deliberately disobeyed some rule while motoring expecting that he would be fined, but he preferred to do it and pay the fine. To his surprise, however, the policeman said, "I'm not going to get you fined, but I'm going to ask you to do something in place of the fine. I'm going to ask you to take some copies of these rules and give them to your friends, and if you have a chance, talk them over with them." Now, my friend would much rather have paid the fine, but he was intelligent enough to see that the policeman had found a better way of treating the matter. Instead of considering the rule against speed, or whatever it was, as an arbitrary rule from outside which one either obeyed, or disobeyed and took the consequences, he tried to get my friend inside the situation, the total situation of the needs of other motorists, of pedestrians and so on.

It is the same with orders. You have to get people within the situation, within the same picture, not issue commands to them from outside. They must somehow be made to feel that you and they are on the same job, are co-workers, even if your part is that of explaining the work, informing them of standards, and theirs is the carrying out, two equally important parts of the same thing. I think if we could do this, it might be the solution of the difficult problem of supervision. Many workers object to being watched. In a case in Scotland arising under the Minimum Wage Act an overman was called in to testify whether a certain workman did his work properly. He said he could not tell, for, as he stated, "They always stop work when they see an overman coming and sit down and wait until he has gone, even take out their pipes if it's a mine free from gas."

Again, in a Clyde engineering works during the War, one of the blacksmiths became enraged when the managing director in his ordinary morning walk through the works stopped for five minutes or so and watched his fire. The matter was taken up by the trade union, a deputation was sent to the director, and he had practically to say that he would not watch the men's work. To be sure that was during the War when everyone was on edge. Also, I should think probably that particular general manager had not been very tactful, and tact is certainly an important consideration for the giving of directions and the supervision of work.

Moreover, I think a good deal of our language will have to be changed. I don't think that any of us would like to be "watched." I think we shall have to substitute another word for that, just as we are substituting other words for "order." A good deal of the language of personnel relations in industry could, I think, with benefit, be changed. For instance, Ford has "trouble specialists," which I think all wrong. Many companies have "grievance committees" or a "complaints department." I think that these "trouble specialists" and "grievance committees" are needed, but I don't think they should be called that. I don't think we should be looking for trouble. And what is called a grievance may be a misunderstanding. What is called a complaint may be the stating of some difficulty. I think these words arouse the wrong reaction and should therefore not be used.

And that brings me to almost my last topic, the need for executives to be trained in the giving of orders—taught how to anticipate reactions, how to arouse the right reactions, and so on. This means an understanding of the psychology of the matter, and that subject would take an hour in itself, but I can give a hint of what I mean. If a man under you is to do his work in a certain way, he has to acquire a certain set of habits or attitudes. There are three things you can do about this: (1) prepare the way for orders by creating in advance when possible the attitudes which will ensure their being carried out; (2) provide some stimulus for the adoption of the methods suggested (the whole question of incentives comes in here); (3) give opportunity for those methods to become a habit.

In psychological language we should say create attitudes, augment attitudes and release attitudes. There is, therefore, much to think about in making out a new instruction card. It should be so worded that it does not require too abrupt a change of habit, and it should find a way of making an appeal. Moreover, the approach to a new method must sometimes be indirect. A direct approach may put a man on the defensive. We cannot be too careful of the power of previous ideas.

And if we come to realise that the following of directions is from one point of view the acquiring of habits, then we shall realise also that we must be patient until the habits are acquired. Many a time an employer has been angry because an employee wouldn't, as he expressed it, do so and so, when as a matter of fact he couldn't, actually couldn't, do as told because he could not at once go contrary to life-long habits. Couldn't even if he had accepted the direction and wanted to follow it. A general manager in America said to me once: "There's a curious thing. I find sometimes that one of my executives will accept the suggestion and then not seem to be able to carry it out." But it is not curious at all. The most elementary knowledge of psychology gives us the reason for this. None of us can change our mental habits in a minute however much we may wish to.

Of course; many rules could be made for the giving of orders. Don't preach when you give orders. Don't discuss matters already settled unless you have fresh data. Make your direction so specific that there will be no question whether they have been obeyed or not. Find out how to give directions and yet to allow people opportunity for independent thinking, for initiative. And so on and so on. Order-giving requires just as much study and just as much training as any other skill we wish to acquire.

The head of a factory told me that in his experience when foremen swaggered and blustered, it was not usually because it was their disposition to swagger and bluster, but merely that they didn't know how to give orders, didn't know how to get work done. It has been suggested that men wishing to become foremen should be specifically trained for their job, and that this should go beyond classes in foremanship, which consist merely of lectures. It has been suggested that they should work for a few weeks under a number of foremen whose methods they should analyse and discuss, and that they should then be given practice in substitute jobs, that is, when a regular foreman is ill or on holiday, before they are considered capable of being put on a regular job. This is, I think, a very good idea.

Business management is gaining something of an accepted technique, but there still remains, as part of the training of executives, the acquiring of skill in the application of that technique. Managerial skill cannot be painted on the outside of executives—it has to go deeper than that. Just as in the case of manual workers, so managerial workers have to acquire certain habits and attitudes.

I can sum up this whole talk in one sentence: orders come from the work, not work from the orders. They have their roots in the activities of the people who are obeying them. There is an active principle in obedience. Obedience is not a passive thing, for it is a moment in a process. There is, as a rule, a very elaborate and complex process going on. At one moment in that process something happens which we call obedience. I have said that it was an advantage to get agreement to instructions, yet it is a fallacy to think that an order gets its validity from consent. It gets its validity long before that, from the whole process to which both order-giver and order-receiver have contributed.

I have written this paper having chiefly in mind the orders given by executives and foremen to those on the operating jobs in the factory, the assistants in the shop, or clerical workers, but all that I have said applies equally well to directions given by upper executives to under executives. Applies even, we might say, more conspicuously to these. For here it is even more obvious that co-operation should be sought in the preliminary study of situations, reasons for policies discussed, the purposes of the company explained, reactions anticipated, and training provided.

I hope, however, there is nothing in what I have said that sounds dogmatic. For while we are trying to get away from a haphazard, hit-or-miss way of performing executive duties to scientifically determined procedure, still not enough study has yet been given to business management as a science for us to be sure that we have worked out the best methods in any one particular. But this we can say, that in business we have always a chance of experimenting, of testing our principles. This is what makes business so interesting. Take our subject of this evening. I am not so much urging you to admit the principles I have put before you as suggesting that you should try them out and decide for yourselves. I am urging that we should all of us take a conscious and responsible attitude toward our experience. In the matter of order-giving this means first that we shall be conscious of the different methods of order-giving, secondly, that we should feel some responsibility in the matter, that is, that we should decide deliberately which of these methods we think the best, thirdly, that we should then follow those methods as far as the customs of our firm permit, and fourthly that we should very carefully watch results. We should try experiments and note whether they succeed or fail. And one of the most interesting things about business to me is that I find so many business men who are willing to try experiments.

I should like to tell you about two evenings I spent last winter and the contrast between them. I went one evening to a drawing-room meeting where economists and M.P.'s talked of current affairs, of our present difficulties. It all seemed a little vague to me, did not seem really to come to grips with our problem. The next evening it happened that I went to a dinner of twenty business men who were discussing the question of centralisation and decentralisation. There was no academic talk about the necessity for centralisation or the advantages of decentralisation. Each one had something to add from his own experience of the relation of branch firms to the central office, and the other problems included in the subject. There I found hope for the future. There men were not theorising or dogmatising, they were thinking of what they had actually done and they were willing to try new ways the next morning, so to speak. I had felt the night before after the drawing-room meeting, that we had all separated at the end of the evening just the same people as when we had entered that house. But the next evening, with the twenty business men, I felt that we had all learned new possibilities, that at nine o'clock the following morning those men could do things, test out some of the things they had heard, and I felt that some of them were ready to do that.

Business, therefore, because it gives us the opportunity of trying new roads, of blazing new trails, because, in short, it is pioneer work, pioneer work in the organised relation of human beings, seems to me to offer as thrilling an experience as going into new country and building railroads over new mountains. For whatever problems we solve in business management may help toward the solution of world problems, since the principles of organisation and administration which are discovered as best for business can be applied to government or international relations. Indeed the solution of world problems must eventually be built up from all the little bits of experience wherever people are consciously trying to solve problems of relation. And this attempt is being made more consciously and deliberately in industry than anywhere else.

One of the best thinkers on business management, Mr. John Lee, formerly Controller of the Central Telegraph Office here, told us: "The old discipline has passed. We are probing a new realm of human relationships which is to take the place of the old relation of subordination and yet is to include subordination (rightly understood)." Mr. Lee died before he could carry this idea further, but he and all the deeper thinkers on business management have for some years been feeling the way for this "new realm of human relationships."

Business men may be making useful products but beyond this, by helping to solve the problems of human relations, they are perhaps destined to lead the world in the solution of those great problems of co-ordination and control upon which our future progress must depend.

NOTES

1. *The Problem of Organisation and Co-ordination in Business.*

FIVE

+⇌ ⇌+

The Basis of Authority

WE HAVE considered the question of order-giving. That obviously is only an aspect of the subject of authority. All through books on business administration you find the word authority constantly used. We hear of supreme authority, of ultimate authority, of final authority. We hear of the delegation of authority, of the division of authority, of the limit of authority. These expressions are current phrases in the business world. But it seems to me that some of these expressions are a survival of former days. And are consequently misleading. For they do not describe business as conducted today in many plants. Business practice has gone ahead of business theory, business practice has gone ahead of business language.

In the best managed plants today there is a tendency for each man to have the authority which goes with his particular job rather than that inhering in a particular position in a hierarchy. The most fundamental idea in business today, that which is permeating our whole thinking and business organisation, is that of function. Research and scientific study are coming more and more to determine function. And we are coming more and more to think that a man should have just as much, no more and no less, authority as

Note: This chapter is reprinted from L. Urwick, ed. *Freedom & Co-ordination: Lectures in Business Organisation by Mary Parker Follett* (London: Management Publications Trust, Ltd., 1949), pp. 34–46.

141

goes with his function or task. People often talk about the limit of authority when it would be better to speak of the definition of task.

When each man's function is defined by scientific research, when the form of organisation is such that he has the authority which belongs to his function, we automatically get rid of that kind of authority which puts one man "over" another because he is higher up on the page in an organisation chart. I know a man in a factory who is superintendent of a department which includes a number of sub-departments. He tells me that in many cases he says to the head of a sub-department, that is, to a man in a subordinate position to his own, "With your permission I shall do so and so." This is a decided reversal of the usual method, is it not? In the old hierarchy of position, the head of the sub-department would be "under" the superintendent of the department, the "lower" would take orders from the "higher." But this man recognised that authority should go with knowledge and experience, that that is where obedience is due no matter whether it is up the line or down the line. Where knowledge and experience are located, there, he says, you have the key man of the situation. If this has begun to be recognised in business practice, we have here the fore-runner of some pretty drastic changes in our thinking on business management.

I was having a talk a little while ago with the head of a large corporation. His telephone bell rang. He took up the receiver and said in answer to some question, "My secretary decides that, she knows much more about it than I do." Just the other day the head of a big organisation here in London came to one of his heads of departments, this woman told me, and said, "I've come for my orders." She was much amused, but this wasn't a pleasantry on his part. It was simply a recognition that she knew more about the matter in hand than he did.

Perhaps sometime it may seem advisable to get rid of the words "over" and "under." We find a growing dislike to these words in many places. A few years ago my nurse in hospital said to me, "Did you notice that nurse in the operating room? Didn't she look black?" I innocently said, "Perhaps one of the surgeons had reprimanded her for something." To which my nurse replied, "Why, he couldn't. The doctors are not over us. They have their work and we have ours." Now while it is not true that a doctor cannot reprimand a nurse for a mistake, while a doctor certainly has the right to expect his directions in regard to a patient to be obeyed, yet on speaking of this occurrence to several doctors, I was told that there is a growing tendency, on the part of nurses to consider that they are following the standards of their profession rather than merely obeying orders from someone over them. And these doctors said that while this attitude obviously has drawbacks, there may be a good side to it, for it may indicate on the part of the nurses a greater pride in their profession, a greater interest in their work, and a willingness to take responsibility. This should be a matter of further observation, I think, before we form an opinion.

The testimony before the Coal Commission a few years ago threw much light on this question. We heard there stated explicitly the dislike of being "under some one," the dislike of the feeling of "subordination," the dislike of being "at the will of another." One man said: "It's all right to work with anyone: what is disagreeable is to feel too distinctly that you are working under anyone."

This objection to being under we find among executives as well as among the rank and file. A business man here in London talking to me of two of his executives said: "Mr. A. will take instructions from Mr. B. but will not admit that he is under him." Well, perhaps that is all right. I don't know that it makes us under a person to take instructions from him. We are all of us, as a matter of fact, taking instructions from people all the time. I take instructions from my plumber, my electrician, but I am not under them. Or perhaps I am in a sense and to an extent.

I say that executives as well as workers object to being under anyone. I have found among chief executives an objection to being over others and a feeling that these words over and under are unfortunate. One general manager said to me, "I don't know whether I'm at the head or the bottom and I wish there were some way of making out a chart that didn't put the general manager at the top." Another general manager tells me that he thinks the use of the terms "higher," "superior," in an organisation is unwise, that a meaning is attached to them which they ought not to have. The head of a large business in the north of England told me that one of the things which was retarding the unification of his plant was this feeling of over and under. The head of another English firm said to me, "I don't like all this over and under talk. I have a lot of able executives all doing their work well. My work is different from theirs, but I don't see why I should be considered over them."

I think one difficulty about this matter, one reason why people object so strongly to being "under" others, is that there has been too much pomp attached to the idea of being over someone, of giving orders. I am convinced that we have to change our thinking very radically in this respect. I am convinced that any feeling of exaltation because we have people under us should be conquered, for I am sure that if we enjoy being over people, there will be something in our manner which will make them dislike being under us. And often there is not sufficient ground for any feeling of superiority. Indeed, if I give instructions to someone who knows less about a matter than I do, he probably knows more than I about some other matter. I know more about the composition of menus than my cook, but she knows more about cooking and the management of the kitchen range. So we can all be over and under at the same time.

There is an amusing story of a teacher who went into a new school. There were certain rules in regard to the disposal of small pieces of chalk, of erasers that needed cleaning, and so on, but she disregarded these rules as she had been in a school where there were no rules for such matters. In a little while she was taken to task by the caretaker of the building who remarked that evidently she wasn't used to working under a caretaker. She was, naturally, much amused, but perhaps she was under him in regard to left-over pieces of chalk.

I know a lady who had one maid for the work of her little summer cottage. One summer she was very tired mentally and decided that instead of the maid she would engage someone to run her cottage for her, and she took one of the students from a college which taught household economics. This girl obviously couldn't do the planning and buying and all the work too, so the lady did part of the work. She had the physical exercise and the mental rest she needed, and was only too pleased to be told what to do by the household economics girl.

In the conduct of business there have been many changes in recent years which have tended to make them feel less pompous about being over others. I heard a man at the head of a factory in the West of England say, "You can call me General Manager, but any kid can come along with a chit and I have to do what it says." The most marked difference in this respect we find among foremen. I remember the wife of a foreman who said with pride, "John has seventy in his department that he's boss over." There is much now that is hastening the disappearance of that phrase, notably newer methods of dismissal. When employment managers were first introduced into a business, the foremen were almost invariably jealous. One of the duties of the employment manager is, as you know, to hire and dismiss, of course with the concurrence of the foreman, but the foreman thought that this took away from their authority. They had to be led to see that it is merely a division of duties, just as one of the general manager's jobs is often nowadays given to some specialist engaged to do that particular thing. Moreover, when dismissals are made after consultation between foreman and employment manager, or between foreman, employment manager and psychologist, that is, when it is decided that a man has not the qualifications for a particular job, such dismissals may come in time to be looked at in the same way as when a doctor says a man's heart is too weak for a certain kind of work. That decision does not mean that the doctor is over anyone. It is only capricious firing, firing that is unfounded, that makes a man over another, and that kind of firing is disappearing. One of the differences between the old-time foreman and the present is that the former was thinking in terms of his authority; he thought he could not keep up his dignity before his men unless he had this thing he called authority. Many foremen today are learning to think in terms of responsibility for definite tasks.

Indeed there are many indications in the present reorganisation of industry that we are beginning to rid ourselves of the over and under idea, that we are coming to a different conception of authority, many indications that there is an increasing tendency to let the job itself, rather than the position occupied in a hierarchy, dictate the kind and amount of authority. An incident in my own experience brought this vividly home to me. One morning in America I wanted to telephone a certain bank. I could not get them. I tried repeatedly without success. I knew of course that the switchboard of a large bank was not dead at the busiest time of the day. I therefore tried, by calling first one official of the telephone company and then another, to see if someone couldn't get that number for me. I did at length get the bank, but before the incident was closed, I learned a good deal about the organisation of that Telephone Company. For one thing each official seemed to be thinking more in terms of his job than of his position. The first thing that struck my attention was the minor importance of hierarchy of each. This was rather a good joke on me. For, forgetting all my beautiful theories, all my preaching against one man having power over another, forgetting all this, the mental habits of a life-time asserted themselves without my being aware of it, and I started out on a hunt for someone in authority over another. When the operator didn't get my number, I called the chief operator, then I called the exchange manager because I thought he was over the chief operator. I then asked for a superintendent because I thought he was over the exchange manager. But I found that the officials of the Telephone Company did not seem to be thinking in those terms. When I said to the superintendent: "Are you over the exchange manager?" he replied in rather bewildered tones, "No, I'm not over him." When in the afternoon a superintendent who wished to investigate the matter rang me up, the first thing I said to him was "Are you over the superintendent I talked with this morning?" He replied, "Oh, no, I'm not over him." You see, in spite of all my principles, I was so used to the old way of thinking that I couldn't adjust myself quickly to a different way of thinking. I wanted someone who had the authority to boss, so I kept straight on in this search for someone above others instead of asking: "What particular job is this?"

And later on (for the President of the Company, when he found I was studying organisation, asked me to investigate theirs) later on I found that this lack of emphasis on hierarchy of rank went right through the whole organisation. There was either no position which as such carried with it the right to boss, or else no-one took advantage of such a position. Everyone seemed to be thinking not so much in terms of to whom he was responsible as for what he was responsible—a much healthier attitude of mind.

When I finally had a talk with the President, part of what he said is I think worth quoting in full. "The kind of management we are aiming at," he said, "is management with authority all down the line, as contrasted with management by edict from a central source. We are trying to teach our men what their jobs are, what the underlying principles of these jobs are, and then we are trying to get them to exercise the authority of their job with the idea that they shall use their brains, their discretion, having in mind these fundamental principles. We teach people what their job is, and then insist that they shall exercise the authority and responsibility which goes with that job instead of relying on the fellow above them."

In many companies we find this emphasis on the job rather than on the hierarchy of position. For one thing, as management is becoming more and more specialised, the policies and methods of a department tend more and more to rest on that department's special body of knowledge. We find authority with the head of a department or with an expert or with a staff official. The despatch clerk has more authority in despatching work than the general manager. The balance of stores clerk, as he is called in some places, will tell the purchasing agent when to act, although the purchasing agent is above him in the official scale.

Moreover, some firms have planning departments, and these, it is obvious, lessen arbitrary authority.

Again, all that I said of the order being found by research, of executives or workers being asked to co-operate in the forming of rules for the job—all this takes away from arbitrary authority.

Moreover, we are not now drawing the line so sharply as formerly between those who manage and those who are managed. A close analysis of jobs shows us many which occupy a place at the bottom of the organisation chart which yet contain some degree of management, which carry with them some degree of authority. That is, there is authority all down the line: the driver of a delivery van has authority as he decides on the order of deliveries.

Instead then of "supreme control," "ultimate authority," we might perhaps think of cumulative control, cumulative authority.

What has been keeping us back in our thinking on this subject is, I think, what I have called elsewhere the fallacy of finals. The final moment in a process may be the most striking, the most dramatic, but it may not be any more important than all the other moments. What we have to recognise about authority is that it is a process. To recognise this gives us a thoroughly realistic view of our subject. The old theory of authority I call unrealistic because it tends to ignore the process by which authority is generated. Perhaps it will help us to destroy the illusion of final authority if we consider for a moment executive decisions, if we ask ourselves where a decision really comes from.

It is often supposed that the administrative head receives facts from his heads of departments and that then from the facts thus gained he makes his decisions, constructs his policies. But it is a matter of everyday experience to top executives that their heads of departments pass up to them more than mere facts. They give interpretations of facts, the conclusions they have drawn from these facts, yes, and often judgments too, so that they contribute very largely to final authority, supreme control.

The various experts too, the staff officials, the planning department—all these give more than mere facts. The planning department, to be sure, is still so much of a novelty that there are many different ideas as to its place in the plant. It may be asked for only statistical information. For instance, in the case of a decision pending for the sales department, it may be asked only for a record of past sales with analyses in regard to volume, localities, and so on. Usually, however, it is asked for more than this, for the probable future development of certain localities, what the future demand will probably be, the probable effect of the raising of price. By the time this has all been passed up to the head, this decision is already largely pre-determined.

Hence, while the board of directors or executive committees may be theoretically the governing body, practically, as many of our large businesses are now organised and operated, before their decisions are made there has already taken place much of the process of which these decisions are but a last step.

Moreover, both as to conclusions and judgments handed up from executives it is often not possible for the chief executive or the board of directors to reject them. For these conclusions and judgments are already, to a certain extent, woven into the pattern, and in such a way that it would be impossible to get them out.

For instance, suppose the question comes up in a board of directors or executive committee in a factory whether a psychologist shall be engaged. Much has gone on before that question comes up. It has been felt desirable by many to have better tests for hiring, promoting and dismissing, to have studies in fatigue, and so on. But there has been at the same time many other influences at work.

The foremen perhaps think that their methods of testing applicants are sufficient, the older men among the upper executives may oppose what they call "new-fangled" notions, the workers may think that fatigue studies will tend only to more work being required of them, and so on. It is obvious, is it not, that the decision in regard to engaging a psychologist will be the cumulative result of all these interacting influences. The decision will be a moment pregnant with much experience, with many emotions, with many interests. When you hear someone say that there are not so many one-man decisions in scientifically managed plants as in others, they do not mean necessarily that the decisions in those plants are made by committees, but rather that the decisions are part of a process of interacting influence made possible by the form of organisation, and these interacting influences gather force until comes the moment which we call the decision. The fallacy of finals has too long blinded us to the true nature of decisions.

In summary of this matter I think we may say that so much goes to contribute to executive decisions before the part which the executive head takes in them, that the conception of final authority is losing its force in the present organisation of business. And this is as true of other executives as of the head. Here, too, final decisions have the form and the force which they have accumulated. I have seen an executive seem a little self-important over a decision he had made when it had really come to him ready made.

I do not of course want to imply that there is no such thing as final authority. There are some questions which have to be decided by the head alone. Moreover, the head must decide when there is disagreement between executives which these executives cannot manage to deal with themselves. I am not denying the existence of final authority. I am speaking only against its over-emphasis, against ignoring the fact that decisions are usually reached through a process. The growth of a decision, the accumulation of authority, not the final step, is what we need most to study.

What I have wanted to try to make clear is that authority is not something from the top which filters down to those below. I hoped it would help us to understand this if we considered how decisions were really made. There is something else which may help us to understand this very important point, and that is the relation of departmental policy to general policy.

In books on business management we sometimes find this sentence, "General policy dictates departmental policies." But when the Board of Directors want to decide on a general policy, have they not to take into consideration the policy of the sales department, of the manufacturing department, the views of the financial department and of those dealing with the human element, the personnel department? You will find that general policy is made up of all the departmental policies. Is it then wrong to say that general policy dictates departmental policy? No, because after general policy is formulated by the Board of Directors or Executive Committee, then the various departments have to see that their various policies conform to it. The flow goes both ways. They contribute to general policy and then they must conform to general policy. They follow what they have helped to construct. But this latter part is what we forget when we say that general policy dictates departmental policies. We forget that general policy is not an air plant, but has its roots in all that is going on in the business.

Mr. Gerard Swope, President of the General Electric, told me, "It is the greatest mistake to think that a business is run from the President's chair, that there is constantly flowing out of my office a stream of directions. In fact the flow is just the other way. I sit all day in my office and receive my upper executives who come to me with plans and suggestions for my acceptance." I said, "What then is the need of you? What is your particular job?" He had his answer to that all ready, but I am not going to give it to you until later in our talks when we consider the function of the chief executive more particularly. All that I am calling your attention to now is the flow from executives up to the General Manager. I do not say that the General Manager's consent is not important. It is very important, but it is only one part of the process.

The whole science of business management today tends to be based on the linking of one part with another, on the contribution of some narrower aspect of the work to a broader aspect. When I am told that sales planning is but a division of business planning, when I am told that sales research is only part of a broader function which might be designated commercial research, then I say that we have got out of the region of finals and absolutes, that we are going beyond our old notion of supreme authority.

If we accept the statement that authority is a process, we find that the phrase delegation of authority is a little misleading. What is the fallacy here? Suppose we consider what actually happens when we wish to start a new business. We probably call in an expert organiser to organise it. One executive is given authority over one thing, another over something else. When I say "is given" I do not mean that the expert gives it, but that the form of organisation decides the matter. The form of organisation decides what authority the general manager shall have. Therefore we do not talk about the delegation of authority, because that would seem to imply that someone had the right to all the authority, but that for purposes of convenience he delegated some of it.

It becomes still more obvious that this is not true if you consider the creation of new functions. The head of a large concern told me that he knew nothing about merchandising and must therefore engage a merchandise manager. Obviously he was not giving up any of his authority, but a certain amount of authority would belong to that job.

It is just the same with the separation of functions as with the creation of new ones. For instance, in a small bank the head in addition to his other duties, looks after the new business. As the business of the bank increases, a separate man is given responsibility for new business: exchange, deposits, credit loans, and so on. Here we see very clearly that the separation of function does not mean the delegation of authority. Authority follows the function. When one man had the job he had the authority. When the job went to someone else, the authority went with it. Authority belongs to the job and stays with the job.

We have been confused in theory on this point because we have never got over the eighteenth-century way of thinking when men were always thinking about their rights. And so we have gone at this subject from the angle of rights, tried to see what authority belonged by right to certain people. But this has only been in theory. In practice it all works out quite naturally. For instance, to take another illustration from banking, the head of a branch bank may decide on small loans, while large loans may have to go up to the executive committee. This is not because the matter of large loans belongs by "right" to the executive committee, but because it is recognised that the combined judgment of executive committee and the head of the branch bank is probably better than that of either alone.

That we are beginning now to get away from the notion of rights, that we are beginning to think more and more in terms of the job, is why I call the treatment of authority I am presenting to you a realistic one. We are beginning in business management to rid ourselves of many theories, abstract notions, mere clichés, of conceptions which have become meaningless, and nowhere is this more marked than in the case of my subject this evening. For we are trying to think out the form of organisation whereby authority may go with three things: knowledge, experience, and the skill to apply that knowledge and experience.

It is perhaps due to the fact that arbitrary authority, the authority of mere position, is diminishing, more than to anything else, that business management is approaching a science.

To sum up: all this question of decisions, of responsibility, of authority has been made, I think, too personal. The important thing about a decision is not who makes it but what gets into it. The important thing about responsibility is not to whom you are responsible, but for what you are responsible. The important thing about authority is that real authority and official authority shall coincide.

You will see by this time that I believe in authority. Those writers who think people should rebel against authority seem to me to have a wholly wrong idea of the matter. Submission to authority does not imply, as these writers seem to think, a lack of freedom. On the contrary, it is by an understanding of the laws which govern the process by which authority is generated that we gain our freedom, freedom in any true sense of the word. For authority, genuine authority, is the outcome of our common life. It does not come from separating people, from dividing them into two classes, those who command and those who obey. It comes from the intermingling of all, of my work fitting into yours and yours into mine, and from that intermingling of forces a power being created which will control those forces. Authority is a self-generating process. To learn more of that process, the process of control, is what we all think the world today most needs.

COMMENTARY

Mary Parker Follett's View on Power, the Giving of Orders, and Authority: An Alternative to Hierarchy or a Utopian Ideology?

Nitin Nohria

I FIRST read "The Giving of Orders" as a graduate student at MIT. But I truly discovered Mary Parker Follett only about three years ago, toward the end of a project that I was doing with Bob

Eccles, a colleague at the Harvard Business School. In 1988, when I joined the Harvard faculty, Bob and I were both convinced, as many continue to be today, that the hierarchical bureaucracy—the dominant organizational model since the turn of this century—was rapidly becoming obsolete. We were convinced that because of the waning of the archetype of industrial bureaucracy a new model would be required for organizations of the next century.

Even though the field was crowded, Bob and I joined the fray. We placed our bets on what we called the "network" organization. We eagerly set out to elaborate and develop this idea that we hoped would eventually supplant the increasing number of competing ideas for the new organization such as the postbureaucratic organization, the information-based organization, the cluster organization, the virtual organization, the metanoic organization, and so forth.

We began by looking where we thought we were most likely to find this new organization. We decided to study organizations in knowledge-intensive contexts—where value was added primarily through "brainpower," not "machine power"—because it was widely held that one of the major forces driving the obsolescence of bureaucracy was the transition from an industrial to a knowledge-based society.

Two years and hundreds of interviews later, we wrote up what we had learned. The product was a paper with the awkward title "The Poststructuralist Organization." In it we set forth what we felt were some of the defining characteristics of the new organization that would inevitably replace hierarchy. But like everyone else writing about the new organization, we could not say that we had actually studied even one organization that exhibited all the characteristics we had identified. Thus our model was more on the order of an "ideal type"—a conceptual archetype akin to Weber's bureaucracy.

After we had let the paper sit for some time, we developed a gnawing sense that, even though we were writing about the advent of a new organization based on an extensive study of "new-age" organizations, not much of what we had found was actually new. Although we were describing the features of an organization that we felt was at the cutting edge (and indeed, "was destined to become the dominant organizational model in the century ahead"), many of the features we had outlined were disturbingly reminiscent of models of organization we had seen earlier. We were not sure, for instance, how our model of the new organization truly differed from the model of the "organic" organization proposed by Burns and Stalker (1961) 30 years earlier. It was then that I recalled the papers by Mary Parker Follett, which had been gathering dust in the attic of my mind.

Our unease about whether we were saying anything new led us to carefully reexamine the early literature on organizations. We wanted to determine exactly when the quest to identify a new organization that was to replace bureaucracy was born and how this quest had evolved over time. You can only imagine our surprise when we found that every one of the features of the new organization that we (and so many others) were so giddily proclaiming as cutting-edge and revolutionary had been anticipated by Mary Parker Follett at the same time as bureaucracy was ostensibly being ensconced as the dominant organizational model for the twentieth century.

As many of the other commentators in this book have noted, we were struck by how clearly, cogently, and comprehensively Mary Parker Follett had articulated the principles of organization that are in vogue today. Consider, for instance, her essays on power, authority, and the giving of orders. In them Follett captures the essence of contemporary thinking on these topics.

Follett's argument hinges on reframing the way we commonly think of power and authority. In "Power," she highlights the many ways in which we use the term "power" and draws our attention to the distinction between power "over" and power "with": "Whereas power usually means power-over, the power of some person or group over some other person or group, it is possible to develop the conception of power-with, a jointly developed power, a co-active, not a coercive power."[1] Follett argues that firms can be more effective if they emphasize power-with rather than power-over. To translate this ideology into practice, Follett recommends that the way to develop power-with is to organize and manage so "that you can influence a co-manager while he is influencing you, so that a workman has an opportunity of influencing you as you have of influencing him."[2] Ignoring her gender-biased writing style (ironic, given that she was one of the most influential women in the field of management in her time), I find that Follett offers contemporary readers, especially those who may be as puzzled as I am, one of the clearest statements of what the current buzzword "empowerment" really means.

Similarly, with respect to authority Follett writes: "Authority should go with knowledge and experience, that is where obedience is due no matter whether it is up the line or down the line."[3] Instead of organizations where authority is based primarily on hierarchical position and people can be separated into two classes, those who command and those who obey, Follett recommends that we "think out the form of organization where by authority may go with three things: knowledge, experience, and the skill to apply that knowledge and experience." Thus, in her essay on authority, Follett anticipates much of what organizational theorists (including agency theorists) preach today—that we should recognize that knowledge does not reside solely at the top of the organization; that knowledge specific to the performance of a task may lie with those who are most intimately involved in doing the task; that workers should thus be valued not only for their labor but also for their knowledge; and that by treating everyone as a knowledge-worker and creating a learning organization, we can more fully realize the potential of any organization.

In "The Giving of Orders" Follett further elaborates her vision of a mode of organizing that stands in sharp contrast to the Weberian bureaucracy. In this essay her primary thesis is that orders should not be based on positional authority. In most organizations, she laments, there is a class system defined by one class of order givers and another of order takers. This creates a system of obedience and control—those who receive orders are expected to obey them and, in addition to giving orders, the order givers must ensure compliance. Such a control-oriented system, according to Follett, has several disadvantages. It loses "what we might learn from the man actually on the job."[4] It "ignores one of the fundamental facts of human nature, namely the wish to govern one's own life."[5] It forgets that "the worker is often . . . equally interested . . . in [doing] the best of which he is capable."[6] And it "decreases the worker's sense of responsibility."[7]

To overcome the disadvantages of a command-and-control system, Follett recommends a system in which the giving of orders is based on the "law of situation." In such a system orders are depersonalized. Orders are given not because the person giving the order wants something done, but because it is demanded by the task or the situation at hand. Follett believed that in any situation, reasonable people could come to an agreement of who needed to do what to achieve the best possible results. Orders could be naturally generated by focusing on the demands of the situation. Orders that emanate from the law of the situation, Follett argues, are less likely to be resented and more likely to be followed. Furthermore, since the orders are based on the logic of the task and incorporate the input of all those whose expertise is relevant to performing the task, the task can inevitably be performed more effectively.

Follett's ideas on the giving of orders define the behavioral principles that are at the heart of contemporary wisdom on high-performance teams. Recent research suggests that the division of work and responsibility in high-performance teams is usually based on an assessment of what the situation demands and how that matches up with the skills of the team members. Coordination and other supervisory tasks can be assigned to an informal team leader, but the role of the leader in this setting is oriented toward serving as a facilitator or coach rather than someone who gives orders. Orders in these teams, as Follett recommended so many years ago, flow from the task or problem at hand and not from positional authority. Indeed, in most cases the team meets at the beginning of every workday, or whenever there is a problem, to discuss the situation at hand; it develops a shared plan of action and then takes responsibility for making sure the plan is implemented. In sum, contemporary research supports Follett's premise that organizations perform best when they operate on the basis of shared responsibility and not arbitrary command and obedience.

I could highlight many other ideas from Follett's essays that resonate with contemporary thinking. Her emphasis on employee training and education and on finding integrative solutions in negotiation are just examples of why she richly deserves the title— "prophet of management." Like many of the other commentators here, I think it is time we acknowledged our debts and paid tribute to this forgotten prophet.

But even as I join in the long overdue celebration of Mary Parker Follett's contributions to management practice, I feel compelled to raise some concerns. Follett was, no doubt, the first modern management thinker to propose a mode of organization that could serve as an alternative to the traditional bureaucratic hierarchy. And even though the ideology she espoused and the principles she advocated seem especially relevant to our contemporary quest for the new organization, it is worth noting that Follett's ideas have not remained dormant until now. There have been at least two other periods when ideas similar to Follett's flourished. The first was the participative management school of thought that flourished in the 1950s and 1960s. The essence of this ideology was captured by Douglas McGregor (1960) in his famous distinction between Theory X and Theory Y. Although the advocates of a Theory Y approach to management did not acknowledge Follett's legacy (there is not one reference to Follett's work in McGregor's *Human Side of Enterprise*), they echoed the same themes she had struck more than two decades earlier (I urge you to read Chapter 2, "Methods of Influence and Control," in McGregor's book to see how similar his ideas were to Follett's).

The second period during which ideas resonant with Follett's principles flourished was in the 1970s, when job enrichment, employee involvement, job redesign, workplace democracy, and quality of work life became the vaunted ideas of the time. Again, Follett's legacy went largely unrecognized. While it is sad that we have waited so long to honor Follett, what really concerns me is that neither of these movements had a lasting impact. Both had a short half-life. Their popularity waned as quickly as it waxed.

Now for a third time we are trying to reinvent organizations. With the republication of some of Mary Parker Follett's papers, we have at least been more careful to acknowledge our intellectual debt. But can we be sanguine that this time we will finally be able to create organizations that enduringly embody the principles laid down by Follett? Will our new organizations last any longer than some of the earlier experiments I've mentioned?

Certainly the calls for change are more strident today than they were during the two earlier revivals, and the extent to which the ideology is espoused is more widespread. There are, no doubt, enabling information technologies that offer unprecedented organizing possibilities. And there are many experiments that might point the way. But, frankly, I think that contemporary efforts to create new organizations that reflect Follett's ideas are no more likely to endure tomorrow than they did yesterday.

I am pessimistic for the following reasons. First, although I agree with Follett that we can think of power and authority in many ways—and that a more productive view of power might well be to view it as power-with, not as power-over—I fear that as long as there are people who seek power, as Follett herself noted, "as a means to end or as end in itself," it will be hard to sustain a system based on the former view of power. Trust, as others wiser than I have noted, is a fragile thing. It is hard to build and easy to destroy.

All it takes to destroy trust is a few people who are driven to acquire power-over as opposed to power-with. And since Follett admits that it is unlikely that "we shall ever get rid of power-over," I think organizations based on the principle of empowerment or power-with will always remain fragile and especially susceptible to reversion to a command-and-control system during times of change in their leadership.

Second, I am not sure that authority can be based on the "law of situation." While Follett is right in pointing out that it might be useful to depersonalize authority or the giving of orders by focusing on the task at hand and not on the person, there are unfortunately few situations where the best course of action can be unambiguously determined. Indeed, most situations are ambiguous and uncertain, and it is not at all straightforward, even for well-intentioned individuals, to derive orders based on the law of the situation.

Indeed, if there is any law of the situation that is universal, it is Michel's iron law of oligarchy. After reviewing numerous efforts at true egalitarian reform, Michel begrudgingly concluded: "The majority of human beings, in a condition of eternal tutelage, are predestined by tragic necessity to submit to the dominion of a small minority, and must be content to constitute the pedestal of an oligarchy." I believe Michel found the Achilles heel of Follett's argument. The evidence overwhelmingly supports Michel's view that all organizations eventually become divided into a minority of directors and a majority of directed. I fear that's what inevitably happens to efforts to introduce a more egalitarian and participative system of authority and explains the short half-life of earlier attempts to create organizations that presented an alternative to hierarchy.

A third reason why I believe that Follett's principles may be more idealistic than pragmatic is that there exist situations that are truly zero-sum, where it is not possible to find an integrative solution. In such situations someone has to suffer. A classic case is downsizing. It is hard to arrive at a decision to lay off 20 percent of a workforce through a participative process. In situations where distributive considerations become paramount, someone has to make a tough decision, a decision that inevitably will be contested by those who lose out. It is not clear how an organization built on Follett's principles can either make such decisions on a timely basis or survive once such a decision has to be made.

For all these reasons, I think Follett's ideas for a different kind of organization to serve as an alternative to bureaucracy may well be a utopian ideal that we can never actually realize. But I do not imply that we should either abandon the quest or let Follett's ideas be forgotten. To the extent that Follett provides a vision of an organization that we could all feel better about working in, I think we should continue to cherish and use her ideas for their rhetorical force—as a beacon for change that we can keep striving for and at times—albeit imperfectly and, alas, fleetingly—achieve.

A final word about this beacon. To view Follett's ideas from a rhetorical perspective is to realize that the primary task of managers is to mobilize organized action. Thus, if we adopt a rhetorical perspective, the periodic search for a new organization that is an alternative to bureaucracy need not be viewed cynically. It can be understood as an attempt to lend new energy to organizations that find themselves, like many do today, in situations of doubt and realignment. For such organizations, Follett's vision provides the energy to move forward. And for that we must always be thankful.

NOTES

1. Mary Parker Follett, "Power," in *Dynamic Administration: The Collected Papers of Mary Parker Follett,* Elliot M. Fox and L. Urwick, eds. (London: Pitman, 1973), p. 72.
2. Ibid., p. 76.
3. Mary Parker Follett, "The Illusion of Final Authority," in *Freedom and Coordination,* L. Urwick, ed. (London: Management Publications Trust, 1949), p. 2.
4. Ibid., p. 19.
5. Ibid., p. 20.
6. Ibid., p. 21.
7. Ibid.

+≒ ≒+

The Essentials of Leadership

I HAVE tried to show you certain changes which are creeping in to our thinking on business management. As I have said in the more progressively managed businesses an order was no longer an arbitrary command but—the law of the situation. A week ago I defined authority as something which could not really be conferred on someone, but as a power which inhered in the job. Now I want to show the difference between the theory of leadership long accepted and a conception which is being forced on our attention by the way in which business is today conducted.

What I call the old-fashioned theory of leadership is well illustrated by a study made a few years ago by two psychologists. They worked out a list of questions by which to test leadership ability. Here are some of the questions:

At a reception or tea do you try to meet the important persons present?

At a lecture or entertainment do you go forward and take a front seat?

At a hairdresser's are you persuaded to try a new shampoo or are you able to resist?

Note: This chapter is reprinted from L. Urwick, ed. *Freedom & Co-ordination: Lectures in Business Organisation by Mary Parker Follett* (London: Management Publications Trust, Ltd., 1949), pp. 47–60.

If you make purchases at Woolworths, are you ashamed to have your friends know it?

If you are at a stupid party do you try to inject life into it?

If you hold an opinion the reverse of which the lecturer has expressed do you usually volunteer your opinion?

Do you find it difficult to say No when a salesman is trying to sell you something?

What do you do when someone tries to push in ahead of you in a line at the box office?

When you see someone in a public place whom you think you have met, do you go up to him and enquire whether you have met?

And so on—there are a good many more. But what on earth has all this to do with leadership? I think nothing whatever. These psychologists were making tests, they said, for aggressiveness, assuming that aggressiveness and leadership are synonymous, assuming that you cannot be a good leader unless you are aggressive, masterful, dominating. But I think, not only that these characteristics are not the qualities essential to leadership, but, on the contrary, that they often militate directly against leadership. I knew a boy who was very decidedly the boss of his gang all through his youthful days. That boy is now forty-eight years old. He has not risen in his business or shown any power of leadership in his community. And I do not think that this has been in spite of his dominating traits, but because of them.

But I cannot blame the psychologists too much, for in the business world too there has been an idea long prevalent that self-assertion, pugnacity even, are necessary to leadership. Or at any rate, the leader is usually supposed to be one who has a compelling personality, who can impose his own will on others, can make others do what he wants done.

One writer says that running a business is like managing an unruly horse, a simile I particularly dislike. Another writer says, "The successful business man feels at his best in giving orders. . . . The business man tends to lay down the law—he feels himself to be an individual source of energy." While this is undoubtedly true of many business men, yet there are many today of whom it is not true. It is no longer the universally accepted type of administrative leadership. We saw two weeks ago that in scientifically managed plants, with their planning departments, their experts, their staff officials, their trained managers of the line, few "orders" are given in the old sense of the word. When therefore we are told that large-scale ability means masterfulness and autocratic will, some of us wish to reply: But that is the theory of the past, it is not what we find today in the best-managed industries.

This does not however denote that less leadership is required than formerly, but a different kind. Let me take two illustrations, one of the foreman, one of the salesman. We find in those plants where there is little order-giving of the old kind, where the right order is found by research, that the foreman is not only as important but more important than formerly. He is by no means less of a leader; indeed he has more opportunities for leadership in the sense of that word which is now coming to be accepted by many. This is because his time is freed for more constructive work. With the more explicitly defined requirements made upon him— requirements in regard to time, quality of work and methods—he has a greater responsibility for group accomplishment. In order to meet the standards set for group accomplishment, he is developing a technique very different from the old foreman technique. The foreman today does not merely deal with trouble, he forestalls trouble. In fact we don't think much of a foreman who is always dealing with trouble; we feel that if he were doing his job properly, there wouldn't be so much trouble. The job of the head of any unit—foreman or head of department—is to see that conditions (machines, materials, etc.) are right, to see that instructions are understood, and to see that workers are trained to carry out the instructions, trained to use the methods which have been decided on as best. The test of a foreman now is not how good he is at bossing, but how little bossing he has to do, because of the training of his men and the organisation of their work.

Now take the salesman. If the foreman was supposed to dominate by aggressiveness, the salesman was supposed to dominate by persuasiveness. Consider the different demand made on salesmen today. Salesmen are being chosen less and less for their powers of persuasion, but for their general intelligence, for their knowledge of the goods handled, and for their ability to teach prospective customers the best way to use the goods. A business man said to me: "The training of salesmen . . . is being carried on with increasing elaboration, and always with more emphasis on knowledge of the product and its uses, and distinctly less on the technique of persuasion. . . ." For the firms who sell production equipment, this means sending men who sometimes act as consulting engineers for their customers.

We find this same doctrine taught in the salesmanship classes held in the big shops. The shop assistants are told not to over-persuade a customer, else when the customer gets home she may be sorry she has bought that article and may not come to that shop again. The saleswoman may have made one sale and lost a dozen by her persuasiveness. Her job is to know her goods and to study the needs of her customer.

To dominate, either by a masterful or a persuasive personality, is going out of fashion. People advertise courses in what they call "applied psychology" and promise that they will teach you how to develop your personality and thus become leaders, but wiser teachers say to their students, "Forget your personality, learn your job."

What then are the requisites of leadership? First, a thorough knowledge of your job. And this fact is keenly appreciated today as business is becoming a profession and business management a science. Men train themselves to become heads of departments or staff officials by learning all that goes with the particular position they wish to attain.

Consider the influence which it is possible for the cost accountant to exercise because of his special knowledge. Where there is cost-accounting and unit budgeting, the cost accountant is in a position to know more about the effect of a change in price than anyone else. His analyses and his interpretations may dictate policy to the chief executive.

Moreover, we find leadership in many places besides these more obvious ones, and this is just because men are learning special techniques and therefore naturally lead in those situations. The chairman of a committee may not occupy a high official position or be a man of forceful personality, but he may know how to guide discussion effectively, that is, he may know the technique of *his* job. Or consider the industrial-relations-man now maintained in so many industries. This man is an adept at conciliation. He has a large and elaborate technique for that at his command.

When it is a case of instruction, the teacher is the leader. Yet a good instructor may be a poor foreman. Again, some men can make people produce, and some are good at following up quality who could never make people produce.

There is also individual leadership which may come to the fore irrespective of any particular position; of two girls on a machine, one may be the leader. We often see individual leadership, that is, leadership irrespective of position, springing up in a committee. There was an instance of this in a sales committee. The chairman of the committee was the sales manager, Smith. Smith was narrow but not obstinate. Not being obstinate, Jones was able to get Smith to soften his opinion on the particular matter in question, and there was then an integration of the opinion of that committee around Jones' leadership.

I think it is of great importance to recognise that leadership is sometimes in one place and sometimes in another. For it tends to prevent apathy among under-executives. It makes them much more alert if they realise that they have many chances of leadership before they are advanced to positions which carry with them definitely, officially, leadership. Moreover, if such occasional leadership is exercised with moderation without claiming too much for oneself, without encroaching on anyone's official position, it may mean that that person will be advanced to an official position of leadership.

But let us look further at the essentials of leadership. Of the greatest importance is the ability to grasp a total situation. The chief mistake in thinking of leadership as resting wholly on personality lies probably in the fact that the executive leader is not a leader of men only but of something we are learning to call the total situation. This includes facts, present and potential, aims and purposes and men. Out of a welter of facts, experience, desires, aims, the leader must find the unifying thread. He must see a whole, not a mere kaleidoscope of pieces. He must see the relation between all the different factors in a situation. The higher up you go, the more ability you have to have of this kind, because you have a wider range of facts from which to seize the relations. The foreman has a certain range—a comparatively small number of facts and small number of people. The head of a sub-department has a wider range; the head of a department a wider still, the general manager the widest of all. One of the principal functions of the general manager is to organise all the scattered forces of the business. The higher railway officials may not understand railway accounting, design of rolling stock, and assignment of rates as well as their expert assistants, but they know how to use their knowledge, how to relate it, how to make a total situation.

The leader then is one who can organise the experience of the group—whether it be the small group of the foreman, the larger group of the department, or the whole plant—can organise the experience of the group and thus get the full power of the group. The leader makes the team. This is pre-eminently the leadership quality—the ability to organise all the forces there are in an enterprise and make them serve a common purpose. Men with this ability create a group power rather than express a personal power. They penetrate to the subtlest connections of the forces at their command, and make all these forces available and most effectively available for the accomplishment of their purpose.

Some writers tell us that the leader should represent the accumulated knowledge and experience of his particular group, but I think he should go far beyond this. It is true that the able executive learns from everyone around him, but it is also true that he is far more than the depository where the wisdom of the group collects. When leadership rises to genius it has the power of transforming, of transforming experience into power. And that is what experience is for, to be made into power. The great leader creates as well as directs power. The essence of leadership is to create control, and that is what the world needs today, control of small situations or of our world situation.

I have said that the leader must understand the situation, must see it as a whole, must see the inter-relation of all the parts. He must do more than this. He must see the evolving situation, the developing situation. His wisdom, his judgment, is used, not on a situation that is stationary, but on one that is changing all the time. The ablest administrators do not merely draw logical conclusions from the array of facts of the past which their expert assistants bring to them, they have a vision of the future. To be sure, business estimates are always, or should be, based on the probable future conditions. Sales policy, for instance, is guided not only by past sales but by probable future sales. The leader, however, must see all the future trends and unite them. Business is always developing. Decisions have to anticipate the development. You remember how Alice in Wonderland had to run as fast as she could in order to stand still. That is a commonplace to every business man. And it is up to the general manager to see that his executives are running as fast as they can. Not, you understand, working as hard as they can—that is taken for granted—but anticipating as far as they can.

This insight into the future we usually call in business anticipating. But anticipating means more than forecasting or predicting. It means far more than meeting the next situation, it means making the next situation. If you will watch decisions, you will find that the highest grade decision does not have to do merely with the situation with which it is directly concerned. It is always the sign of the second-rate man when the decision merely meets the present situation. It is the left-over in a decision which gives it the greatest value. It is the carry-over in a decision which helps develop the situation in the way we wish it to be developed. In business we are always passing from one significant moment to another significant moment, and the leader's task is pre-eminently to understand the moment of passing. The leader sees one situation melting into another and has learned the mastery of that moment. We usually have the situation we make—no one sentence is more pregnant with meaning for business success. This is why the leader's task is so difficult, why the great leader requires the great qualities—the most delicate and sensitive perceptions, imagination and insight, and at the same time courage and faith.

The leader should have the spirit of adventure, but the spirit of adventure need not mean the temperament of the gambler. It should be the pioneer spirit which blazes new trails. The insight to see possible new paths, the courage to try them, the judgment to measure results—these are the qualifications of the leader.

And now let me speak to you for a moment of something which seems to me of the utmost importance, but which has been far too little considered, and that is the part of the followers in the leader-ship situation. Their part is not merely to follow, they have a very active part to play and that is to keep the leader in control of a situation. Let us not think that we are either leaders or—nothing of much importance. As one of those led we have a part in leader-ship. In no aspect of our subject do we see a greater discrepancy between theory and practice than here. The definition given over and over again of the leader is one who can induce others to follow him. Or that meaning is taken for granted and the question is asked: "What is the technique by which a leader keeps his followers in line?" Some political scientists discuss why men obey or do not obey, why they tend to lead or to follow, as if leading and following were the essence of leadership. I think that following is a very small part of what the other members of a group have to do. I think that these authors are writing of theory, of words, of stereotypes of the past, that they are, at any rate, not noticing the changes that are going on in business thinking and business practice. If we want to treat these questions realistically, we shall watch what is actually happening, and what I see happening in some places is that the members of a group are not so much following a leader as helping to keep him in control of a situation.

How do we see this being done? For one thing, in looking at almost any business we see many suggestions coming up from below. We find sub-executives trying to get upper executives to install mechanical improvements, to try a new chemical process, to adopt a plan for increasing incentives for workers, and so on. The upper executives try to persuade the general manager and the general manager the board of directors. We have heard a good deal in the past about the consent of the governed; we have now in modern business much that might be called the consent of the governing, the suggestions coming from below and those at the top consenting. I am not trying to imitate Shaw and Chesterton and being paradoxical; there is actually a change going on in business practice in this respect which I want to emphasise to you at every point.

How else may a man help to keep those above him in control? He may, instead of trying to "get by" on something, instead of covering up his difficulties so that no one will know he is having any, inform his chief of his problems, tell him the things he is not succeeding in as well as all his wonderful achievements. His chief will respect him just as much for his failures as for his successes if he himself takes the right attitude towards them.

Another way is to take a wrong order back for correction. It may have been an error, or it may be that it was all right once, but that it must be changed to meet changing conditions. The worker has not met his responsibility by merely obeying. Many a worker thinks that the pointing out of a wrong order is a gratuitous thing on his part, a favour he generously confers but which he need not because it is not really his job, his job is to obey. As a matter of fact, however, obeying is only a small part of his job. One general manager told me that what they disliked in his factory was what they called there the Yes, yes man. The intelligent leader, this man said, does not want the kind of follower who thinks of his job only in terms of passive obedience.

But there is following. Leader and followers are both following the invisible leader—the common purpose. The best executives put this common purpose clearly before their group. While leadership depends on depth of conviction and the power coming therefrom, there must also be the ability to share that conviction with others, the ability to make purpose articulate. And then that common purpose becomes the leader. And I believe that we are coming more and more to act, whatever our theories, on our faith in the power of this invisible leader. Loyalty to the invisible leader gives us the strongest possible bond of union, establishes a sympathy which is not a sentimental but a dynamic sympathy.

Moreover, when both leader and followers are obeying the same demand, you have, instead of a passive, an active, self-willed obedience. The men on a fishing smack are all good fellows together, call each other by their first names, yet one is captain and the others obey him; but it is an intelligent, alert, self-willed obedience.

The best leaders get their orders obeyed because they too are obeying. Sincerity more than aggressiveness is a quality of leadership.

If the leader should teach his followers their part in the leadership situation, how to help keep their chief in control, he has another duty equally important. He has to teach them how to control the situations for which they are specifically responsible. This is an essential part of leadership and a part recognised today. We have a good illustration of this in the relation between upper executives and heads of departments in those firms where the Budget is used as a tool of control. Suppose an upper executive is dissatisfied with the work of a department. When this happens it is either because quality is too poor or costs are too high. The old method of procedure was for the upper executive simply to blame the head of the department. But in a plant where the departments are budgeted, an upper executive can ask the head of a department to sit down with him and consider the matter. The Budget objectifies the whole situation. It is possible for an upper executive to get the head of the department to find out himself where the difficulty lies and to make him give himself the necessary orders to meet the situation.

Many are coming to think that the job of a man higher up is not to make decisions for his subordinates but to teach them how to handle their problems themselves, teach them how to make their own decisions. The best leader does not persuade men to follow his will. He shows them what it is necessary for them to do in order to meet their responsibility, a responsibility which has been explicitly defined to them. Such a leader is not one who wishes to do people's thinking for them, but one who trains them to think for themselves.

Indeed the best leaders try to train their followers themselves to become leaders. A second-rate executive will often try to suppress leadership because he fears it may rival his own. I have seen several instances of this. But the first-rate executive tries to develop leadership in those under him. He does not want men who are subservient to him, men who render him an unthinking obedience. While therefore there are still men who try to surround themselves with docile servants—you all know that type—the ablest men today have a larger aim, they wish to be leaders of leaders. This does not mean that they abandon one iota of power. But the great leader tries also to develop power wherever he can among those who work with him, and then he gathers all this power and uses it as the energising force of a progressing enterprise.

If any of you think I have under-estimated the personal side of leadership, let me point out that I have spoken against only that conception which emphasises the dominating, the masterful man. I most certainly believe that many personal qualities enter into leadership—tenacity, sincerity, fair dealings with all, steadfastness of purpose, depth of conviction, control of temper, tact, steadiness in stormy periods, ability to meet emergencies, power to draw forth and develop the latent possibilities of others, and so on. There are many more. There is, for instance, the force of example on which we cannot lay too great stress. If workers have to work overtime, their head should be willing to do the same. In every way he must show that he is willing to do what he urges on others.

One winter I went yachting with some friends in the inland waterways of the southern part of the United States. On one occasion our pilot led us astray and we found ourselves one night aground in a Carolina swamp. Obviously the only thing to do was to try to push the boat off, but the crew refused, saying that the swamps in that region were infested with rattlesnakes. The owner of the yacht offered not a word of remonstrance, but turned instantly and jumped overboard. Every member of the crew followed.

So please remember that I do not underestimate what is called the personal side of leadership, indeed there is much in this paper, by implication, on that side. And do not think that I underestimate the importance of the man at the top. No one could put more importance on top leadership than I do, as I shall try to show you next week when we consider the part of the chief executive in that intricate system of human relationship which business has now become.

I might say as a summary of this talk that we have three kinds of leadership: the leadership of position, the leadership of personality and the leadership of function. My claim for modern industry is that in the best managed plants the leadership of function is tending to have more weight and the leadership of mere position or of mere personality less.

Please note that I say only a tendency. I am aware how often a situation is controlled by a man either because his position gives him the whip hand and he uses it, or because he knows how to play politics. My only thesis is that in the more progressively managed businesses there is a tendency for the control of a particular situation to go to the man with the largest knowledge of that situation, to him who can grasp and organise its essential elements, who understands its total significance, who can see it through—who can see length as well as breadth—rather than to one with merely a dominating personality or in virtue of his official position.

And that thought brings me to my conclusion. The chief thing I have wanted to do in this hour is to explode a long-held superstition. We have heard repeated again and again in the past, "Leaders are born, not made." I read the other day "Leadership is a capacity that cannot be acquired." I believe that leadership can, in part, be learned. I hope you will not let anyone persuade you that it cannot be. The man who thinks leadership cannot be learned will probably remain in a subordinate position. The man who believes it can be, will go to work and learn it. He may not ever be president of the company, but he can rise from where he is.

Moreover, if leadership could not be learned, our large, complex businesses would not have much chance of success, for they require able leadership in many places, not only in the president's chair.

Leadership is a part of business management and there is a rapidly developing technique for every aspect of the administration and management of a business.

I urge you then, instead of accepting the idea that there is something mysterious about leadership, to analyse it. I think that then you cannot fail to see that there are many aspects of it which can be acquired. For instance, a part of leadership is all that makes you get on most successfully in your direct contacts with people— how and when to praise, how and when to point out mistakes, what attitude to take toward failures. All this can of course be learned. The first thing to do is to discover what is necessary for leadership and then to try to acquire by various methods those essentials. Even those personal characteristics with which we were endowed by birth can often be changed. For instance, vitality, energy, physical endurance, are usually necessary for leadership, but even this is not always beyond us. Theodore Roosevelt was a delicate lad and yet became an explorer, a Rough Rider, a fighter, and by his own determined efforts. You have seen timid boys become self-confident. You have seen bumptious little boys have all that taken out of them by their schoolmasters.

Leadership is not the "intangible," the "incalculable" thing we have often seen it described. It is capable of being analysed into its different elements, and many of these elements can be acquired and become part of one's equipment.

My paper has been concerned with functional leadership and with multiple leadership. Our present historians and biographers are strengthening the conception of multiple leadership by showing us that in order to understand any epoch we must take into account the lesser leaders. They tell us also that the number of these lesser leaders has been so steadily increasing that one of the most outstanding facts of our life today is a widely diffused leadership. Wells goes further and says that his hope for the future depends on a still more widely diffused leadership. In the past, he says, we depended on a single great leader . . . today many men and women must help to lead. In the past, he says, Aristotle led the world in science, today there are thousands of scientists each making his contribution.

Industry gives to men and women the chance for leadership, the chance to make their contribution to what all agree is the thing most needed in the world today.

Business used to be thought of as trading, managing as manipulating. Both ideas are now changing. Business is becoming a profession and management a science and an art. This means that men must prepare themselves for business as seriously as for any other profession. They must realise that they, as all professional men, are assuming grave responsibilities, that they are to take a creative part in one of the large functions of society, a part which, I believe, only trained and disciplined men can in the future hope to take with success.

COMMENTARY

Thoughts on "The Essentials of Leadership"
Warren Bennis

I TAKE mild exception to Peter Drucker's characterization of Mary Parker Follett as a "nonperson." She wasn't to me. Not at all. My mentor, Doug McGregor, referred to her constantly, and in a 1942 article on collective bargaining he cited her distinction between "genuine collaboration and adversarial collective bargaining." Later, in a book I helped edit, I referred to her "law of the situation," of which she wrote, prophetically as usual: "When there is identification with organizational goals, the members tend to perceive what the situation requires and to do it whether the boss exerts influence to have it done or not. In fact, he need not be present or even aware of the immediate circumstances." This sounds suspiciously like—even identical with—what leadership and organizational theorists are saying today. No, Mary Parker Follett wasn't a nonperson to me, but she was a cult figure during the formative years of my academic upbringing.

One of the most striking things to observe about Follett's life and career is that she lived as long in the nineteenth century as she did in the twentieth! She was born only three years after the end of the Civil War. A central concern of nineteenth-century female writers—Jane Austen, George Eliot, the Brontes, as well as some of the men—was female dependency. With the move to the cities and the loosening of family ties, women were thrown into a new and threatening situation, sometimes one of abandonment; most were left in a form of emotional and economic dependency. Not Follett. Which was probably why she was such a pioneer, a swash-buckling advance scout of management thinking.

Just about everything written today about leadership and orga-nizations comes from Mary Parker Follett's writings and lectures. They are dispiritingly identical—or if not identical, they certainly rhyme—with the most contemporary of writings. Whether the sub-ject is the shift in paradigms from a command-and-control, hierar-chically driven organization to a more empowered and democratic type or the significance of a shared vision or the importance of achieving an "integrated picture of the situation" or the need for "expert" rather than coercive power, Follett was there first. It makes you wince when you sincerely believe, as I do, that what you have written about leadership was already literally bespoke by another 40 years before your precious and "prescient" sentences saw the light of day.

I'll give just one example of her extraordinary capacity to foresee issues of leadership, one that only recently have I seen its utmost significance. She writes:

> And now let me speak to you for a moment of something which seems to me of the utmost importance, but which has been far too little considered, and that is the part of followers in the leadership situation. . . . Let us not think that we are either leaders or—nothing of much importance. As one of those led we have a part in leadership. In no aspect of our subject do we see a greater discrepancy between theory and practice than here. . . .[1]

It is probably inevitable that a society as starstruck as ours should focus on leaders in analyzing why organizations succeed or fail. As a long-time student and teacher of management, I, too, have tended to look at leadership for the clues on how organizations achieve and maintain institutional health. But the longer I study effective leaders, the more I am persuaded of the underappreciated importance of effective followers. In rereading Follett's essay, I was inspired to try to answer the inevitable follow-up question: What makes an effective follower? So, with a low bow to my role model, I will try to answer that question in what follows.

The single, most important characteristic may well be a willingness to tell the truth. In a world of growing complexity and speed (some call it "raplexity"), leaders are increasingly dependent on their subordinates for good information, whether they want to hear it or not. Followers who tell the truth and leaders who listen to it are an unbeatable combination.

Like portfolios, organizations benefit from diversity. Effective leaders stifle the urge to hire only those people who look or sound or think just like themselves, what I call the Doppelgänger, or ghostly double, effect. Effective leaders look for good people from many molds, and they encourage them to speak out, even to disagree. Aware of the pitfalls of institutional unanimity, some leaders wisely build dissent into the decision-making process.

Like good leaders, good followers understand the importance of speaking out. More important, they do it. Almost 35 years ago, when Nikita Khrushchev came to America, he met with reporters at the Washington Press Club. The first written question he received was: "Today you talked about the hideous rule of your predecessor, Stalin. You were one of his closest aides and colleagues during those years you now denounce. What were you doing all that time?" Khrushchev's face grew red. "Who asked that?" he roared. No one answered. "Who asked that?" he insisted. Again, silence. "That's what I was doing," Mr. Khrushchev said.

Even in democracies, where the only gulag is the threat of a pink slip, it is hard to disagree with the person in charge. Several years ago TV's John Chancellor asked former presidential chiefs of staff how they behaved on those occasions when the world's most powerful leader came up with a damned fool idea. Several of the aides admitted doing nothing. Ted Sorenson revealed that John F.

Kennedy could usually be brought to his senses by being told, "That sounds like an idea Nixon would have."

Quietism, in a more pious age called the sin of silence, often costs organizations—and their leaders—dearly. President Ronald Reagan suffered far more at the hands of so-called friends who refused to tell him unattractive truths than from his ostensible enemies.

It is the good follower's obligation to share his or her best counsel with the person in charge. And silence—not dissent—is one answer that leaders should refuse to accept. History contains dozens of cautionary tales on the subject, none more vivid than the murder of Thomas à Becket. "Will no one rid me of this meddlesome priest?" Henry II muttered, after a contest of wills with his former friend.

The four barons who then murdered Becket in his cathedral were the antithesis of good followers they thought themselves to be. At the risk of being irreverent, the right answer to Henry's question—the one that would have served his administration best— was "No," or at the very least, "Your liege, can we not discuss it?"

Like modern-day subordinates who testify under oath that they were only doing what their leader wanted them to do, the barons were guilty of remarkable chutzpah. The barons failed by not making the proper case against the king's decision. But Henry failed even more by not making his position clear and by creating an atmosphere in which followers would rather kill than disagree with him.

Effective leaders reward dissent, as well as encourage it. They understand that whatever momentary discomfort they experience as a result of being told from time to time that they are wrong is more than offset by the fact that "reflective back talk" increases a leader's ability to make good decisions.

Executive compensation should go far toward salving the pricked ego of the leader whose followers speak their minds. But what's in it for the follower? The good follower may indeed have to put his or her job on the line when speaking up. But consider the price he or she pays for silence. What job is worth the enormous psychic cost of following a leader who values loyalty in the narrowest sense?

Perhaps the ultimate irony is that the follower who is willing to speak out shows precisely the kind of initiative that leadership is made of.

The idea of Good Followership is only one of so many insights that Follett proffered. I could have written on any of them. In conclusion, what's even more important to consider is why it has taken so long for Mary Parker Follett to be acknowledged as one of the most seminal thinkers of management theory as well as a precursor for so many of management practices today. I have a small clue. In 1939, the poet W. H. Auden wrote a memorial to Freud: "To us he is no more a person/Now but a whole climate of opinion." It may possibly be that Mary Parker Follett's remarkable body of writing was not only ahead of her time but was at an angle to the time she was writing about.

Is the "climate of opinion" today, the zeitgeist, any more congenial today than it was during her heyday, 60 or 70 years ago? Perhaps, perhaps. But it would be helpful if a few more of us got behind her ideas and gave them a little push here and there. How much better that would be for our theories and our practices.

NOTE

1. L. Urwick, ed., *Freedom & Co-ordination: Lectures in Business Organisation by Mary Parker Follett* (London: Management Publications, Ltd., 1949), p. 54.

SEVEN

+≈   ≈+

Co-ordination

I HAVE said that we find responsibility for management shot all
through a business, that we find some degree of authority all along
the line, that leadership can be exercised by many people besides
the top executive. All this is now being increasingly recognised,
and the crux of business organisation is how to join these varied
responsibilities, these scattered authorities, these different kinds of
leadership. For a business, to be a going concern, must be unified.
The fair test of business administration, of industrial organisation,
is whether you have a business with all its parts so co-ordinated,
so moving together in their closely knit and adjusting activities, so
linking, interlocking, inter-relating, that they make a working unit,
not a congerie of separate pieces. In the businesses I have studied, the
greatest weakness is in the relation of departments. The efficiency of
many plants is lowered by an imperfectly worked-out system of
co-ordination. In some cases all the co-ordination there is depends
on the degree of friendliness existing between the heads of departments, on whether they are willing to consult; sometimes it depends
on the mere chance of two men coming up to town on the same
train every morning.

I spoke to you last week of a recent conference here in London
of Works Managers and Sales Managers. The object of the confer-

Note: This chapter is reprinted from L. Urwick, ed. *Freedom & Co-ordination:
Lectures in Business Organisation by Mary Parker Follett* (London: Management
Publications Trust, Ltd., 1949), pp. 61–76.

ence was to discuss ways in which Works Managers and Sales Managers could work more closely together. We heard a great deal about the lack of co-operation between them. We heard a great deal of the necessity of understanding each other's problems, that the production department should know more of customers' demands, why they liked one product, why they complained of another; that the sales department, on the other hand, should know more of the difficulties of production, the difficulty, for instance, of producing what the customer wants within the price the customer is willing to pay. And so on. Many instances were given of the way in which Sales Managers and Works Managers could help each other by a greater understanding of each other's work. We heard that neither side should lead, that they should work together, that they should make a team.

I thought this one of the best conferences I had ever attended. I thought it was bound to do a lot of good. But one thought persisted uppermost in my mind all day and just at the end of the afternoon one man voiced this thought when he rose and said: "But surely co-ordination is a problem of management." There was no discussion of this point and quite rightly. These were Works Managers and Sales Managers and they were considering how, as industry is generally organised, they could co-operate more effectively. But surely it is obvious that many of the capital suggestions made at that Conference, suggestions for voluntary co-operation, were things that could be required of the sales and production department. Two men thought it desirable that the heads of these departments should lunch together frequently. One trembles to think of the success of industry depending on such a mere chance as that. Surely regular meetings between production department and sales department could be required at which they could inform each other of all the things which were mentioned at this conference as essential each should know of the other.

And indeed a good many companies are considering co-ordination a question of management and organisation and the problem is met in different ways. In some cases regular meetings between departments is required. Some companies have a co-ordinating department whose special function it is to bring into closer relation the work of the various departments. Some have a planning department which serves also as a co-ordinating agency. A department of sales research, separate from the selling department as such, may act as a link with production. Research as to future lines of production must necessarily be linked up with sales research. The merchandise department to a certain extent links production and sales. And so on. I give these merely as illustrations. If I were to describe to you all the ways in which co-ordination is being effected in industry that would be a talk on organisation, and, besides the fact that that would take all winter, it is not what I have undertaken to do. I have, therefore, chosen three things which seem to me to make for the greater unity of an enterprise. I might express this more forcefully and say that I think they embody the fundamental principle of unity.

One, which I consider a very important trend in business management is a system of cross-functioning between the different departments. Let me take, as providing an example of this trend, the Telephone Company of which I have already spoken to you, although of course there are many other companies which would do equally well for illustration. Here we find the four departments—traffic, engineering, commercial and plant—conferring with one another and all together. These conferences are often informal but they are expected of all officials. Each department is expected to get in touch with certain others. The district traffic manager asks the wire chief from the plant department to talk some matter over with him, or if it is a commercial matter, he calls in the commercial manager of that district, or if it is a question of blue prints or costs, he asks the engineering department if they will send a man over. They may settle it among themselves. If not, the district traffic manager puts the matter up to the superintendent of the traffic department. The superintendent of the traffic department may consult the superintendent of the plant or the commercial department.

Here, you see, we have a combination of going both across the line and up the line. When one of the exchanges was cut in two (such questions come up every day, I mention this only because it occurred while I was making my investigation), the question came up whether to cut thirty-five a day or five hundred in a blanket order one night. This affected all four departments—traffic, engineering, commercial and plant. They agreed after discussion on the blanket order. If they had disagreed they would have taken it up to the general superintendent of each department—up the line, note. Then the four superintendents would have consulted, now across the line. If they had agreed the matter would have ended there. If not, it would have had to go to the General Manager—up the line.

This combination of across and up exists, as I have said, in many plants today. Many businesses are now organised in such a way that you do not have an ascending and descending ladder of authority. You have a degree of cross-functioning, of inter-relation of departments, which means a horizontal rather than a vertical authority. That means in this case that a problem which occurs at X which concerns Y does not have to be taken up the line from X and then taken down the line to Y.

A telephone company sells service rather than a product, but you can have the same cross-functioning anywhere. If you have it in a company which both manufactures and sells a product, instead of all that the selling department knows of customers' demands going up the line to the general manager and then going down the line from him to the manufacturing department, and the problems of the manufacturing department going up the line to the general manager and then from him down the line to the sales department, instead of this you can have a system of cross-relations which gives opportunity for direct contact between Sales Manager and Production Manager. Where you have this direct contact there is much less chance of misunderstanding, there is opportunity of explaining problems and difficulties each to the other. This seems to me very important. Direct contact of the responsible people concerned is, indeed, one of the four vital principles of organisation which I shall speak of later.

I should like to say incidentally that where we see a horizontal rather than a vertical authority, we have another proof of what I said two weeks ago, namely that we are now finding in business practice less of that kind of authority which puts one man over another. We have conferences of parallel heads.

But there are companies who get this horizontal authority, as I have called it, by another method. These companies think that the methods which I have been describing to you, where each man decides for himself when he needs to discuss a matter with another, is not sufficient for the steadily continuous binding together of the different parts of a business. These companies, therefore, have a system of committees composed of men who have closely related problems who meet regularly to discuss these problems. I do not, however, propose to consider the question of committees in industry here, it is too large and too controversial a subject. I mention them because they are a form of cross-functioning, and cross-functioning was one of the ways of unifying a business of which I wished to speak to you.

But all this matter of consultation, of discussion of problems, whether it be done officially and formally or informally, means that there will be constantly antagonistic policies, antagonistic methods, confronting each other, each wanting right of way. Before we can hope for the most effective co-ordination, we shall have to learn how best to deal with all the differences of opinion that arise day by day, hour by hour, in any enterprise. They may be between the members of the Board of Directors, between executives, or between executives and workers, but daily they tend to produce discord, daily they threaten to be a disintegrating influence, if we do not know the best method of dealing with them. This seems to me of the utmost importance and I shall therefore spend a large part of my hour considering this point.

There are three ways of settling differences: by domination, by compromise, or by integration. Domination, obviously, is a victory of one side over the other. This is not usually successful in the long run for the side that is defeated will simply wait for its chance to dominate. The second way, that of compromise, we understand well, for that is the way we settle most of our controversies—each side gives up a little in order to have peace. Both these ways are unsatisfactory. In dominating, only one way gets what it wants; in compromise neither side gets what it wants. We are continually hearing compromise praised. That is the accepted, the approved, way of ending controversy, yet no one really wants to compromise, because that means giving up part of what he wants. Is there any other way of dealing with difference?

There is a way beginning now to be recognised at least and sometimes followed, the way of integration. Let me take first a very simple illustration. In a University library one day, in one of the smaller rooms, someone wanted the window open, I wanted it shut. We opened the window in the next room where no one was sitting. There was no compromise because we both got all we really wanted. For I did not want a closed room, I simply did not want the north wind to blow directly on me; and he, the man in the room with me, did not want that particular window open, he merely wanted more air in the room. Integration means finding a third way which will include both what A wishes and what B wishes, a way in which neither side has had to sacrifice anything.

Let us take another illustration. A Dairymen's Co-operative League almost went to pieces on the question of precedence in unloading cans at a creamery platform. The creamery was on the side of a hill. The men who came down the hill thought they should not be asked to wait on a downgrade and that therefore they should unload first. The men who came up the hill thought equally that they should unload first. They had a hot row about it, so hot that it almost broke up the League. Both sides, you see, were thinking of just those two possibilities: should the uphillers or downhillers unload first? But then an outsider suggested that the position of the platform should be changed so that up-hillers and down-hillers could unload at the same time. This suggestion was accepted by both sides. Both were happy. But neither was happy because he had got his way. They had found a third way. Integration involves invention, the finding of the third way, and the clever thing is to recognise this and not to let one's thinking stay within the boundaries of two alternatives which are mutually exclusive. In other words, never let yourself be bullied by an either-or situation. Never think you must agree to either this or that. Find a third way.

And the extraordinarily interesting thing about this is that the third way means progress. In domination you stay where you are. In compromise likewise you deal with no new values. By integration something new has emerged, the third way, something beyond the either-or.

Take now an illustration from business. I am making a good deal of this point because I think it about the most important thing in the world. If you go into business you will have to integrate with someone almost every day. When you marry you surely will. And can we have any peace between nations until we learn this? We all recognise that Germany is right in wanting equality of status, and France right in wanting security. International states must discover how both these objects can be attained.

Now for my illustration from industry. The purchasing agent in a factory said that he had found a material for a certain product which he could buy at less cost than that being used. The head of the manufacturing department said that the cheaper material would not produce as good results, he preferred to keep to the material then in use. What was to be done? The general manager at first thought he had a struggle on his hands between these two men, but then he met the difficulty by suggesting that the purchasing agent should continue his hunt for a cheaper material, but should try to find one which would fill the requirements of the head of the manufacturing department. The purchasing agent succeeded in doing this and both he and the head of the manufacturing department were satisfied. This could not have happened if they had stayed within an either-or situation, if they had thought that either the purchasing agent must have his way or the head of the manufacturing department his way. And that integration was obviously good for the business. If the purchasing agent had had his way, quality would have suffered. If the head of the manufacturing department had had his way, costs would have remained unnecessarily high. But as it was, they got at the same time quality and reduced costs. The integration created something new. Hence difference can be constructive rather than destructive if we know what to do with it. It may be a sign of health, a prophecy of progress.

I have told you what I think integration is and how necessary it is in business. I have not spoken of how to get integration, but I will speak further of this. For the moment all that I can do is to point out that there *is* a technique for integration. And the person who should know most about this is the chief executive. I think that books on business management sometimes make a mistake here, for they sometimes tell us that in the case of a difference of opinion between executives, the chief executive acts as arbitrator, decides between the executives. But I know chief executives who do not decide between their executives. And let me say here, what perhaps I should have called your attention to before, that in these talks I am not moralising to you, telling you what I think ought to be done, or theorising to you, telling you what I think might be done, I am merely telling you the things I have seen in practice in industry. And I am saying now that I know chief executives who do not act as umpire and decide between their executives. They try to integrate the different points of view, for they know that if they take A's and reject B's, they will lose whatever advantage there might be in B's view. The clever administrator wants to get the advantage of both A's and B's views and so he tries to secure such an interplay of their different experience and different knowledge as will bring them into co-operating agreement.

If a chief executive cannot integrate the different policies in his business, that is, if he cannot make his executives unite wholeheartedly on a certain policy, the suppressions will work underground and be a very strong factor against the success of his business. For suppression means dissatisfaction, and that dissatisfaction will go on working underneath and increasing, and may crop up at any moment in some place where we least desire to see it, in some place where it will give us more trouble than if we had dealt with it in the first instance.

We find the same thing in cases of disputes between nations. The nation which has had a decision go against it in an arbitrated matter, simply waits for some further chance of getting what it wants, and during that time, embittered by its disappointment and its sense of unfair dealing, the trouble grows.

Professor Brierley of Oxford who, I have been told, is the best international lawyer in England, goes to Geneva and urges the method of integration. He tries to convince people that this is better than arbitration. He of course is not, any more than any of us, opposed to arbitration. We all recognise that arbitration is better than war. But there is something even better than arbitration offering. The best business practice is on this point in line with the best modern thinking in general.

Of course you will understand that all I have said on this subject in regard to the general manager applies equally to any executive who has conflicting suggestions made to him by under executives or to a foreman who has the conflicting claims of two workmen to deal with. Many in such positions are coming to see that it is better not to decide between, but to try when possible to integrate the conflicting claims. It is not always possible, that must be fully recognised, but many are coming to think that it is well worth trying, that when it is possible the gains are great.

I have so far been speaking chiefly of the co-ordination of departments, or of departments and the regular staff officials. But there is another co-relation to be made, that between executive and expert—the expert who is a staff official, or the expert who may not be a regular staff official. And just here there is an important change going on, hardly noticed as yet, a change in regard to the place of an expert in a business, a change indeed in regard to our conception of his function—advice. We used to think that the different heads gave orders, that the various experts gave advice, but we have seen emerging in recent years something which is neither orders nor advice. This is an extraordinarily interesting point. For instance, a staff man, an expert, may be responsible for seeing that machines are taken care of, but the line man, the man, that is, at the head of a department, takes care of them. Now suppose the staff man tells a line man that a certain machine needs attention. Is that an order? No, because the line man does not take orders from this man. Is it then advice? No, because one of the characteristics of advice, as we have been accustomed to use that word, is that advice can be rejected, and this cannot be rejected without taking it higher up. The line man, the man in charge of that department, has either to attend to the machine or else take the matter to someone higher up the line.

You see why I think this so extraordinarily interesting. It is because something is coming into business which is neither orders nor advice, and we have not any word for it yet.

It is not advice as we have been accustomed to use that word, for in ordinary usage advice involves a take-it-or-leave-it attitude. If I ask a friend to give me his advice about something, we both have a take-it-or-leave-it attitude about what he may say. That is, I do not feel any obligation to take his advice and he does not expect me to feel any obligation in the matter. But those who give advice in business are usually such an integral part of the organisation that one cannot have a take-it-or-leave-it attitude towards their suggestions.

Yet we do not want the executive to be dominated by the expert. While the executive should give every possible value to the information of the expert, no executive should abdicate thinking because of the expert. The expert's opinion should not be allowed automatically to become a decision. On the other hand, full recognition should be given to the part the expert plays in decision making. Our problem is to find a method by which the opinion of the expert does not coerce and yet enters integrally into the situation. Our problem is to find a way by which the specialist's kind of knowledge and the executive's kind of knowledge can be joined. And the method should, I think, be one I have already advocated, that of integration.

And I should like to point out that when there is a difference of opinion with an expert, we often take that method without realising that we are doing so. Let me try to make this clear by a very simple illustration. An electrician comes to wire my house for electric lighting. I say that I want it done in a certain way. He says that there are mechanical difficulties about doing it in that way. I suggest another way. He tells me that the laws in regard to safeguarding against fire do not permit that way. Then he tells me how he thinks it shall be done. Do I accept his suggestions? No, because I have a very decided objection for aesthetic reasons or reasons of convenience. We continue our discussion until we find a way which meets the mechanical difficulties and the laws in regard to fire safeguards and at the same time satisfies me.

Now I believe the reason that we integrate so often with the expert without knowing that we are doing such a difficult thing as I am told integration is, is that we do not usually think of our relation with the expert as that of a fight. We expect to be able to unite a difference of opinion with him. We have gone to him for that purpose.

So with the general manager or any executive. They recognise that the specialist has one kind of knowledge and they another and they expect to be able to unite them.

To conclude then a matter so important that it should have a whole paper to itself, namely, the expert's place in business organisation, I should say that the tendency is in recent years to give the expert a real place in the game. Lord Cecil said the other day: "The expert must be on tap but not on top." Well I certainly do not want him on top, but I think he is coming to be a more constituent part of an enterprise than is implied by saying that he must be merely on tap. Any study of business administration shows us that the expert in industry is not merely on tap when the executive wants to turn him on to a question, but that he is becoming an integral part of the decision-making machinery.

I have spoken of two things which will help to unify a business, namely, some system of cross-functioning and an understanding of integration. There remains a third equally important and bound up with the other two. Present business practice shows an increased sense of collective responsibility. One evidence of this has a special interest for us. Many companies have now what is called a functional form of organisation. This in itself makes a joint responsibility imperative. The functional development in industry means, as you know, that in many plants we have now, in addition to the different departments, a number of special functions recognised, each of which serves all the departments. For instance, formerly the head of each department looked after its own machines; now the equipment department looks after the machines in all the departments. Formerly each department dealt with its own labour problems; now we have a labour manager who deals with labour problems in all the departments. Purchasing has become a special function; the purchasing department purchases for all the manufacturing processes. And so on.

Now what new demand is made on us in the way of joint responsibilities by the functional development in industry? Suppose the head of the production department wants a new machine. Before the degree of specialisation which we have now come to, this man would have made his decision himself, and then made his recommendations to the general manager. Now in those plants where there is a special department for mechanical equipment, the head of this special department and the head of the manufacturing department have to agree before the recommendation can go to the general manager. They share the responsibility.

Such instances might be multiplied indefinitely. Is it the head of a production department who is responsible for the quality of a food product or is it the consulting chemist? Or both together? Or if a certain method proves a failure, who is responsible? The expert who suggested it? Or the head of the department who accepted it? Or both?

This interlocking responsibility exists indeed under any form of organisation, but we have much more of it wherever the functional form has been introduced.

You will have noticed that the Telephone Company I spoke of has a functional form of organization, for it is organised both by areas, the different districts, and by functions—traffic, engineering, etc.

A second tendency in present business practice which is helping to increase the sense of collective responsibility is the development of group responsibility. In a certain large shop all the men on the lifts have regular meetings at which are considered how this department, the men who run the lifts, can help the general manager, can help the charge office, can help the floor superintendent, can help the information bureau, and so on. I knew another instance where the drivers of the delivery vans undertook as a group certain responsibilities toward the firm.

You remember the little girls in the chocolate factory who were shown how their work affected the sale of chocolate and hence the success of the whole business. A salesman in the north of England told me that he had reckoned that there were seventy men whose continuation in their jobs depended on the number of sales he made. Such awareness of interdependence is surely an asset for any business.

A man said to me once, a man working on a salary as the head of a department in a factory, "I'm no wage-earner, working so many hours a day; if I wake up at midnight and have an idea that might benefit the factory, it belongs to the factory." That was a very proper sentiment for him to have, but his implication was that wage-earners would not feel this. Organisation engineers, however, expert organisers who go into a business to organise or re-organise, are paying a good deal of attention to this point. They are trying to devise ways by which everyone concerned in an enterprise should feel responsible for its success.

And wherever men or groups think of themselves not only as responsible for their own work, but as sharing in a responsibility for the whole enterprise, there is much greater chance of success for that enterprise. Take the question of waste and think how often we have failed to cure that. Over and over again in the past we have heard it said to workmen, "If this were your material, you wouldn't waste it," and over and over again that admonition has failed to produce any results. But when you can develop a sense of collective responsibility then you find that the workman is more careful of material, that he saves time in lost motions, in talking over his grievances, that he helps the new hand by explaining things to him, and so on.

We have been preached to times without number that everyone should do conscientiously his particular piece of work, and this has perhaps tended to make us forget that we are also responsible for the whole. This is a very interesting point. There was an amusing story in *Punch* a few weeks ago, amusing but suggesting a very fundamental truth. A man said that he wanted to get rid of the feeling that he owed money to America and for his part he was thinking of washing out his debts. He had divided the amount of the American debt by the number of inhabitants in Great Britain and he found that each individual owed American twelve shillings, and he was going to send Mr. Hoover twelve shillings and be through with the matter. Of course this was meant to be merely amusing, but it is interesting, is it not, to think that he could not be through with the matter by sending Mr. Hoover twelve shillings, that he could not thus wash out his debt to America, that after he had sent his twelve shillings he would have been exactly as much in debt to America as before. *Punch* gave us a profound truth there, for we cannot get rid of our joint obligation by finding the fraction of our own therein, because our own part is not a fraction of the whole, it is in a sense the whole. Wherever you have a joint responsibility, it can only be met jointly.

I have now spoken of three things which will help to unify a business—an understanding of integration as a method of settling differences, some system of cross-functioning, and a sense of collective responsibility. Let me now give an example which will illustrate all three of these. Suppose a firm is selling frigidaires. The production department has decided on a certain design, best from the engineering point of view. If the production and sales departments of that firm are given opportunities of consulting together, the sales department may say: "Yes, that's a nice tidy design, but my customers tell me that the dishes they use in which to put food away do not fit that design so well as if your ice cubes were in this place and your shelves in that." But then the engineering department might have a good deal to say about condensation of moisture, direction of draughts for the passing off of odours, and so on. What has to be done obviously is to find a design which will satisfy both the engineers' requirements and customers' demand. Neither must be given up, they must find a third way.

Think also of the different way of looking at the question of the amount of electricity consumed. The engineer's job is to see that his frigidaire does the greatest amount of work on the least amount of electricity. But then the salesman's point of view on this matter is that he must be able to tell customers that the frigidaire of this firm does not consume any more electricity than some other make. But then the engineer may say to him, "Can't you show your customers that for a little more electricity with our make they get better service?" And so it may go, backwards and forwards, each modifying the other until we have a truly integrated plan for a frigidaire.

In regard to my second point, the advantage of some form of cross-functioning is obvious here. When you have a purely up and down the line system of management, those who sell frigidaires have to take all their requirements up to the general manager and he communicates them, if he considers them worth-while suggestions, to the production department. And in the same way the production department takes its problems up to the general manager and he may pass them down to the sales department. But then you lose all the advantage of that first-hand contact, that process of backwards and forwards, that process of reciprocal modification.

Again, the third point of this paper, collective responsibility, is also very well illustrated I think by the frigidaire case. It has often been thought in the past, as I pointed out a few moments ago, when I told the story from *Punch*, that I need be concerned only with doing my part well. It has been taken as self-evident, as a mere matter of arithmetic like 2 and 2 making 4, that if everyone does his best, then all will go well. But one of the most interesting things in the world is that this is not true, although on the face of it it may seem indisputable. Collective responsibility is not some-thing you get by adding up one by one all the different responsibilit-ies. Collective responsibility is not a matter of adding but of interweaving, a matter of the reciprocal modification brought about by the interweaving. It is not a matter of aggregation but of inte-gration.

We see this very clearly in the frigidaire illustration. A frigidaire company needs much more from its salesmen than that they shall know how to sell, much more from its engineers than that they shall know how to design. These two departments must know how to integrate their different kinds of knowledge and experience. It isn't enough—I cannot repeat too often, since the success of any enterprise depends largely on an understanding of this point—it isn't enough to do my part well and leave the matter there. My obligation by no means stops at that point. I must study how my part fits into every other part and change my work if necessary so that all parts can work harmoniously and effectively together.

The most important thing to remember about unity is—that there is no such thing. There is only unifying. You cannot get unity and expect it to last a day—or five minutes. Every man in a business should be taking part in a certain process and that process is unifying. Every man's success in business depends largely, I believe, on whether he can learn something of this process, which is one neither of subordination nor of domination, but of each man learning to fit his work into that of every other in a spirit of co-operation, in an understanding of the methods of co-operation.

COMMENTARY

Some Fresh Air for Management?
Henry Mintzberg

I AGREED with enthusiasm to write this commentary because of two recent experiences.

One was a paper I wrote early in 1992, "Some Fresh Air for Canada," based on a speech I gave at Queen's University in Kingston, Ontario, as part of its one hundred fiftieth anniversary celebration. At that time the country was going through the agonies of constitution making, and I thought the approach being taken by the government, and supported by virtually all the major establishment figures, was an aberration from beginning to end. And I knew exactly how to make my point.

"Compromise" was the watchword of this constitutional exercise; anyone attuned to the media or participating in the actual process heard it many times a day. As I said at the time—and continue to believe—Canadians are truly the great compromisers. It is one of our great strengths—we are a tolerant people, ready to adjust to the needs at hand. (That is probably why we have such a good record as United Nations peacekeepers.) But compromise wasn't going to work this time, as the results of the October 1992 referendum later made dramatically clear. Despite the almost unanimous support of all the major political figures and political parties in the country, the population at large rejected the proposal—collectively and pervasively.

The metaphor from which I drew the title of my paper came directly from Mary Parker Follett, in words she wrote more than half a century ago. When you read them, I think you will be struck by just how contemporary her writings truly are. This commentary repeats some of her material from the chapter that follows, but frankly I am inclined to agree with her assessment of it: it may well be "the most important thing in the world."

As I told my audience in Kingston, politics is the art of compromise. But was compromise, and politics, the best way—even a possible way—to resolve the kind of difficulties Canada was encountering in 1992? I pointed out that in the essay that follows, Mary Parker Follett explained long ago that differences can be settled in three ways, which she called "domination," "compromise," and "integration." I quoted her at length.

> Domination, obviously, is a victory of one side over the other. This is not usually successful in the long run for the side that is defeated will simply wait for its chance to dominate. The second way, that of compromise, we understand well, for that is the way we settle most of our controversies—each side

gives up a little in order to have peace. Both these ways are unsatisfactory. In dominating, only one way gets what it wants; in compromise neither side gets what it wants. . . . Is there any other way of dealing with difference?

There is a way beginning now to be recognised at least and sometimes followed, the way of integration. Let me take . . . a very simple illustration. In a University library one day, in one of the smaller rooms, someone wanted the window open, I wanted it shut. We opened the window in the next room where no one was sitting. There was no compromise because we both got all we really wanted. For I did not want a closed room, I simply did not want the north wind to blow directly on me; and he, the man in the room with me, did not want that particular window open, he merely wanted more air in the room. Integration means finding a third way which will include both what A wishes and what B wishes, a way in which neither side has had to sacrifice anything.[1]

Domination has sometimes been used in Canada—for example, over the French schools in Manitoba in the last century and the English signs of Quebec more recently. It has never been acceptable. Mostly, however, Canadians have relied on compromise. And it has often worked—more or less. But compromise would not resolve the constitutional crisis in 1992. We had already tried to create one constitution by domination; when that failed, having alienated many people in Quebec, we tried to create two more by compromise. These efforts failed too, succeeding only in alienating everyone. "If we get only compromise," Follett added, "the conflict will come up again and again in some other form, for in compromise we give up part of our desire, and because we shall not be content to rest there, sometime we shall try to get the whole of our desire." It seemed to me that our one possibility, therefore—indeed our great opportunity—was her "third way": "when two desires are integrated."

Integration means moving the debate to another place, going back to basics to find a common ground. As Follett puts it, "Integration involves invention . . . and the clever thing is to recognize this and not to let one's thinking stay within the boundaries of two alternatives which are mutually exclusive. In other words, never let yourself be bullied by an either-or situation . . . . Find a third way." Fresh air without the draft—a nice metaphor for Canada, her approach literally and her solution figuratively. Hence the title.

I did not quote Mary Parker Follett that day just because the ideas and the metaphors fitted so well. I quoted her because the eloquence and the inspiration of her words set the tone for a people who had lost their way. I know of nothing written before or since that comes anywhere close to this. I recount all this here to show how relevant Mary Parker Follett's writings are to today's problems—really, to *every* day's problems.

The second experience that encouraged me to write this commentary was my more recent need to respond to a French professor's criticism of my study of managerial work. The author resurrected Henri Fayol, or at least condemned me for having had the gall to criticize the French master.[2] Reacting to the critic (a chore compared to writing this!) reminded me of how out-of-date Fayol really is. Managers who believe they plan, organize, command, coordinate, and control are not technically wrong, they are just misguided. These are not the managers who see themselves in the role of facilitating the work of other adult human beings, or who build organizations predisposed to flexible learning, or who are open to interesting thoughts unfolding in their own peculiar ways. Follett's concepts of "integration," "constructive conflict," "cross functioning," "collective responsibility," and "reciprocal modification," likely have little meaning for these people. Instead, they see themselves perched atop metaphorical hierarchies, there to impose the control of their "superior" minds over everyone else, the "subordinates."

Of course, we might argue that Fayol wrote in another time. Things were different. How can we fault him for seeing organizations as they were then?

Well, Follett wrote in another time too, not long after Fayol and overlapping with him for a period, in fact.[3] But we have no need to make such excuses for her; quite the contrary, in fact. Peter Drucker points out in his introduction that her work got lost not long after it was written, and stayed lost for decades. Just look at the dates of publication of her major works: years, even decades, after her death. Imagine if we had spent most of this century heeding Follett instead of Fayol!

Peter Drucker also mentions the central role of the citizen in Follett's work. The citizen of the corporation might well be a natural extension of this, for especially in the essay that follows, Follett plays down the commanding role of the manager (so important to Fayol) and plays up the cooperating role of the employee.

All that we make such a fuss about these days—currently the words are "empowerment" and "total quality management," although not long ago they were "participative management" and "quality of work life"—are crystal clear in Follett's work. "All of this is now being increasingly recognized," she writes at the outset of this essay, her optimism perhaps clouding her judgment. Indeed, having not read some of these works for a long time, I was taken aback by her discussion of "group responsibility" and the example of the elevator operators—total quality management, long before even the Japanese!

There may be nothing new under the sun, but one person seeing it does not necessarily illuminate the vision of others. We are still mesmerized with hierarchy, after Fayol, and are all too often blind to the insights of the cooperation of equals, that wonderful concept of "collective responsibility," after Follett.

Will the republication of Follett's work change things? Even though we need her message now more than ever, in American business no less than in Canadian politics, will enough of the powers that be *really* listen? I don't mean some hype in the business press, trendy reviews in the best newspapers, or glitzy lectures about Follett's teaching that are forgotten on the way home. I mean a real change in attitudes.

I wonder. For we live in a world in which the most superficial among us, those supposed wizards of Wall Street, still have immense influence; in which barely experienced MBAs still command high salaries to command and control (albeit through empowerment or reengineering or whatever is the latest fad, the medium inevitably drowning out whatever may be valuable in the message); in which business school academics are mesmerized with a theory that is based on "opportunism," specifically "self-interest seeking with guile," to the explicit preclusion of "trust."[4] Compare these crude, negative, atomistic views of the world with that of a woman who wrote that "Everyone in an enterprise should feel responsible for its success," or "Our own part is not a fraction of the whole, it is in a sense the whole," or of "each man learning to fit his work into that of every other in a spirit of co-operation . . . . "

Integration requires understanding, in-depth understanding. It requires serious commitment and dedication. It takes effort, and it depends on creativity. There is precious little of all of these qualities in too many of our organizations today. But there are other kinds of people too, and other kinds of organizations, including those willing to invest the effort to republish this wonderful work. Let us only hope that a sizable number of readers will make the corresponding efforts to appreciate a set of messages that remain so critical in this world.

NOTES

1. L. Urwick, ed., *Freedom & Co-ordination: Lectures in Business Organisation by Mary Parker Follett* (London: Management Publications, Ltd., 1949) pp. 65–66.

2. Henri Fayol (1841–1925) was a mining engineer by training and managing director of a French mining company between 1888 and 1918. In 1916, the *Bulletin de la Societé de l'Industrie Minerale* published Fayol's *Administration Industrielle et Générale—Prévoyance, Organisation, Commandement, Coordination, Contrôle*. This work first appeared in English in 1949, with the title *General and Industrial Management*. As the French title of his work suggests, Fayol conceived of managers as engaged in five essential tasks: planning, organizing, commanding, coordinating, and controlling.
3. Mary Parker Follett lived from 1868 to 1933, and the essays collected in this volume were, for the most part, written in the 1920s.
4. Oliver E. Williamson, *Markets and Hierarchies: Analysis and Antitrust Implications* (New York: Free Press, 1975); also *The Economic Institutions of Capitalism* (New York: Free Press, 1985).

COMMENTARY

Reflections on Design and the Third Way
Angela Dumas

A MONG the many lessons that Mary Parker Follett provided me with was the one of describing things simply and honestly. Tell the truth of the situation without overdue embellishment, she urged; that way insights and concepts will be clearer.

There are things in this chapter on coordination that are becoming ever more critical to us. To merely marvel at Mary Parker Follett's insights all those many years ago is almost a self-indulgence; what we have to do is face the consequences of their meanings.

Humility and humanity are two words that spring to mind when I think of Mary Parker Follett. There has been too much arrogance in our world of management and not enough humility to enable us to understand or see more clearly. Human groups can, and do, produce great things when their energies are in a proper dynamic. This can't come about when an industrial organization is merely what Mary Parker Follett calls a "congerie of separate pieces." She speaks of the need to find the third way through integration and collective responsibility. The role of the expert and the way in which this role affects organizations and therefore integration is key to her thinking.

> we do not want the executive to be dominated by the expert. While the executive should give every possible value to the information of the expert, no executive should abdicate thinking because of the expert . . . Our problem is to find a method by which the opinion of the expert does not coerce and yet enters integrally into the situation. Our problem is to find a way by which the specialist's kind of knowledge and the executive's kind of knowledge can be joined. And the method should, I think be one . . . of integration.[1]

I began my working life not as a manager or an academic, but as one of a group of designers responsible for commercial building interiors—office blocks and hospitals. In this role I found that relationships with clients often placed us in situations where we were unable to contribute fully to the job. There was little or none of Mary Parker Follett's integration. Sometimes clients accepted our proposals without question and then, at a later date, were dismayed when we hadn't known something that only they could have known. At other times they placed such constraints on us that we were little more than an additional pair of hands. Either way was unsatisfactory. What began as a frustration led to an overriding need to find out what could be done. As a result, I became an academic. My first couple of years of field research (which was based at London Business School) led me to see that there was a lot more design activity going on in organizations than was acknowledged. The activities of managers making design-related decisions went entirely unacknowledged just because these were not the activities of an expert with the title "designer."

In the 1980s, many U.K. companies adopted new approaches to design, based on the views of an expert brought in to manage design. In fact, frequently these new approaches did not provide opportunities for integration. Companies would declare that they were to be design led and they would adopt a formal policy toward design. But I observed that far from getting better, the actual process of design could, and did, get worse. Obviously, this was not the intention, but it did point to the importance of those design activities of the unacknowledged group that were unwittingly pushed away, devalued, or suppressed by the new policies.

An example of how the lack of design integration could backfire was a large retailer that I once did some research for. The company had recently reorganized and adopted a formal policy on design— allying design more directly with marketing and physically moving the design activities next to the marketing activities. I was in an area called Functional Packaging and was able to talk to people across the organization: the development director, a buyer, and the new marketing director.

Functional Packaging worked with the buyer to determine how the merchandise should be displayed and packaged: whether it needed to be hung or boxed. This department had to decide the correct dimensions for packs relative to shelf size, the best way to protect merchandise while making it accessible to the customer, and whether to pack at the factory or at the distribution warehouse. It was clear to me that between the decisions taken by the buyers and those taken by Functional Packaging lay a high proportion of the activities that turn the idea (of a product) into a material thing (the actual product). Yet none of these activities was classified by the organization as a design decision. I remember meeting the designer in her new office, which was now sited next to marketing. "It's crazy really," said the designer. "They hire me to put the pictures on the boxes! Since I know the people in Functional Packaging, I know when to go to them, but when I leave next month that connection will end. We already work at opposite ends of the building."

In this example, the formal policy of the organization was that design was largely a graphic activity, best managed by marketing. Before the design policy and the reorganization, design, though unacknowledged, had been integral. In not knowing where to look for its real range of design activities, the company had devalued its design activity. It had placed only one aspect of design in the expert category.

The adoption of the retailer's overly narrow definition of design overlooked the real process of turning ideas into things and excluded those individuals inside the organization with the most and the best expertise. Instead of the reorganization bringing about integration and improving design, it left many people feeling of little consequence to the new initiative, their knowledge devalued. This was an instance of the domination of one group over another, caused by an abdication of thinking among the senior executives. Experts from the world of design had been involved in developing the new design policy. These experts had acted in a way that was consistent with the way they worked, but not consistent with the way the retail organization worked.

During my observations I came to realize that there are two senses of design. There is the sense of design when we see or use a thing and we say this is a good design. This is the sense of design we are most likely to associate with the expert, who may be an aesthetic designer or engineering designer. But there also is the sense of design for which we don't have words: a silent sense of design. This is the internal dynamic that, as Mary Parker Follett suggests, is the interweaving of all the knowledges. This was what was at work in the example I gave, between Functional Packaging and the buyer. This silent sense of design is at work when Mary Parker

Follett asks, "Is it the head of a production development who is responsible for the quality of a good product or is it the consultant chemist? Or both together?" The more we convene cross-functional teams, the more collective responsibility exists. However, we need to do more than put people together. "Collective responsibility is not something you get by adding up one by one all the different responsibilities. Collective responsibility is not a matter of adding but of interweaving, a matter of reciprocal modification brought about by the interweaving. It is not a matter of aggregation but of integration."[2]

This insight is critical, not only to an understanding of how cross-functional teams are active in the silent sense of design, but also to knowing more about how the silent sense of design enables us to develop new techniques to help cross-functional teams, to achieve "the third way" and integration.

It is necessary to think about designing in a broader way, and to do that we have to return to basics. To the idea that design is at some levels the simple process of turning ideas in the mind into material things. By using the example of a simple product such as a chair, we can see how the interweaving of knowledges works.

Suppose I am a maker of chairs and I have an idea to make a chair with a soft back. I know a lot about my context, of course. Otherwise, I would not have the idea to make a soft-back chair. Perhaps I noticed someone rub their back, or I heard them say something about their chair. The idea for a chair with a soft back might jump into my head rapidly or it might slowly emerge; either way, as it comes into being, I begin to see it in my mind's eye. I see perhaps bits of it and I cannot quite grasp other bits but the time is right to help the idea along with some sketches, maybe a mock-up. Looking over the timber at my workbench, I ponder the construction details. How would it work? Thinking about how I attach the soft part, I go and look at other things—things I don't have in my workshop.

Later I say to the man who I saw rubbing his back, "I have a design that might interest you." I show him the mock-up. He is thrilled—he orders my chair.

The process of the chair maker has been dynamic and interactive with its context and environment, but much of it has been internal. The situation is simply that the chair maker has internal conversations with him- or herself. A diagram may help here.

Idea for soft back chair
Knowledge of materials
Available machinery
Construction requirements
Knowledge of the market

The lines don't run straight; they interweave—the chair comes out of the dynamic of the interweaving. The design is taking place all the while. The chair maker created a new chair by the interweaving of all his knowledges, which span the knowledge needed for the concept and the knowledge needed for implementation—he cannot separate them: "Integration involves invention, and the finding of the third way."[3] We tend to refer to this activity these days as "innovation." Yet the process whereby we achieve innovation is the interweaving of knowledges, which is a process of design. The example with the chair is simple, but our organizations face the complex task of interweaving so many knowledges. The challenge they face is to find the third way. The way of integration is the challenge to our organizations, a challenge that many have taken up and succeeded in. However, we still need new techniques to open the gateways to the "third way" for cross-functional teams. The realities expressed by large cross-functional teams are far removed from the rhetoric.

The interweaving of knowledges cannot happen rapidly when a cross-functional team sets out to work on a new project. The process of interweaving, which we all understand and have experience of as an internal dynamic, is different when it must occur externally in the social domain. "I must study how my part fits into every other part and change my work if necessary so that all parts can work harmoniously and effectively together. The most important thing to remember about unity is that there is no such thing. There is only unifying."[4]

We need new techniques—soft technologies that help integrate and unify knowledges. One such technique is to build object-based metaphors, or totems, that operate to build collective responsibility. But this is merely one way; to unify, we need many more ways to metaphorically heap the knowledges into a pile that we can sift through together to achieve a harmonious and effective fit. One final quote from Mary Parker Follett sums up what we must do for the future: ". . . for we cannot get rid of our joint obligation by finding the fraction of our own therein, because our own part is not a fraction of the whole, it is in a sense the whole. Wherever you have a joint responsibility, it can only be met jointly."[5] A good design is usually found in a simple solution, but we often have to go through much complexity to arrive there. Mary Parker Follett is sitting there waiting for us.

NOTES

1. L. Urwick, ed., *Freedom & Co-ordination: Lectures in Business Organisation by Mary Parker Follett* (London, Management Publications, Ltd., 1949), p. 70.
2. Ibid., p. 75.
3. Ibid., p. 66.
4. Ibid., p. 76.
5. Ibid., p. 74.

+≓   ≓+

The Process of Control

OUR SUBJECT in this chapter is the process of control. Of course that is what we have been talking about all along—when we were considering orders or authority or leadership or co-ordination. This final talk therefore may be considered partly as a summary of the other four.

In our best managed industries, we notice two points about control:

(1) Control is coming more and more to mean fact-control rather than man-control;

(2) Central control is coming more and more to mean the co-relation of many controls rather than a super-imposed control.

In regard to the first point, notice how often the word control is used in the sense of fact-control. We hear, for instance, of inventory control. We used to think the Inventory helped us in our control, we did not talk of it as if it were in itself a control. We hear, again, of Budgetary Control. This means that where you have cost-accounting and unit-budgeting, the general manager and the head of a department are both subject to an impersonal control. The

---

Note: This chapter is reprinted from L. Urwick, ed. *Freedom & Co-ordination: Lectures in Business Organisation by Mary Parker Follett* (London: Management Publications Trust, Ltd., 1949), pp. 77–89.

head of a department does not receive an arbitrary order from the general manager, but both study the analyses and interpretations which cost-accounting and unit-budgeting have made possible.

Control is becoming less personal in the old-fashioned sense; control and fact-control are becoming synonymous.

My second point was the co-relation of controls. The ramifications of modern industry are too widespread, its organisation too complex, its problems too intricate for it to be possible for industry to be managed by commands from the top alone. This being so, we find that when central control is spoken of, that does not mean a point of radiation, but the gathering of many controls existing throughout the enterprise.

Genuine control, then, that is, fact-control and co-related control is within the situation.

With this in mind as our guiding thought, namely, that each situation should generate its own control, and in the light of our previous talks, what can we say are the principles of control? This is the same as asking what are the principles of organisation. For the object of organisation is control, or we might say that organisation is control.

Four fundamental principles of organisation are:

(1) Co-ordination as the reciprocal relating of all the factors in a situation.

(2) Co-ordination by direct contact of the responsible people concerned.

(3) Co-ordination in the early stages.

(4) Co-ordination as a continuing process.

My first principle, co-ordination as the reciprocal relating of all the factors in a situation, shows us just what this process of co-ordination actually is, shows us the nature of unity. We have considered unity, but I want to penetrate further into its meaning. We have seen the process by which any two people may combine their different kinds of knowledge and experience. I compared it to a game of tennis. Let us now take more than two. There usually are more than two concerned in any decision. Take four heads of departments. You cannot envisage accurately what happens between them by thinking of A as adjusting himself to B and to C and to D. A adjusts himself to B and also to a B influenced by C and to a B influenced by D and to a B influenced by A himself. Again he adjusts himself to C and also to a C influenced by B and to a C influenced by D and to a C influenced by A himself—and so on. One could work it out mathematically. This sort of reciprocal relating, this interpenetration of every part by every other part and again by every other part as it has been permeated by all, should be the goal of all attempts at co-ordination, a goal, of course, never wholly reached.

You will understand that I am simplifying when I speak of A, B, C and D adjusting themselves to one another. They are of course at the same time adjusting themselves to every other factor in the situation. Or it would be more accurate to say that all the factors in the situation are going through this process of reciprocal relating.

If anyone finds this principle difficult to accept, I would suggest that it is a principle which he has already accepted in regard to facts. Any fact gains its significance through its relation to all the other facts pertaining to the situation. For instance, if you have increased sales, you are not too pleased until you find out whether there has been an increased sales cost. If there has been, or one out of proportion to sales, your satisfaction disappears. Merchandising shows you this principle at work. For merchandising is not merely a bringing together of designing, engineering, manufacturing and sales departments, it is these in their total relativity.

This may seem a rather clumsy phrase, total relativity, but I am trying to express a total which shall include all the factors in a situation not as an additional total but as a relational total—a total where each part has been permeated by every other part.

The possible examples from business management of the working of this fundamental principle are innumerable. Take a situation made by credit conditions, customers' demand, output facilities and workers' attitude. They all together constitute a certain situation, but they constitute that situation through their relation to one another. They don't form a total situation merely by existing side by side.

It is necessary to emphasize this because while it is customary nowadays to speak of "the total situation"—you find that phrase often in articles on business management—that phrase, total situation, means to many people merely that we must be sure to get all the factors into our problem. But that is by no means enough for us to do, we have to see these factors each one affecting every one of the others.

Many examples of this come to mind at once. Take an instance of a social worker. She is dealing with a girl of a difficult temperament, who has a nagging stepmother, is working at a job for which she is not fitted, and has evening recreations of not the most wholesome character. It is obvious that here you have a situation, a whole, made up not of its parts but of the interacting of the parts. Perhaps it is because the girl is working at something she is not interested in that makes her seek over-excitement in the evening. And so on. The most successful social worker is not the one who deals with these separately, but who sees them in relation to one another.

This is the first requirement of statesmanship. We shall get no control over economic conditions until we have statesmen who can meet this requirement. American life is stagnant at present for lack of any such statesman. Here we say Buy British, but then the foreigner will not be able to buy our goods if we do not buy of him, and where are we then? I do not say we shouldn't Buy British. I do not know; personally I have been doing so. I say only that we shall get no grip on our economic affairs until we acquire a greater capacity than we seem to have at present for understanding how economic factors affect one another at every point.

I am talking in all this of the nature of a unity. This, which is a matter of everyday experience to business men in their problems of co-ordinating, happens to be considered by some scientists the most important thing in present scientific thinking. The most interesting thing in the world to me is the correspondence between progressive business thinking and certain recent developments in the thinking of scientists and philosophers. Such biologists as J. B. S. Haldane, such philosophers as Whitehead, such physiologists as Sherrington, are telling us that the essential nature of a unity is discovered not alone by a study of its separate elements, but also by observing how these elements interact.

I could give you many examples from the sciences. I am going to take a moment to give you one, although it may seem far from my subject, simply to bring home to you this remarkable correspondence in thinking in such entirely different fields. I found this in an article in a Journal of Zoology—a very different subject from business management! The article was on the local distribution of wild mice, and the whole point of the article was that this distribution, while controlled by food and water supply, by nesting material, by climatic conditions, and by antagonism between species, while controlled by these, was controlled by them only as they were related to one another, that the behaviour of the wild mice was governed by an environmental complex, that it was not influenced by these various factors one by one.

I thought this expression, "environmental complex," strikingly like what I have been trying to say to you in describing the nature of unities, very much like what I called a relational total as distinct from an additional total. And business men, as I have said, see this every day. The ablest business man, or social worker, or statesman, the ablest worker in any field, looks at an "environmental complex," sees the solution of his problem depending on the interacting of the elements of that complex.

This seems to me a principle of the utmost importance for industry or for any joint endeavour. This seems to me as important a principle for the social sciences as Einstein's theory of relativity has been for the natural sciences. They are both, it may be noticed in passing, concerned with relativity. I believe that the principle of relativity in the realm of social theory will displace as many of our old ideas in the social sciences as Einstein's has in the natural sciences. And I think it greatly to the honour of progressive business thinking that it is taking a lead here—a lead which I am sure must be followed eventually by statesmen, national and international.

Before I leave this point, let me call particularly to your attention that this reciprocal relating, co-ordinating, unifying, is a process which does not require sacrifice on the part of the individual. The fallacy that the individual must give up his individuality for the sake of the whole is one of the most pervasive, the most insidious, fallacies I know. It crops up again and again in one place after another. In some of the businesses I have studied, I have been told that the head of a department should subordinate the good of his department to the good of the whole undertaking. But of course he should do no such thing. His departmental point of view is needed in the whole. It must indeed be reconciled with all the other points of view in the business, but it must not be abandoned. Just as we have been told by an eminent authority in international matters that men should not de-nationalise themselves but inter-nationalise themselves, so I should say to the heads of departments that they should not de-departmentalise themselves but inter-departmentalise themselves. In other words, departmental policy should be an integral part of what is known as "general policy." General policy is not an imaginary "whole," an air-plant, it is the interweaving of many policies. Whether we are talking of the individual man, or individual department, the word should never be sacrifice, it should always be contribution. We want every possible contribution to the whole.

My second principle was co-ordination by direct contact of the responsible people concerned. We saw last week that in some industrial plants, control is exercised through cross relations between heads of departments instead of up and down the line through the chief executive. This seems sensible as these are the people closest to the matter in hand. Moreover, if my first principle was right, if the process of co-ordination is one of interpenetration, it is obvious that it cannot be imposed by an outside body. It is essentially, basically, by its very nature, a process of auto-controlled activity. It is the same as with the individual. We know that every individual has many warring tendencies inside himself. We know that the effectiveness of an individual, his success in life, depends largely on these various tendencies, impulses, desires, being adjusted to one another, being made into one harmonious whole. Yet no one can issue a fiat by which I am adjusted, I can only be helped to adjust myself. It is the same with a group, with a group of executives for instance. Here too the process is one of self-adjustment. This being so, it is essential that they should have the opportunity for direct contact.

My third principle was co-ordination in the early stages. This means that the direct contact must begin in the earliest stages of the process. We see how this works in the co-relation of policies in a business. If the heads of departments confront each other with finished policies, agreement will be found difficult. Of course they then begin to "play politics," or that is often the tendency. But if these heads meet while they are forming their policies, meet and discuss the questions involved, a successful co-relation is far more likely to be reached. Their thinking has not become crystallized. They can still modify one another. I should say that one of the fundamental ideas for business management is that the making of decisions and the co-relating of decisions should be one process. You cannot, with the greatest degree of success for your undertaking, make policy forming and policy adjusting two separate processes. Policy adjusting cannot begin after the separate policies have been completed.

I speak of the co-relation of departmental policies, yet the principle of early stages should, I believe, begin to be operative far earlier than with the heads of departments—with heads of sub-divisions, with foremen, and, where you have union-management co-operation, with the workers themselves. In the union-management plan of the Baltimore & Ohio Railroad, the adjustment of trade unions and management begins down in the lowest shop committees. We see this also in the Canadian railways. The same principle should guide us where we have shop stewards or employee representatives on committees. That is, we shouldn't put to these representatives of the workers finished plans in order merely to get their consent. We should bring them into the game while the plan is still in a formative stage. If we do not, one or two things is likely to happen, both bad: either we shall get a rubber-stamp consent and thus lose what they might contribute to the problem in question, or else we shall find ourselves with a fight on our hands—an open fight or discontent seething underneath.

I do not mean by this that I think workers should be consulted on all questions, only on those on which they are competent to have some opinion. To that extent I think they should have a share in management. If control is the process of the inter-functioning of the parts, if the most perfect control is where we have the inter-functioning of all the parts, then I think the workers should have a share, not from any vague idea of democracy, not because of their "rights," but simply because if you leave out one element in a situation you will have just that much less control. It has been found that piece-rates cannot be wholly decided by an expert, that the question of fatigue cannot be wholly decided by psychologists, that the cost of living cannot be wholly decided by statisticians. And so on.

And it is because of this conception of control which I have been giving you that I cannot believe in "workers' control" as advocated by some in the Labour Party. I think managers and workers should share in a joint control.

These two principles, direct contact and early stages—I have given you three principles now, reciprocal relating, direct contact and early stages—these last two, direct contact and early stages, which I have seen in operation in some of our industries, governed some of the Allied co-operation during the War, and are vigorously advocated by Sir Arthur Salter in his *Allied Shipping Control*. He thinks that adjustments between nations should be made not through their Foreign Offices, but between those who exercise responsible authority in the matters concerned, that is, between departmental ministers. This corresponds, you see, to what I have said of the cross-relations between departments in a business. And in regard to the principle of early stages, Sir Arthur shows us most convincingly that a genuine international policy cannot be evolved by first formulating your national policy and then presenting it as a finished product to confront the policies of other nations. For the only process, he tells us, by which completed policies can be adjusted is that of bargaining and compromise; if you want integration, he says, the process of the interpenetration of policies must begin before they are completed, while they are still in the formative stage.

It seems to me extraordinarily significant that we should find these principles recognised in such different fields as those of business management and international relations. It means that our ablest thinkers, men who are at the same time thinkers and doers, have found a way of making collective control collective self-control. That is a phrase used by Sir Arthur Salter and I think it a remarkably good one—collective self-control.

My fourth principle was co-ordination as a continuous process. Just as I think that co-ordination cannot be enforced on us, that it must be a self-activity, just as I think it must begin in the earliest stages, so I think it must go on all the time. I do not think that the various people concerned should meet to try to unite only when difficulties arise. I think that continuous machinery for this purpose should be provided.

One reason for this is that there is then a greater incentive to discover the principles which can serve as guides for future similar cases. If we make some classification of problems, then when a fresh one arises we can see the points in which that resembles a certain class of case, and we can ask "Have we evolved any principles for dealing with cases of this kind?" One of the interesting things about the League of Nations as one watches its work at Geneva, is that many in the Secretariat are trying deliberately to discover the principles underlying the decisions made in order that they may be taken as precedents in similar cases arising later. A member of the political section of the Secretariat said to me: "Our treatment of every question is two-fold:

(1) An attempt to solve the immediate problem;

(2) The attempt to discover root causes to help our work in the future."

Another advantage of continuous machinery for co-ordination is that then the line is not broken from planning to activity and from activity to further planning. A mistake we often tend to make is that the world stands still while we are going through a certain adjustment. And it does not. Facts change, we must keep up with the facts; keeping up with the facts changes the facts. In other words, the process of adjustment changes the things to be adjusted. If you want an illustration of this, consider the financial and economic adjustments between nations. When one financial adjustment is made, that means only that we have a fresh financial problem on our hands, the adjustment has made a new situation which means a new problem. We pass from situation to situation. It is a fallacy to think that we can solve problems—in any final sense. The belief that we can do so is a drag upon our thinking. What we need is some process for meeting problems. When we think we have solved one, well, by the very process of solving, new elements or forces come into the situation and you have a new problem on your hands to be solved. When this happens men are often discouraged. I wonder why; it is our strength and our hope. We do not want any system that holds us enmeshed within itself.

In order, however, to get the fullest benefit of continuous machinery for co-ordinating, in order to utilise our experience, get the advantage of precedents, be able to formulate principles, we must learn how to classify our experience. I do not think any satisfactory method for that has yet been worked out. I was present once at a meeting of heads of departments in a large shop, and heard one of these heads say in regard to a case they were discussing, "We had a problem like this two or three years ago. Does anyone remember how we treated that?" No one did! We talk much about learning from experience, but we cannot do that unless we

(1) observe our experience,

(2) keep records of our experience, and

(3) organise our experience, that is, relate one bit to another.

Unrelated experience is of little use to us; we can never make wise decisions from isolated bits, only as we see the parts in relation to one another.

I have given four principles of organisation. These principles show the basis of control, show the process of control, show that control is a process. They show us control as self-generated through a process of the interweaving of the parts. The degree of co-relation is the measure of control; the more complete the reciprocal adjusting, the more complete the control.

We find this principle also in the sciences. I said a few moments ago that scientists are finding that the nature of the unities they deal with is governed by a certain principle and that that is the same principle which we find in the co-ordinations that appear in the running of a business. I want now to go further and say that both scientists and business men find that this principle of unity is the principle of control, that is, that organisation is control.

Biologists tell us that the organising activity of the organism is the directing activity, that the organism gets its power of self-direction through being an organism, that is, through the functional relating of its parts.

On the physiological level, control means co-ordination. I cannot get up in the morning, I cannot walk downstairs without that co-ordination of muscles which is control. The athlete has more of that co-ordination than I have and therefore has more control than I have.

On the personal level I gain more and more control over myself as I co-ordinate my various tendencies.

This is just what we have found in business. Let me remind you how often we have noticed this even in the few illustrations I have had time to give you in these talks. We have seen that if the price of a certain article has to be lowered, the situation will not be controlled by the production manager's solution of the problem, nor by the sales manager's. The situation will be controlled when these two men, and the others concerned, unite their different points of view. We saw that if the personnel manager tries to force his opinion of a worker on the foreman, or the foreman tries to force his opinion on the personnel manager, the situation will not be controlled.

The question of the debt to America will find no satisfactory solution if either America tries to force her will on England or England tries to force her will on America. We shall have control of the situation only if England and America are able to unite their different points of view, only if we can find what I have called in these talks an integration. A writer in the *Observer* last Sunday spoke of the divergence between English and American opinion on the debt question, but added that there were indications that we might yet be able to get the hyphen back into Anglo-American opinion. That expresses wittily and concisely what I have taken two hours to say to you. His hyphen is a symbol of my integration. If instead of an English opinion and an American opinion, we can get an Anglo-American opinion, that unity will mean control of the situation.

I come now to my conclusion. We aim at co-ordination in industry because we know that through unity an enterprise generates its own driving force. And this self-generated control does not coerce. But I do not think that this kind of control is sufficiently understood. Everyone knows that our period of *laissez-faire* is over, but socialists wish to give us in its place state control and they mean by that state coercion—we find again and again in their pamphlets the words force, coerce. Those using these words are making the fatal mistake, I believe, of thinking that the opposite of *laissez-faire* is coercion. And it is not. The opposite of *laissez-faire* is co-ordination.

Others who do not believe in state control are urging National Planning Boards of experts to co-ordinate industry. If these boards were to be composed of the heads of industry or their representatives, we might hope to have the kind of self-adjusting, of self-correlating, which I have been describing to you, but I have not seen any plan which allows for this process. Therefore I do not believe that as at present conceived they will bring us any appreciable degree of co-ordination. The policies of our different industrial and economic organisations will have to be adjusted to one another by changes not imposed by an outside authority, but voluntarily undertaken, no, not exactly undertaken, but spontaneously brought about by the process of integration. In order for this to be done, the Planning Boards will have to be composed of the heads of the industries themselves, of course with expert economists on the Board as well. I think the consideration of Planning Boards a splendid step in the right direction. I am only hoping that before we establish such Boards we shall see that both their composition and their functions are in line with the more progressive thinking on organisation.

The period of *laissez-faire* is indeed over, but I do not think we want to put in its place a forcibly controlled society, whether it be controlled by the state of the socialists or the experts of a planning board. The aim and the process of the organisation of government, of industry, of international relations, should be, I think, a control not imposed from without the regular functioning of society, but one which is a co-ordinating of all those functions, that is, a collective self-control.

If then you accept my definition of control as a self-generating process, as the interweaving experience of all those who are performing a functional part of the activity under consideration, does not that constitute an imperative? Are we not every one of us bound to take some part consciously in this process? Today we are slaves to the chaos in which we are living. To get our affairs in hand, to feel a grip on them, to become free, we must learn, and practise, I am sure, the methods of collective control. To this task we can all devote ourselves. At the same time that we are selling goods or making goods, or whatever we are doing, we can be working in harmony with this fundamental law of life. We can be aware that by this method control is in our power.

I heard an address by the managing director of a certain firm who said in the course of his address that the emphasis in regard to facts used to be on the accuracy with which they were gathered, and the fairness and balanced judgment with which they were interpreted. Now, he said, we are coming to know that we can make facts. It seems to me that there is much food for thought in that sentence. We need not wait on events, we can create events.

I cannot do better than end with some words written by Wells long ago in the first chapter of *The New Machiavelli*. "It is," he said, "the old appeal indeed for the unification of human effort and the ending of confusion. . . . The last written dedication of all those I burnt last night was to no single man, but to the socially constructive passion—in any man."

Surely with the world in its present condition we have a task before us which may indeed appeal to the constructive passion in any man—in every man.

PART TWO

The Individual, the Group, and Society

NINE

The Individual in the Group

THE GROUP AND THE NEW PSYCHOLOGY

Politics must have a technique based on an understanding of the laws of association, that is based on a new and progressive social psychology. Politics alone should not escape all the modern tendency of scientific method, of analysis, of efficiency engineering. The study of democracy has been based largely on the study of institutions; it should be based on the study of how men behave together. We have to deal, not with institutions, or any mechanical thing, or with abstract ideas, or 'man,' or anything but just men, ordinary men. The importance of the new psychology is that it acknowledges man as the centre and shaper of his universe. In his nature all institutions are latent and perforce must be adapted to this nature. Man not things must be the starting point of the future.

But man in association, for no man lives to himself. And we must understand further that the laws of association are the laws of the group. We have long been trying to understand the relation of the individual to society; we are only just beginning to see that there is no 'individual,' that there is no 'society.' It is not strange, therefore, that our efforts have gone astray, that our thinking yields small returns for politics. The old psychology was based on the

Note: This chapter is adapted from *The New State: Group Organization, the Solution of Popular Government* (London: Longmans, Green, 1920), pp. 19–23, 105–121.

229

isolated individual as the unit, on the assumption that a man thinks, feels and judges independently. Now that we know that there is no such thing as a separate ego, that individuals are created by reciprocal interplay, our whole study of psychology is being transformed.

Likewise, there is no 'society' thought of vaguely as the mass of the people we see around us. I am always in relation not to 'society' but to some concrete group. When do we ever as a matter of fact think of 'society'? Are we not always thinking of our part in our board of directors or college faculty, in the dinner party last night, in our football team, our club, our political party, our trade-union, our church? Practically, 'society' is for every one of us a number of groups. The recognition of this constitutes a new step in sociology analogous to the contribution William James brought to popular recognition the truth that since man is a complex of experiences there are many selves in each one. So society as a complex of groups includes many social minds. The craving we have for union is satisfied by group life, groups and groups, groups ever widening, ever unifying, but always groups. We sometimes say that man is spiritually dependent upon society; what we are referring to is his psychic relation to his groups. The vital relation of the individual to the world is through his groups; they are the potent factors in shaping our lives.

Hence social psychology cannot be the application of the old individual psychology to a number of people. A few years ago I went to a lecture on Social Psychology, as the subject was announced. Not a word was said except on the nervous systems and other aspects of individual psychology, but at the last moment the lecturer told us that, had there been time, he would have applied what he had said to social conditions! It reminded me of the mental processes of the man who, when he wanted to know something about Chinese metaphysics, first looked up China in the encyclopedia and then metaphysics and put them together. The new psychology must take people with their inheritance, their 'tendencies,' their environment and then focus its attention on their interrelatings. The most careful laboratory work must be done to discover the conditions which make these interrelatings possible, which make these interrelatings fruitful.

Some writers make 'socially minded' tendencies on the part of individuals the subject of social psychology, but such tendencies belong still to the field of individual psychology. A social action is not an individual initiative with social application. Neither is social psychology the determination of how far social factors determine the individual consciousness. Social psychology must concern itself primarily with the interaction of minds.

Early psychology was based on the study of the individual; early sociology was based on the study of society. But there is no such thing as the 'individual,' there is no such thing as 'society'; there is only the group and the group-unit—the social individual. Social psychology must begin with an intensive study of the group, of the selective processes which go on within it, the differentiated reactions, the likenesses and unlikenesses, and the spiritual energy which unites them.

The acceptance and the living of the new psychology will do away with all the progeny of particularist psychology: consent of the governed, majority rule, external leadership, industrial wars, national wars, etc. From the analysis of the group must come an understanding of collective thought and collective feeling, of the common will and concerted activity, of the true nature of freedom, the illusion of self-and-others, the essential unity of men, the real meaning of patriotism, and the whole secret of progress and of life as a genuine interpenetration which produces true community.

All thinking men are demanding a new state. The question is—What form shall that state take? No one of us will be able to give an answer until we have studied men in association and have discovered the laws of association. This has not been done yet, but already we can see that a political science which is not based on a knowledge of the laws of association gained by a study of the group will soon seem the crudest kind of quackery. Syndicalism, in reaction to the so-called 'metaphysical' foundation of politics, is based on 'objective rights,' on function, on its conception of modes of association which shall emphasize the object of the associated and not the relation of the associated to one another. The new psychology goes a step further and sees these as one, but how can any of these things be discussed abstractly? Must we not first study men in association? Young men in the hum of actual life, practical politicians, the members of constitutional conventions, labor leaders—all these must base their work on the principles of group psychology.

The fundamental reason for the study of group psychology is that no one can give us democracy, we must learn democracy. To be a democrat is not to decide on a certain form of human association, it is to learn how to live with other men. The whole labour movement is being kept back by people not knowing how to live together much more than by any deliberate refusal to grant justice. The trouble with syndicalism is that its success depends on group action and we know almost nothing of the laws of the group.

I have used group in this book with the meaning of men associating under the law of interpenetration as opposed to the law of the crowd—suggestion and imitation. This may be considered an arbitrary definition, but of course I do not care about the names, I only want to emphasize the fact that men meet under two different sets of laws. Social psychology may include both group psychology and crowd psychology, but of these two group psychology is much the more important. For a good many years now we have been dominated by the crowd school, by the school which taught that people met together are governed by suggestion and imitation, and less notice has been taken of all the interplay which is the real social process that we have in a group but not in a crowd . . . Whilst I recognize that men are more often at present under the laws of the crowd than of the group, I believe that the group should be the basis of a progressive social psychology. The group process contains the secret of collective life, it is the key to democracy, it is the master lesson for every individual to learn, it is our chief hope for the political, the social, the international life of the future.

THE GROUP PRINCIPLE AT WORK

Our rate of progress, then, and the degree in which we actualize the perfect democracy depend upon our understanding that man has the power of creating, and that he gets this power through his capacity to join with others to form a real whole, a living group. . . .

The growing recognition of the group principle in the business world is particularly interesting to us. The present development of business methods shows us that the old argument about cooperation and competition is not fruitful. Cooperation and competition are being taken into a larger synthesis. We are just entering on an era of collective living. 'Cut-throat' competition is beginning to go out of fashion. What the world needs today is a cooperative mind. The business world is never again to be directed by individual intelligences, but by intelligences interacting and ceaselessly influencing one another. Every mental act of the big business man is entirely different from the mental acts of the man of the last century managing his own competitive business. There is of course competition between our large firms, but the cooperation between them is coming to occupy a larger and larger place relatively. We see this in the arrangement between most of our large printers in Boston not to outbid one another, in those trades which join to establish apprentice schools, in the cooperative credit system, worked out so carefully in some of the western cities as almost to eliminate bad debts, in the regular conferences between the business managers of the large department stores, in our new Employment Managers' associations in Boston and elsewhere, in the whole spirit of our progressive Chambers of Commerce. When our large stores 'compete' to give the highest class goods and best quality service, and meet in conference to make this 'competition' effective, then competition itself becomes a kind of cooperation! There are now between thirty and forty associations in this country organized on the open-price plan. The Leather Belting Exchange, an excellent example of 'cooperative competition,' was organized in 1915. Some of its avowed objects are: standardization of grades of leather, promotion of use of leather belting by scientific investigation of its possible uses, uniform contract system, uniform system of cost accounting, daily charts of sales, monthly statistical reports, collection and distribution of information relative to cost of raw material and to methods and cost of manufacturing and distribution. How vastly different a spirit from that which used to animate the business world!

Modern business, therefore, needs above all men who can unite, not merely men who can unite without friction, but who can turn their union to account. The successful businessman of today is the man of trained cooperative intelligence. The world as well as the psychologist places a higher value on the man who can take part in collective thinking and concerted action, and has higher positions to offer him in the business and political field. The secretary of a Commission investigates a subject, is clever in mastering details, in drawing conclusions and in presenting them, perhaps far cleverer in these respects than any member of the Commission. But the chairman of the Commission must have another and higher power—the power of uniting these conclusions with the conclusions of others, the power of using this material to evolve with others plans for action. This means a more developed individual and brings a higher price in the open market.

But more important than any of the illustrations yet given is the application of the group principle to the relations of capital and labor. People are at last beginning to see that industrial organization must be based on the community idea. If we do not want to be dominated by the special interests of the capital-power, it is equally evident that we do not want to be dominated by the special interests of the labor-power. The interests of capital and labour must be united.

Even collective bargaining is only a milestone on the way to the full application of the group principle. It recognizes the union, it recognizes that some adjustment between the interests of capital and labor is possible, but it is still 'bargaining,' still an adjustment between two warring bodies, it still rests on the two pillars of concession and compromise. We see now the false psychology underlying compromise and concession. Their practical futility has long been evident: whenever any difference is 'settled' by concession, that difference pops up again in some other form. Nothing will ever truly settle differences but synthesis. No wonder the syndicalists label the 'compromises' made between 'antagonistic interests' as insincere. In a way, all compromise is insincere, and real harmony can be obtained only by an integration of 'antagonistic' interests which can take place only when we understand the method. The error of the syndicalists is in thinking that compromise is the only method; their fundamental error is in thinking that different interests are necessarily 'antagonistic' interests.

Compromise is accepted not only as inevitable and as entirely proper, but as the most significant fact of human association, by those economists who belong to that school of 'group sociologists' which sees present society as made up of warring groups, ideal society as made up of groups in equilibrium. Not only, I believe, is conflict and compromise not the true social process, but also it is not, even at present, the most significant, though usually the largest, part of the social process. The integrating of ideas which comes partly from direct interpenetration and partly from that indirect interpenetration which is the consequence of the overlapping membership of groups, I see going on very largely in the groups to which I belong, and is surely an interesting sign-post to future methods of association.

The weakness of Arbitration and Conciliation Boards, with their 'impartial' member, is that they tend to mere compromise even when they are not openly negotiating between two warring parties. It is probable from what we see on all sides that the more 'concessions' we make, the less 'peace' we shall get. Compulsory Arbitration in New Zealand has not succeeded as well as was hoped just because it has not found the community between capital and labor.

The latest development of collective bargaining, the Trade Agreement, with more or less permanent boards of representatives from employers and workers, brings us nearer true community than we have yet found in industrial relations. The history of these Agreements in England and America is fruitful study. One of the best known in America is Mr. Justice Brandeis' protocol scheme in 1910 for the garment industries of New York, which provided for an industrial court composed of employers and employed to which all disagreements should be brought, and for six years this prevented strikes in the needles trades of New York.

One of the most interesting of the Trade Agreements to be found in the Bulletins of the National Labor Department, and one which can be studied over a long term of years, is that between the Stove Founders' National Defence Association (employers) and the Iron Moulders' Union of North America. It is not only that the permanent organ of 'conference' (employers and employees represented) has brought peace to the stove industry after forty years of disastrous strikes and lock-outs, but that question after question has been decided not by the side which the market rendered strongest at the moment seizing its advantage, but by a real harmonizing of interest. A good illustration is the treatment of the question of who should pay for the bad castings: this was not decided at once as a matter of superior strength or of compromise, but after many months a basis of mutual advantage was found.

For some years Trade Agreements have been coming to include more and more points: not wages and hours alone, but many questions of shop management, discipline etc. are now included. Moreover it has been seen over and over again that the knowledge gained through joint conference is the knowledge needed for joint control:

the workmen ought to know the cost of production and of transportation, the relative value of different processes of production, the state of the market, the conditions governing the production and marketing of the competing product, etc.; the employer must know the real conditions of labor and the laborer's point of view.

The fundamental weakness of collective bargaining is that while it provides machinery for adjustment of grievances, while it looks forward to all the conceivable emergencies which may arise to cause disagreement between labor and capital, and seeks methods to meet these, it does not give labor a direct share in industrial control. In the collective *bargain* wages and the conditions of employment are usually determined by the relative *bargaining* strength of the workers and employers of the industrial group. Not bargaining in any form, not negotiation, is the key to industrial peace and prosperity; the collective contract must in time go the way of the individual contract. Community is the key-word for all relations of the new state. Labor unions have long been seeking their 'rights,' have looked on the differences between capital and labor as a fight, and have sought an advantageous position from which to carry on the fight: this attitude has influenced their whole internal organization. They quite as much as capital must recognize that this attitude must be given up. If we want harmony between labor and capital, we must make labor and capital into one group: we must have an integration of interests and motives, of standards and ideals of justice.

It is a mistake to think that social progress is to depend upon anything happening to the working people: some say that they are to be given more material goods and all will be well; some think they are to be given more 'education' and the world will be saved. It is equally a mistake to think that what we need is the conversion to 'unselfishness' of the capitalist class. Those who advocate profit-sharing are not helping us. The quarrel between capital and labor can never be settled on material grounds. The crux of that quarrel is not profits and wages—it is the joint control of industry.

There has been an increasing tendency of recent years for employers to take their employees into their councils. This ranges from mere 'advisory' boards, which are consulted chiefly concerning grievances, through the joint committees for safety, health, standardization, wages, etc., to real share in the management. But even in the lower form of this new kind of cooperation, we may notice two points: the advisory boards are usually representative bodies elected by the employees, and they are consulted as a whole, not individually. The flaw in these advisory boards is not so much, as is often thought, because the management still keeps all the power in its own hands, as that the company officials do not sit with these boards in joint consultation. There is, however, much variety of method. In some shops, advisory committees meet with the company officials. Some companies put many more important questions concerning conditions of employment before these bodies than other companies would think practical. A few employers have even given up the right to discharge—dismissal must be decided by fellow-employees.

Usually, the management keeps the final power in its own hands. This is not so, however, in the case of Wm. Filene Son's Co., Boston, which has gone further than any other plant in co-management. Here, the employees have the right by a two-thirds vote to change, initiate, or amend any rule that affects the discipline or working conditions of the employees of the store, and such vote becomes at once operative even against the veto of the management. Further, out of eleven members of the board of directors, four are representative of the employees.

The great advantage of company officials and workers acting together on boards or committees (workshop committees, discipline boards, advisory councils, boards of directors, etc.) is the same as that of the regular joint conferences of the Trade Agreement: employers and employed can thus learn to function together and prepare the way for joint control. Workshop committees should be encouraged, not so much because they remove grievances, etc. as because in the joint workshop committee, managers and workers are learning to act together. Industrial democracy is a process, a growth. The joint control of industry may be established by some fiat, but it will not be the genuine thing until the *process* of joint control is learned. To be sure, the workshop committees which are independent of the management are often considered the best for the workers because they can thus keep themselves free to maintain and fight for their own particular interests, but this is exactly, I think, what should be avoided.

The labor question is—Is the war between capital and labor to be terminated by fight and conquest or by learning how to function together? I face fully the fact that many supporters of labor believe in what they call the 'frank' recognition that the interests of capital and labor are 'antagonistic.' I believe that the end of the wars of nations and of the war between labor and capital will come in exactly the same way: by making the nations into one group, by making capital and labor into one group. Then we shall learn to distinguish between true and apparent interests, or rather, between long-run and immediate interests; then we shall give up the notion of 'antagonisms,' which belong to a static world, and see only difference—that is, that which is capable of integration. This is not an idealistic treatment of the labor problem. Increase of wages and reduction in cost of production were once considered an irreconcilable antagonism—now their concurrence is a matter of common experience. If the hope of that concurrence had been abandoned as visionary or idealistic, we should be sadly off today. Many people are now making a distinction, however, between production and distribution in this respect: in the former the interests of capital and labor are the same, it is said, but not in the latter. When that reorganization of the business world, which it is no longer utopian to think of, is further actualized, then in distribution too we shall be able to see the coincident interests of labor and capital.

As the most hopeful sign in the present treatment of industrial questions is the recognition that man with his fundamental instincts and needs is the very centre and heart of the labor problem, so the most hopeful sign that we shall fully utilize the constructive powers which will be released by this psychological approach to industrial problems is the gradually increasing share of the workman in the actual control of industry.

COMMENTARY

The Individual in the Group
Tokihiko Enomoto

I T I S always fascinating to study how ideas are transplanted in different environments. Japan is particularly interesting in this respect. When it opens itself to the outside world, it goes in for determined and conscious importation. However, it does not take it in wholesale. It carefully studies its imports, adapts them to its own needs and purposes, and absorbs them into its own mores and customs. The transformation is so thorough that very quickly the foreign origin is lost sight of and the import, to the outsider, appears to be a typically native Japanese product. This is the case in what has become known as "Japanese-style business management," which is in fact American in origin.

After World War II, the Americans changed our company and labor laws, made trade unions mandatory, and introduced American systems of industrial relations. These involuntary imports were quickly integrated into our hierarchical and bureaucratic structures and fashioned into our own ways of doing things: we use our right to strike, for example, very differently from the way it is used in the U.S.

In addition to these involuntary imports came a great deal of enthusiastic voluntary importation of American management ideas and techniques. After all, the Americans had won the war, so there was a lot for us to learn from them. Our students flocked to the United States for their graduate and postgraduate studies. They studied F. W. Taylor's scientific management (*The Principles of Scientific Management*, interpreted by a Japanese engineer into *Secrets for Eliminating Futile Work and Increasing Production*, had already been a bestseller in Japan in 1911), discovered the American pioneers of the human relations school, and learned about the various management schools that followed. Our economic missions, sent by such agencies as the Japan Productivity Center for Socio-Economic Development, visited U.S. factories and saw firsthand the latest American machinery and techniques at work. They returned determined to achieve high productivity and effective quality control in our early postwar factories.

The bottom-up concept of the quality circle and Toyota's just-in-time system, for example, are direct imports of American management thinking. The quality circle idea was first propounded by an American management expert and the zero-defect movement is based on the work of the American statistician, W. E. Deming. We recognize his invaluable contribution to our business renewal and growth through the Deming Award, the annual quality control award for which our companies compete ruthlessly.

American techniques yes, but Japanese spirit always. The theories were American, but the engineers who systemized them into working practices and the workers and managers who used them, being Japanese, did it their way—painstakingly and patiently adjusting them to the logic of the local situation, developing and improving the concepts to meet their specific needs and purposes, and, in the process, making them truly their own.

In the matter of organization we went for Chester Barnard. His principle of cooperation as the basis for effective organization has affinities with our own feelings for conformity and consensus. So great, in fact, was Barnard's influence on our management thinking that the phenomenon came to be called "the Barnard Revolution."

Our first article on Barnard appeared in 1950; that on Follett in 1951. In studying Barnard's papers, our scholars found that he had read and annotated Follett's works. So they too, in true Japanese fashion of meticulous attention to detail, had to read Follett. In the process they became interested in her teaching in its own right. Very quickly, she was being written up in management books and included in management encyclopedias. Little by little, Follett's work has become part of our teaching on management and is well known to quite a number of the mid- and upper-level managers who staff our government institutions and business organizations.

How is it, one might well speculate, that Follett, still today an unknown quantity in the United States, is known and highly prized in Japanese management circles?

The reasons are many and various. To mention but one of them—we hold a different view of history. We have a strong sense of the past. For us, the past is important and has value. We reach out for the new but do not discard the old. We incorporate the new into the old, in this way renewing the past, evolving it into the new present. Americans, it seems to me, do not have the same feeling for the past. For them, it would appear that the new is all that counts. The new somehow invalidates the past. Therefore there is no need to keep in touch with it. I understand that in management studies anything more than 10 years old is set aside as old hat and not worth looking at. Could there be, perhaps, in American thinking a remnant of Ford's dictum that "History is Bunk"?

The Harvard Business School Press obviously does not share this view. It is clearly respectful of the past; otherwise, it would not be reviving the invaluable teachings of Mary Parker Follett.

Much of what Follett says about individuals and groups reflects to a substantial extent our Japanese views of the place of individuals in groups and by extension their place in society. For Follett, the unit of society is neither the individual in isolation nor the group as an entity, but the group-individual. She sees individuals not as independent selves going their separate ways, but as interdependent, interactive, and interconnecting members of the groups to which they belong. This is something close to the Japanese ethos. We can fully agree with Follett when she writes that "The vital relation of the individual to the world is through his groups."[1]

Another important element of Follett's teaching is integration. For effective group organization, for productive and satisfying results, Follett says we need to bring about integration of differences—of views, of interests. Integration is to be achieved not through power being imposed by one party on the other but by the parties themselves studying their differences and, together, finding the solution that meets their mutual needs and desires. For Follett, this concept of integration applies to all relations—between individuals as they relate within their groups, and between groups as these relate with one another.

In industrial relations, Follett is quite clear: "If we want harmony between labour and capital, we must make labour and capital into one group: we must have an integration of interests and motives, of standards and ideals of justice."[2] This concept of joint action through consensus and integration of interest is also integral to Japanese culture. So we accept as basic common sense what Follett is telling us here. To Western thinking, based on division and control, perhaps it is considered too radical and therefore unacceptable.

As a university professor, I often meet with businesspeople who come to campus to recruit young talent. They come not knowing Follett, but after reading our book *Mary Parker Follett,*[3] most of them learn to appreciate her views on integration and to realize her relevance and importance for their organizations and for the country as a whole. In telephone interviews with former students now in managerial posts in government and business, I found it revealing that Follett's concept of integration is central to their work as managers—although sadly, in our current harsh economic environment and the need for retrenchment, it is not always possible for them to fully integrate needs and aspirations to the satisfaction of all concerned.

Follett's thought, which appears to us simple and basic common sense, is, however, subtle and profound. She shows the way to true democracy: how individuals, to develop their potential and at the same time contribute to their group, must not passively conform to its norms. If they disagree, they must voice their differences and work with the others to bring about a new synthesis and integration. Follett has an interesting phrase: "the dictatorship of the majority." Brought down to the group level, it is "groupism," the pathogeny of the group, when its members fear to go against its accepted wisdom and its traditional ways—something that we, in our society where conforming to usage and tradition is so important, must strive especially to guard against.

Throughout *The New State* and, in particular, in the extracts here, Follett shows how to avoid passive acceptance and the way to true democracy: self-respect and respect for the views and interests of others, and always working together in trust and openness for reciprocal understanding and benefit. Follett is the beacon that lights up the true democratic ideal. This is why I use every opportunity, in research groups and academic conferences, to promote her ideas on democratic governance in the business organization.

It is because Follett's teaching is so important to us that eight years ago, a number of Japanese professors founded The Mary P. Follett Association of Japan. (Is there, I wonder, a Follett Association anywhere else in the world?) Our association now has more than 80 members, a combination of scholars and businesspeople active throughout Japan. The association gives us the opportunity to deepen our understanding of Follett's methodology and study her ideas in relation to her contemporaries (Barnard, Mayo, Whitehead) as well as to current thinkers in management and other fields.

I have no doubt that this Follett compendium will prove inspiring not only to scholars and managers, but also to all who happen to find their way to it.

NOTES

1. Mary Parker Follett, *The New State: Group Organization, the Solution of Popular Government* (London: Longmans Green, 1920), p. 20.
2. Follett, *The New State*, p. 117.
3. Tadashi Mito and Tokihiko Enomoto, *Mary Parker Follett* (Tokyo: Doubunkan, 1986), in Japanese.

TEN

✠ ══╋

The Individual in Society

THE UNITY OF THE SOCIAL PROCESS

We have seen that the common idea and the common will are born together in the social process. One does not lead to the other; each is involved in the other. But the collective thought and the collective will are not yet complete; they are hardly an embryo. They carry indeed within themselves their own momentum, but they complete themselves only through activity in the world of affairs, of work, of government. This conception does away with the whole discussion, into which much ardor has gone, of the priority of thought or action in the social life. There is no order. The union of thought and will and activity by which the clearer will is generated, the social process, is a perfect unity.

We see this in our daily life where we do not finish our thought, construct our will, and then begin our actualizing. Not only the actualizing goes on at the same time, but its reactions help us to shape our thought, to energize our will. We have to digest our social experience, but we have to have social experience before we can digest it. We must learn and build and learn again through the building, or we must build and learn and build again through the learning.

We sit around the council table not blank pages but made up of all our past experiences. Then we evolve a so-called common will, then we take it into the concrete world to see if it will work.

Note: This chapter is adapted from *The New State: Group Organization, the Solution of Popular Government* (London: Longmans, Green, 1920), pp. 50–78.

In so far as it does work, it proves itself; in so far as it does not, it generates the necessary idea to make it 'common.' Then again we test and so on and so on. In our work always new and necessary modifications arise which again in actualizing *themselves,* again modify themselves. This is the process of the generation of the common will. First, it appears as an ideal, secondly it works itself out in the material sphere of life, thereby generating itself in a new form and so on forever and ever. All is a-making. To elevate General Welfare into our divinity makes a golden calf of it, erects it as something external to ourselves, with an absolute nature of its own, whereas it is the ever new adjusting of ever new relatings to one another. The common will never finds perfection but is always seeking it. Progress is an infinite advance towards the infinitely receding goal of infinite perfection.

Democratic ideals will never advance unless we are given the opportunity of constantly embodying them in action, which action will react on our ideals. Thought and will go out into the concrete world in order to generate their own complete form. This gives us both the principle and the method of democracy. A democratic community is one in which the common will is being gradually created by the civic activity of its citizens. The test of democracy is the fullness with which this is being done. The practical thought for our political life is that the collective will exists only through its self-actualizing and self-creating in new and larger and more perfectly adjusted forms.

Thus the unity of the social process becomes clear to us. We now gain a conception of 'right,' of purpose, of loyalty to that purpose, not as particularistic ideas but as arising within the process.

RIGHT

We are evolving now a system of ethics which has three conceptions in regard to right, conscience and duty which are different from much of our former ethical teaching:

1. we do not follow right, we create right;

2. there is no private conscience;

3. my duty is never to 'others' but to the whole.

First, we do not follow right merely; we create right. It is often thought vaguely that our ideals are all there, shining and splendid, and we have only to apply them. But the truth is that we have to create our ideals. No ideal is worthwhile which does not grow from our actual life. Some people seem to keep their ideals all carefully packed away from dust and air, but arranged alphabetically so that they can get at them quickly in need. But we can never take out a past ideal for a present need. The ideal which is to be used for our life must come out from that very life itself. The only way our past ideals can help us is in moulding the life which produces the present ideal; we have no further use for them. But we do not discard them: we have built them into the present—we have used them up as the cocoon is used up in making the silk. It has been sometimes taught that, given the same situation, the individual must repeat the same behaviour. But the situation is never the same, the individual is never the same; such a conception has nothing to do with life. We cannot do our duty in the old sense, that is of following a crystallized ideal, because our duty is new at every moment.

Moreover, the knowledge of what is due to the whole is revealed within the life of the whole. This is above everything else what a progressive ethics must teach—not faithfulness to duty merely, but faithfulness to the life which evolves duty. Indeed 'following our duty' often means mental and moral atrophy. Man cannot live by taboos; that means stagnation. But as one taboo after another is disappearing, the call is upon us deliberately to build our own moral life. Our ethical sense will surely starve on predigested food. It is we by our acts who progressively construct the moral universe; to follow some preconceived body of law—that is not for responsible moral beings. In so far as we obey old standards without interpenetrating them with the actual world, we are abdicating our creative power.

The group consciousness of right thus developed becomes our daily imperative. No mandate from without has power over us. There are many forms of the fallacy that the governing and the governed can be two different bodies, and this one of conforming to standards which we have not created must be recognized as such before we can have any sound foundation for society. When the 'ought' is not a mandate from without, it is no longer a prohibition but a self-expression. As the social consciousness develops, 'ought' will be swallowed up in will. We are some time truly to see our life as positive, not negative, as made up of continuous willing, not of restraints and prohibition. Morality is not the refraining from doing certain things—it is a constructive force.

So in the education of our young people it is not enough to teach them their 'duty'; somehow there must be created for them to live in a world of high purpose to which their own psychic energies will instinctively respond. The craving for self-expression, self-realization, must see quite naturally for its field of operation the community. This is the secret of education: when the waters of our life are part of the sea of human endeavor, duty will be a difficult word for our young people to understand; it is a glorious consciousness we want, not a painstaking conscience. It is ourselves soaked with the highest, not a Puritanical straining to fulfill an external obligation, which will redeem the world.

Education therefore is not chiefly to teach children a mass of things which have been true up to the present moment; moreover it is not to teach them to learn about life as fast as it is made, not even to interpret life, but above and beyond everything, to create life for themselves. Hence, education should be largely the training in making choices. The aim of all proper training is not rigid adherence to a crystallized right (since in ethics, economics or politics there is no crystallized right), but the power to make a new choice at every moment. And the greatest lesson of all is to know that every moment *is* new.

We must breed through the group process the kind of man who is not fossilized by habit, but whose eye is intent on the present situation, the present moment, present values, and can decide on the forms which will best express them in the actual world.

To sum up this point: morality is never static; it advances as life advances. You cannot hang your ideals up on pegs and take down No. 2 for certain emergencies and No. 4 for others. *The true test of our morality is not the rigidity with which we adhere to standards, but the loyalty we show to the life which constructs standards.* The test of our morality is whether we are living not to follow but to create ideals, whether we are pouring our life into our visions only to receive it back with its miraculous enhancement for new uses.

Secondly, I have said that the conception of right as a group product, as coming from the ceaseless interplay of men, shows us that there is no such thing as an individual conscience in the sense in which the term is often used. As we are to obey no ideals dictated by others or the past, it is equally important that we obey no ideal set up by our unrelated self. To obey the moral law is to obey the social ideal. The social ideal is born, grows and shapes itself through the associated life. The individual cannot alone decide what is right or wrong. We can have no true moral judgment except as we live our life with others. It is said: 'Every man is subject only to his own conscience.' But what is my conscience? Has it not been produced by my time, my country, my associates? To make a conscience by myself would be as difficult as to try to make a language by myself.

It is sometimes said, on the other hand, 'The individual must yield his right to judge for himself; let the majority judge.' But the individual is not for a moment to yield his right to judge for himself; he can judge better for himself if he joins with others in evolving a synthesized judgment. Our individual conscience is not absorbed into a national conscience; our individual conscience must be incorporated in a national conscience as one of its constituent members. . . .

What we want is a related conscience, a conscience that is intimately related to the consciences of other men and to all the spiritual environment of our time, to all the progressive forces of our age. The particularistic tendency has had its day in law, in politics, in international relations and as a guiding tendency in our daily lives.

We have seen that a clearer conception today of the unity of the social process shows us:

1. that we are not merely to follow but to create 'right';

2. that there is no private conscience; and

3. that my duty is never to 'others' but to the whole.

We no longer make a distinction between selfishness and altruism. An act done for our own benefit may be social and one done for another may not be. Some twenty or thirty years ago, our 'individual' system of ethics began to be widely condemned and we have been hearing a great deal of 'social' ethics. But this so-called 'social' ethics has meant only my duty to 'others.' There is now emerging an idea of ethics entirely different from the altruistic school, based not on the duty of isolated beings to one another, but on integrated individuals acting as a whole, evolving whole-ideas, working for whole-ideals. The new consciousness is of a whole.

PURPOSE

As right appears with that interrelating, germinating activity which we call the social process, so purpose also is generated by the same process. The goal of evolution most obviously must evolve itself. How self-contradictory is the idea that evolution is the world-process and yet that some other power has made the goal for it to reach. The truth is that the same process which creates all else creates the very purpose. That purpose is involved in the process, not prior to process, has far wider reaching consequences than can be taken up here. The whole philosophy of cause and effect must be rewritten. If the infinite task is the evolution of the whole, if our finite tasks are wholes of varying degrees of scope and perfection, the notion of causality must have an entirely different place in our system of thought.

The question is often asked: 'What is the proposed unity of European nations after the war to be for?' This question implies that the alliance will be a mere method of accomplishing certain purposes, whereas it is the union which is the important thing. With the union, the purpose comes into being, and with its every step forward, the purpose changes. No one would say that the aims of the Allies today are the same as in 1914, or even as in April, 1917. As the alliance develops, the purpose steadily shapes itself.

Every teleological view will be given up when we see that purpose is not 'preexistent,' but involved in the unifying act which is the life process. It is man's part to create purpose and to actualize it. From the point of view of man we are just in the dawn of self-consciousness, and his purpose is dimly revealing itself to him. The life-force wells up in us for expression—to direct it is the privilege of self-consciousness.

LOYALTY

As this true purpose evolves itself, loyalty springs into being. Loyalty is awakened through and by the very process which creates the group. The same process which organizes the group energizes it. We cannot 'will' to be loyal. Our task is not to 'find' causes to awaken our loyalty but to live our life fully and loyalty issues. A cause has no part in us or we in it if we have fortuitously to 'find' it . . . Loyalty to a collective will which we have not created and of which we are, therefore, not an integral part, is slavery. We belong to our community just in so far as we are helping to make that community; then loyalty follows, then love follows. Loyalty means the consciousness of oneness, the full realization that we succeed or fail, live or die, are saved or damned together. The only unity of community is one we have made of ourselves, by ourselves, for ourselves. (In a relation even of two I am not faithful to the other person but to my conception of the relation in the whole. Loyalty is always to the group idea not to the group-personnel. This must change our idea of patriotism).

Thus, the social process is one all-inclusive, self-sufficing process. The vital impulse which is produced by all the reciprocally interacting influences of the group is also itself the generating and the vivifying power. Social unity is not a sterile conception, but an active force. It is a double process—the activity which goes to make the unity and the activity which flows from the unity. There is no better example of centripetal and centrifugal force. All the forces which are stored up in the unity flow forth eternally in activity. We create the common will and feel the spiritual energy which flows into us from the purpose we have made, for the purpose which we seek.

THE INDIVIDUAL

As the collective idea and the collective will, right and purpose, are born within the all-sufficing social process, so here too the individual finds the wellspring of his life. The visible form in which this interplay of relations appears is society and the individual. A man is a point in the social process rather than a unit in that process, a point where forming forces meet straightway to disentangle themselves and stream forth again. In the language of the day, man is at the same time a social factor and a social product.

People often talk of the social mind as if it were an abstract conception, as if only the individual were real, concrete. The two are equally real. Or rather the only reality is the relating of one to the other which creates both. Our sundering is as artificial and late an act as the sundering of consciousness into subject and object. The only reality is the interpenetrating of the two into experience. Late intellectualism abstracts for practical purposes the ego from the world, the individual from society.

But there is no way of separating individuals, they coalesce and coalesce, they are 'confluent' to use the expression of James, who tells us that the chasm between men is an individualistic fiction, that we are surrounded by fringes, that these overlap and that by means of these I join with others. It is as in Norway when the colors of the sunset and the dawn are mingling, when today and tomorrow are at the point of breaking, or of uniting, and one does not know to which one belongs, to the yesterday which is fading or the coming hour—perhaps this is something like the relation of one to another: to the onlookers from another planet our colors might seem to mingle.

The truth about the individual and society has been already implied, but it may be justifiable to develop the idea further because of the paramount importance for all our future development of a clear understanding of the individual. Our nineteenth-century legal theory (individual rights, contract, "a man can do what he likes with his own," etc.) was based on the conception of the separate individual. We can have no sound legal doctrine, and hence no social or political progress, until the fallacy of this idea is fully recognized. The new state must rest on a true conception of the individual. Let us ask ourselves therefore for a further definition of individuality than that already implied.

The individual is the unification of a multiplied variety of reactions. But the individual does not react to society. The interplay constitutes both society on the one hand and individuality on the other: individuality and society are evolving together from this constant and complex action and reaction. Or, more accurately, the relation of the individual to society is not action and reaction, but infinite interactions by which both individual and society are forever a-making: we cannot say whether the individual acts upon and is acted upon, because that way of expressing it implies that he is a definite, given, finished entity and would keep him apart merely as an agent of the acting and being acted on. We cannot put the individual on one side and society on the other, we must understand the complete interrelation of the two. Each has no value, no existence without the other. The individual is created by the social process and is daily nourished by that process. There is no such thing as a self-made man. What we think we possess as individuals is what is stored up from society, is the subsoil of social life. We soak up and soak up and soak up our environment all the time.

Of what then does the individuality of a man consist? Of his relation to the whole, not (1) of his apartness nor (2) of his difference alone.

Of course, the mistake which is often made in thinking of the individual is that of confusing the physical with the real individual. The physical individual is seen to be apart and therefore apartness is assumed of the psychic or real individual. We think of Edward Fitzgerald as a recluse, that he got his development by being alone, that he was largely outside the influences of society. But imagine Fitzgerald's life without his books. It undoubtedly did not suit his nature to mix freely with other people in bodily presence, but what a constant and vivid living with others his life really was. How closely he was in vital contact with the thoughts of men.

We must bear in mind that the social spirit itself may impose apartness on a man; the method of uniting with others is not always that of visible, tangible groups. The pioneer spirit is the creative spirit even if it seems to take men apart to fulfill its dictates. On the other hand, the solitary man is not necessarily the man who lives alone; he may be one who lives constantly with others in all the complexity of modern city life, but who is shut-up or so set upon his own ideas that he makes no real union with others.

Individuality is the capacity for union. The measure of individuality is the depth and breadth of true relation. I am an individual not as far as I am apart from, but as far as I am a part of other men. Evil is non-relation. The source of our strength is the central supply. You may as well break a branch off the tree and expect it to live. Non-relation is death.

I have said that individuality consists neither of the separatedness of one man from the other, nor of the differences of one man from the other. The second statement is challenged more often than the first. This comes from some confusion of ideas. My individuality is difference springing into view as relating itself with other differences. The act of relating is the creating act. It is vicious intellectualism to say 'Before you relate you must have things to relate, therefore the differences are more elemental; there are (1) differences which (2) unite, therefore uniting is secondary! The only fact, the only truth, is the creative activity which appears as the great complex we call humanity. The activity of creating is all. It is only by *being* this activity that we grasp it. To view it from the outside, to dissect it into its different elements, to lay these elements on the dissecting table as so many different individuals, is to kill the life and feed the fancy with dead images, empty, sterile concepts. But let us set about relating ourselves to our community in fruitful fashion, and we shall see that our individuality is bodying itself forth in stronger and stronger fashion, our difference shaping itself in exact conformity with the need of the work we do.

For we must remember when we say that the essence of individuality is the relating of self to other difference, that difference is not something static, something given that it also is involved in the world of becoming. This is what experience teaches me—that society needs my difference, not as an absolute, but just so much difference as will relate me. Differences develop within the social process and are united through the social process. Difference which is not capable of relation is eccentricity. Eccentricity, caprice, put me outside, bring anarchy; true spontaneity, originality belong not to chaos but to system. But separatedness must be coordinated; irrelevancy produces nothing, is insanity. It is not my uniqueness which makes me of value to the whole but my power of relating. The nut and the screw form a perfect combination not because they are different, but because they exactly fit into each other and together can perform a function which neither could perform half of alone or any part of alone. It is not that the significance of the nut and screw is increased by their coming together, they have no significance at all unless they do come together. The fact that they have to be different to enter into any fruitful relation with each other is a matter of derivative importance—derived from the work they do.

Another illustration is that of the specialist. It is not a knowledge of his specialty which makes the expert of service to society, but his insight into the relation of his specialty to the whole. Thus it implies not less but more relation, because the entire value of that specialization is that it is part of something. Instead of isolating him and giving him a narrower life, it gives him at once a broader life because it binds him more irrevocably to the whole. But the whole works both ways. The specialist not only contributes to the whole, but all his relations to the whole are embodied in his own particular work.

Thus difference is only a part of the life process. To exaggerate this part led to the excessive and arrogant individualism of the nineteenth century. It behooves us children of the twentieth century to search diligently after the law of unity that we may effectively marshal and range under its dominating sway all the varying diversities of life.

Our definition of individuality must now be 'finding my place in the whole': 'my place' gives you the individual, 'the whole' gives you society, but by connecting them, by saying 'my place in the whole,' we get a fruitful synthesis. I have tried hard to get away from any mechanical system and yet it is difficult to find words which do not seem to bind. I am now afraid of this expression—my place in the whole. It has a rigid, unyielding sound, as if I were a cog in a machine. But my place is not a definite portion of space and time. The people who believe in their 'place' in this sense can always photograph their 'places.' But my place is a matter of infinite relation, and of infinitely changing relation, so that it can never be captured. It is neither the anarchy of particularism nor the rigidity of the German machine. To know my place is not to know my niche, not to know whether I am cog No. 3 or cog No. 4; it is to be alive at every instant at every finger tip to every contact and to be conscious of those contacts.

We see now that the individual both seeks the whole and is the whole.

First, the individual, biology tells us, is never complete, completeness spells death; social psychology is beginning to show that man advances towards completeness not by further aggregations to himself, but by further and further relatings of self to other men. We are always reaching forth for union; most, perhaps all, our desires have this motive. The spirit craves totality, this is the motor of social progress; the process of getting it is not by adding more and more to ourselves, but by offering more and more of ourselves. Not appropriation but contribution is the law of growth. What our special contribution is, it is for us to discover. More and more, to release the potentialities of the individual means the more and more progressive organization of society, if at the same time we are learning how to coordinate all the variations. The individual in wishing for more wholeness does not ask for a chaotic mass, but for the orderly wholeness which we call unity. The test of our vitality is our power of synthesis, of life synthesis.

But although we say that the individual is never complete, it is also true that the individual is a being who, because his function is relating and his relatings are infinite, is in himself the whole of society. It is not that the whole is divided up into pieces; the individual is the whole at one point. This is the incarnation: it is the whole flowing into me, transfusing, suffusing me. The fullness, bigness of my life is not measured by the amount I do, nor the number of people I meet, but how far the whole is expressed through me. This is the reason why unifying gives me a sense of life and more unifying gives me a sense of more life—there is more of the whole and of me. My worth to society is not how valuable a part I am. I am not unique in the world because I am different from any one else, but because I am a whole seen from a special point of view.

That the relation of each to the whole is dynamic and not static is perhaps the most profound truth which recent years have brought us. We now see that when I give my share, I give always far more than my share, such are the infinite complexities, the fullness and fruitfulness of the interrelatings. I contribute to society my mite, and then society contains not just that much more nourishment, but as much more as the loaves and fishes which fed the multitude outnumbered the original seven and two. My contribution meets some particular need not because it can be measured off against that, but because my contribution by means of all the cross currents of life always has so much more than itself to offer. When I withhold my contribution, therefore, I am withholding far more than my personal share. When I fail some one or some cause, I have not failed just that person, just that cause, but the whole world is thereby crippled. This thought gives an added solemnity to the sense of personal responsibility. To sum up: individuality is a matter primarily neither of apartness nor of difference, but of each finding his own activity in the whole. In the many times a day that we think of ourselves it is not one time in a thousand that we think of our eccentricities, we are thinking indirectly of those qualities which join us to others: we think of the work we are doing with others and what is expected of us, the people we are going to play with when work is over and the part we are going to take in that play, the committee-meeting we are going to attend and what we are going to do there. Every distinct act of the ego is an affirmation of that amount of separateness which makes for perfect union. Every affirmation of the ego establishes my relation with all the rest of the universe. It is one and the same act which establishes my individuality and gives me my place in society. Thus an individual is one who is being created *by* society, whose daily breath is drawn *from* society, whose life is spent *for* society. When we recognize society as self-unfolding, self-unifying activity, we shall hold ourselves open to its influence, letting the Light steam into us, not from an outside source, but from the whole of which we are a living part. It is eternally due us that that whole should feed and nourish and sustain us at every moment, but it cannot do this unless at every moment we are creating it. This perfect interplay is Life. To speak of the 'limitation of the individual' is blasphemy and suicide. The spirit of the whole is incarnate in every part. 'For I am persuaded that neither death, nor life, nor agent, nor principalities, nor powers, nor things present, nor things to come, nor height, nor depth, nor any other creature, shall be able to separate'—the individual from society.

SOCIETY

We have seen that the interpenetrating of psychic forces creates at the same time individuals and society, that, therefore, the individual is not a unit but a centre of forces (both centripetal and centrifugal), and consequently society is not a collection of units but a complex of radiating and converging, crossing and recrossing energies. In other words, we are learning to think of society as a psychic process.

This conception must replace the old and wholly erroneous idea of society as a collection of units, and the later and only less misleading theory of society as an organism.

The old individualism with all the political fallacies it produced—social contract of the seventeenth and eighteenth centuries, majority rule of the nineteenth, etc.—was based on the idea of developed individuals first existing and then coming together to form society. But the basis of society is not numbers: it is psychic power.

The organic theory of society has so much to recommend it to superficial thinking that we must examine it carefully to find its fatal defects. But let us first recognize its merits.

Most obviously, an organic whole has a spatial and temporal individuality of its own, and it is composed of parts each with its individuality yet which could not exist apart from the whole. An organism means unity, each one his own place, every one dependent upon every one else.

Next, this unity, this interrelating of parts is the essential characteristic. It is always in unstable equilibrium, always shifting, varying and thereby changing the individual at every moment. But it is always produced and maintained by the individual himself. No external force brings it forth. The central life, the total life, of this self-developing, self-perpetuating being is involved in the process. Hence biologists do not expect to understand the body by a study of the separate cells as isolated units: it is the organic connection which unites the separate processes which they recognize as the fundamental fact.

This interrelating holds good of society when we view it externally. Society too can be understood only by the study of its flux of relations, of all the intricate reciprocities which go to make the unifying. Reciprocal ordering—subordinating, superordinating, coordinating—purposeful self-unifyings, best describe the social process. Led by James who has shown us the individual as a self-unifying centre, we now find the same kind of activity going on in society, in the social mind. And this interrelating, this unity as unity, is what gives to society its authority and power.

Thus the term organism is valuable as a metaphor, but it has not strict psychological accuracy.

There is this world-wide difference between the self-interrelatings of society and of the bodily organism: the social bond is a psychic relation and we cannot express it in biological terms or in any terms of physical force. If we could, if 'functional combination' could mean a psychological relation as well as a physiological, then the terms 'functional' and 'organic' might be accepted. But they denote a different universe from that of thought. For psychical self-unitings knit infinitely more closely and in a wholly different way. They are freed from the limitations of time and space. Minds can blend, yet in the blending preserve each its own identity. They transfuse one another while being each its own essential and unique self.

It follows that while the cell of the organism has only one function, the individual may have manifold and multiform functions: he enters with one function into a certain group this morning and with another function into another group this afternoon, because his free soul can freely knit itself with a new group at any moment.

This self-detaching, self-attaching freedom of the individual saves us from the danger to democracy which lurks in the organic theory. No man is forced to serve as the running foot or the lifting hand. Each at any moment can place himself where his nature calls. Certain continental sociologists are wholly unjustified in building their hierarchy where one man or group of men is the sensorium, others the hewers and carriers, etc. It is exactly this despotic and hopeless system of caste from which the true democracy frees man. He follows the call of his spirit and relates himself where he belongs today, and through this relating gains the increment of power which knits him anew where he now belongs and so continually as the wind of spirit blows.

Moreover in society every individual may be a complete expression of the whole in a way impossible for the parts of a physical organism. When each part is itself potentially the whole, when the whole can live completely in every member, then we have a true society and we must view it as a rushing of life—onrush, outrush, inrush—as a mobile, elastic, incalculable Protean energy seeking fitting form for itself. This ideal society is the divine goal towards which life is an infinite progress. Such conception of society must be visibly before us to the exclusion of all other theories when we ask ourselves later what the vote means in the true democracy.

PART THREE

Business—the Way Ahead

ELEVEN

═══ ═══

Business in Society

I SAID in the preceding lecture
that for most people the word
"profession" connotes a foundation of science and a motive of
service. It would be well, therefore, for us to examine the idea of
service. I do not wholly like the present use of that word. In the
first place, it has been so over-used that we are tired of it—"Service
is our motto," "Service with a smile," and so on. Moreover, this
word is often used sentimentally, or at least vaguely, to express
good intentions, or even, like charity, to cover a multitude of sins.
"Public service" is not always genuine service; public service corporations are not wholly self-sacrificing associations. "Social service"
often means the work necessary to make up for certain defects in
society, as pure-milk stations. It is well to have healthy babies; but
we are looking forward to the time when the making of healthy
babies will not devolve on extra-social agencies, on agencies which
would be unnecessary if society were what we hope it will some
day become. You see, I do not call pure-milk stations social agencies,
as do most people, but extra-social; and the distinction I am making
here seems to me to have some value. Business is, and should be
considered, truly a social agency.

Note: This chapter is reprinted from Elliot M. Fox and L. Urwick, eds., *Dynamic
Administration: The Collected Papers of Mary Parker Follett* (London: Pitman,
1973), pp. 103–116. This paper, originally titled "How Must Business Man-
agemant Develop in Order to Become a Profession?," was first presented before
a Bureau of Personnel Administration conference group in November 1925.

THE MEANING OF SERVICE—FUNCTION

Underneath all the various current uses of the word "service," there is the idea of service as expressing man's altruism, labour performed for another, doing good to others. I think there is a more profound meaning to service than this. Let us look at the matter historically. Is there any foundation in the development of our early communities for the notion of business based on altruistic service? A group of people settling in a new region first plant and sow. But other things have to be done. One buys groceries and sells to his neighbours. He does this expecting someone else in the community to build his store and house and keep them in repair, and someone else to make his shoes, and someone else to look after him when he is ill, and so on. This is an exchange, or interchange, of services. When we say "reciprocal service" it seems to me that we are nearer the facts and also that we are expressing that give-and-take of life which is its noblest as it is its most profound aspect. That person is intellectually or morally defective who is not taking part in the give-and-take of life.

With this understanding of the word "service," I think it a good word. Its connotation of self-sacrifice, of the recognition of other aims than private gain, makes it a high motive for individual lives and a social asset. If a man thinks of his business as a service, he will certainly not increase private profits at the expense of public good. Moreover, "business as service" tends to do away with one conception which was very unfortunate. There was a notion formerly that a man made money for himself, a purely selfish occupation, in the daytime, and rendered his service to the community by sitting on the school board or some civic committee at night. Or he might spend his early and middle life in business, in getting money, and then do his service later by spending his money in ways useful to the community—if he did not die before that stage arrived! The much more wholesome idea, which we have now, is that our work itself is to be our greatest service to the community.

There is, however, a word which gives us a truer idea of the place of business in society than even the expression "reciprocal service." I refer, of course, to the word you have been thinking of as you have been reading this paper, the word "function." A business man should think of his work as one of the necessary functions of society, aware that other people are also performing necessary functions, and that all together these make a sound, healthy, useful community. "Function" is the best word because it implies not only that you are responsible for serving your community, but that you are partly responsible for there being any community to serve.

For some time there has been emerging a sense of industry as a function. And this among employees as well as among employers. Someone who attended the La Follette Convention told me that the reason the locomotive engineers had so much influence there was that they had a sense of railroads as functional instruments and brought in a programme which resulted, not in oratory, but in discussion. A good many unionists are beginning to see that labour's stake in industry is not its stake in collective bargaining, but its stake in maintaining a useful enterprise. This is an understanding of function. And this gives actual, not evangelical, value to the idea of service.

I said that the chief reason we often hesitate to use the word "service" is that it has been abused. But so was the word "efficiency," which preceded it, and so certainly is this word "function" which is succeeding it. We need all these words—efficiency, service, function—but we need to use all three discriminatingly.

Assuming, then, that a profession (1) is exercised as one of the necessary functions of society, not purely for private gain, (2) that it is the application of a proved and systematic body of knowledge; recognizing, that is, that it rests on the double foundation of science and service, reciprocal service—what are some of the other implications involved in regarding an occupation as a profession?

One is certainly love of the work. A doctor or a lawyer, a teacher, a chemist, or an engineer usually cares greatly for his work, chooses it usually for that reason, voluntarily goes through the training necessary for it, often a long and strenuous training. But many a boy drifts into a business without having felt any particular urge to do that particular thing.

And love of work usually includes satisfaction in work well done. Craftsman and artist and professional man have aimed at this satisfaction, and more and more this is becoming true of business men. There is an expression which I like very much, "honest" work. We speak of a certain carpenter or plumber as giving us honest work. It would be profitable, I think, for each one of us to scrutinize his own work rigorously to see if it is as "honest" as, say, the surgeon's standard. In a recent book, the author speaks of the business man's zeal for service, and says that long after the clerks have departed from the office of a big corporation you can see lights burning in the rooms of the executives. Much fun has been made of this sentence, but I think a good deal of overtime work is done, if not for service, at any rate with the craftsman's love of doing a job well. And it seems to me that this is too fine an aim to be made second even to that of service, which sometimes narrows us down to too meagre an ethics. The *whole* grandeur of life is not there. It is indeed a noble word, but so also is self-expression, the love of work, the craftsman's and artist's joy in work well done. It seems to me, in short, that some people have their imagination aroused by the idea of service, others by high standards of accomplishment; that usually these go together; and that no occupation can make a more worthy appeal to the imagination, either from the point of view of the service it can perform or from the tremendous interest of the job itself, than that of business management.

PROFESSIONAL STANDARDS DEVELOPED AND EFFECTED THROUGH GROUP ORGANIZATION

Men have been greatly helped in developing standards and in adhering to standards by combining into some form of association. Each profession has its association. While I object to the idea that individual professional men have necessarily a higher code than individual business men, I do think that the professions are ahead of business in the fact that their codes are group codes. The errors of the personal equation are thus often corrected. Moreover, members know that they cannot have the respect of their group unless they follow its standards. But business, too, has begun to develop group codes. We can see how various trade associations, begun chiefly for such objects as central credit records or to secure legislation favouring their particular industry, have already improved trade practices and raised trade standards. And managers have now their associations, too. This is a step toward management's becoming a profession.

A professional association is an association with one object above all others. The members do not come together merely for the pleasure of meeting others of the same occupation; nor do they meet primarily to increase their pecuniary gain; although this may be one of the objects. They have joined in order better to perform their function. They meet:

To establish standards.

To maintain standards.

To improve standards.

To keep members up to standards.

To educate the public to appreciate standards.

To protect the public from those individuals who have not attained standards or wilfully do not follow them.

To protect individual members of the profession from each other.

These objects of a professional association may be summed up by saying that a profession provides a corporate responsibility. As most of the objects speak for themselves, I shall refer further to only three: corporate responsibility for maintenance of standards, for the education of the public, and for the development of professional standards.

In regard to the first, maintenance of standards, business can certainly learn a lesson from the professions, where the ideal is loyalty to the work rather than to the company. An architect feels primarily that he belongs to a certain profession, only secondarily that he is working for a particular firm. He may change his firm; but he remains permanently bound to the standards of his profession. I recognize that there is very serious trouble when the standards of one's firm and one's profession clash—*there* is indeed a difficult integration for you. What I am emphasizing here is that in the profession it is recognized that one's professional honour demands that one shall make this integration. If business management were a profession and had its own recognized code, differences between executives and company heads could perhaps be more easily adjusted. I know a man who recently left a Southern firm because, he told me, he could not reconcile his principles with the way that firm conducted business. When he put the matter to the firm, his principles were treated as a purely individual matter. If he had been a doctor, or if business management were a profession, he could have prevented the matter becoming personal by referring to the accepted standards or methods of the profession.

When, therefore, I say that members of a profession feel a greater loyalty to their profession than to the company, I do not mean that their loyalty is to one group of persons rather than to another; but that their loyalty is to a body of principles, of ideals;

that is, to a special body of knowledge of proved facts and the standards arising therefrom. What, then, are we loyal to? To the soul of our work. To that which is both in our work and which transcends our work. This seems to me the highest romance as it is the deepest religion, namely, that by being loyal to our work we are loyal to that which transcends our work. The great romance of business is not, as sometimes supposed, the element of chance. That spells adventure only for him with the gambler's temperament. The high adventure of business is its opportunity for bringing into manifestation every hour of the day the deeper thing within every man, transcending every man, which you may call your ideal, or God, or what you will, but which is absent from no man.

In regard to the second point mentioned above, responsibility for the education of the public, it is considered one of the duties of a profession to train the public by sticking to professional standards instead of merely giving the public what it wants. An architect, to be sure, may put cupolas and gimcracks on a house he is building, a portrait painter may get rich by painting portraits flattering his sitters, but when architect or portrait painter does these things he is outside professional standards, outside the accepted tradition of a group of people. If business management is to become a profession, business management, too, will have to think of educating the public, not merely of giving it what it asks for. The head of a string of restaurants, one who thinks of business as a public service and is trying to give wholesome food as a public health measure, was trying to reduce the bacterial count in ice cream. A customer asked one day, "Why doesn't the ice cream taste as it used to?" "We are trying," said the waitress, "to reduce the bacterial count." "Oh, give us our old bugs. We liked 'em," said the customer.

Oliver Sheldon says, "Management acknowledges as master the public will of the community alone." I do not agree with that. The public will of a particular community may have to be educated to appreciate certain standards. That is exactly what is going to make business management a profession: to realize that it is responsible to something higher than the public will of a community, that its service to the public does not lie wholly in obeying the public.

And this brings us to our third point. One of the aims of the professional man is not only to practise his profession, to apply his science, but to extend the knowledge upon which that profession is based. A profession means, not only a tradition, but a developing tradition. There would be no progress if men merely lived up to the standards of their profession. The judge makes a decision which not only disposes of the case in hand, but becomes a precedent. A lawyer often handles a case in such fashion that certain principles are established or strengthened. The doctor not only cures a particular person, but has something to tell his profession about that particular disease. Business lags behind the professions in this respect. You know how often you hear the expression "get by"—"I guess we can get by on that." Men tide over certain situations without doing that which means a progressive policy for their business, or that which helps to establish a standard for business management.

There is one thing which I think all executives should remember every hour of the day. You are not helping to develop your profession only when you are discussing its demands in the managers' association. The way in which you give every order, the way in which you make every decision, the way in which you meet every committee, in almost every act you perform during the day, you may be contributing to the science of management. Business management cannot become a profession unless business men realize fully their part in making it such. All professions have been developed by the work of their own members. If there were people somewhere in the world creating executive technique, and you were applying it, your job would be big; but it is just twice as big as that, for there is no one else in the world but yourselves to create the science, the art, the profession of business management. This is pioneer work and difficult, but it has always been pioneer work to which men have responded with courage and vigour.

We have been speaking of professional standards as formed and developed through group association. Is there not something in the manner in which those ideals are followed which we have hitherto connected more closely with the professions than with business? There is a word which means a great deal to me; I wonder if it does to you. That is "style." Whatever a man does, whether he is a statesman or artisan, whether he is poet or tennis player, we like his activity to have the distinction of something we call style. Style, however, is a difficult thing to define. I have seen it defined variously as adapting form to material, as calculation of means to end, as restraint, as that which is opposed to all that is sloppy and bungling, the performance of an act without waste. Others speak of style as broad design, noble proportion. A manager's job performed with style would have all these characteristics.

I have looked for style in literature and art, games and statesmanship. It is interesting to watch polo from this point of view. In all the games of polo I have seen, the best players have usually had style: no waste of muscle, calculation of means to end, yes, and proportion and design, too. Again, watch a good actor when his acting has the distinction of style. There is restraint, calculation of means to end, no waste of energy. A physiologist watching a scene of agony on the stage will, if the acting is of the first order, tell you that he sees no waste of muscular force. In poor acting, however, there is such waste. Such acting lacks, among other things, style.

Professor Whitehead gives attainment and restraint as the two chief elements of style and says:

"Style is the fashioning of power, the restraint of power. The administrator with a sense of style hates waste, the engineer with a sense of style economizes his material, the artisan with a sense of style prefers good work. Style is the ultimate morality of mind."

And further:

"With style, the end is attained without side issues, without raising undesirable inflammations. With style, you attain your end and nothing but your end. With style, the effect of your activity is incalculable, and foresight is the last gift of gods to men. With style, your power is increased, for your mind is not disturbed with irrelevances, and you are more likely to attain your object. Now style is the exclusive privilege of the expert. Whoever heard of the style of an amateur poet, of an amateur painter? Style is always the product of specialist study, the contribution of specialism to culture."

That is an interesting phrase, "the contribution of specialism to culture." Then you need not, according to this definition, give your daytime hours to a low thing called business, and in the evening pursue culture. Through your business itself, if you manage it with style, you are making a contribution to the culture of the world. It makes business management interesting, doesn't it? I take it that you are taking this course throughout the winter to learn how to give to your work of management the distinction of style.

I have left to the last what seems to me the chief function, the real service, of business: to give an opportunity for individual development through the better organization of human relationships. Several times lately I have seen business defined as production, the production of useful articles. But every activity of man should add to the intangible values of life as well as to the tangible, should aim at other products than merely those which can be seen and handled. What does "useful" mean, anyway? We could live without many of the articles manufactured. But the greatest usefulness of these articles consists in the fact that their manufacture makes possible those manifold, interweaving activities of men by which spiritual values are created. There is no over-production here.

Suppose the doctors should tell us that it would be more healthy to go barefoot, and we should all take their advice. What would become of all the shoe factories? Of course, the manufacturers would find out how much of their equipment could be used in making something else, and they would turn to the manufacture of that other article. In that case, must they consider their previous work of no value? Must an old man who has been a shoe manufacturer think he has wasted his life in producing something actually injurious to the community? I think he would have to, if all he had produced was boots and shoes, the material product. But not if the men who worked in that factory, managerial or manual workers, had through their work become more developed human beings. And the tendency today in many plants is, most happily, to make that development one of the objects of the industry. It is the development of the individual involving the progress of society, that some of our finer presidents are aiming at, not pecuniary gain only; not service in the sense of supplying all our present crude wants, but the raising of men to finer wants. If the aim of the lawyer is justice, if the aim of the doctor is health, if the aim of the architect is beauty, business, I am sure, may have as noble an aim. There are business men today who perceive that the *process* of production is as important for the welfare of society as the *product* of production. This is what makes personnel work in industry the most interesting work in the world.

If business offers so large an opportunity for the creation of spiritual values, and I think it offers a larger opportunity than any single profession in the possibilities of those intimate human interweavings through which all development of man must come; if many business men are taking advantage of that opportunity, should we any longer allow the assumption which I have seen stated three times since last summer, that the professions are for service and business for pecuniary gain? I have seen the expression "the greed of the business man." I have seen it stated that the business man's test of an undertaking is, "Will it increase income?" while the professional man's test is, "Will it increase the sum of human welfare?" But I do not think this distinction valid. I object to dividing us off into sheep and goats and putting all the goats on the side of business. Professional men as well as business men used to think less of pecuniary gain. But that is *their* responsibility. Ours, it seems to me, is to redeem the word "business." We are told that business should have a professional conscience. Why not a business conscience? Why not business pride as well as professional pride?

It is unfair to think that all business men have only as high a code as is compatible with keeping profits at a certain level. I have known business men who were willing to make sacrifices to maintain certain standards. Napoleon called England a "nation of shopkeepers." That was an epitome of his own character. Shopkeeping did not have the pomp and glory of *his* trade. It had none of the deceptive values on which his life was based.

We have progressed in a hundred years beyond Napoleon's notion of shopkeeping; yet in an interview reported in the *Boston Herald* the artist, Cecilia Beaux, said in effect, "The business man aims at success in the sense of wealth or prominence; the artist's idea of success is the satisfactory development of an idea." If I were a business man, I would not let business lie any longer under this stigma. It is true that the artist or the professional man undertakes to solve his problems, he does not try to "get by." He would rather be lamely and blunderingly trying to solve his problem than brilliantly escaping it. But why should not the business man have the same attitude? Cecilia Beaux said in this interview, "The artist grips his idea and will not let it go until it has blessed him, as the angel blessed Jacob."

I see no reason why business men should have lower ideals than artists or professional men. Let us, indeed, do everything possible to make business management a profession, but while we are doing it, I think we may feel that business men can make as large a contribution to professional ideas as the so-called learned professions. I think, indeed, that the business man has opportunities to lead the world in an enlarged conception of the expressions "professional honour," "professional integrity." That phrase which we hear so often, "business integrity," is already being extended to mean far more than a square deal in a trade.

I have tried to show in this and the previous lecture that business management has already acquired some of the essentials of a profession, that it is on the way to acquire others. By far the most significant sign that business management is becoming a profession is that the old idea of business as trading has begun to disappear. The successful business man of the past was thought to be the one who could get the best in a trade. This required neither great intelligence nor special training. A man used to think that if his boy was not clever enough for a profession he must be put into business. Today we think that business management needs as high an order of intelligence, as thorough a training as any of the "learned" professions.

It seems to me very significant that we seldom hear today the expression so common twenty or even ten years ago—"captains of industry." While all captains of industry did not fly the black flag, still in the nineteenth century ruthlessness and success too often went together; buccaneering and business were too often synonymous. Even when this was not so, the captain of industry was at best a masterful man who could bend all wills to his own. This is beginning to change. Success is now seen to depend on something other than domination. It is significant that two ideas which so long existed together are disappearing together—namely, business as trading, and managing as manipulating.

As arbitrary authority in the management of business has decreased, as authority has come to be associated less with mere position and more with actual capacity, the whole executive force has more opportunities to exercise creative ability in contributions to organization. Please bear in mind that by the word "organization" I mean far more than constructing a system. As Mr. Dennison has told us, "We have to reorganize every day." By which he means, I think, that many of the daily executive duties contribute to a developing organization.

Organization is the word most often heard today in all discussions of business development. The greatest weakness in most industrial plants is seen to be organization. The organization engineer is the one most in demand. Do you not think that the recognition of organization as the chief need of business is rather interesting when we remember that conscious organization is the great spiritual task of man? We speak of the "composition" of a picture; it is the way the artist has organized his material. The harmony of a piece of music depends on the way the musician has organized his material. The statesman organizes social facts into legislation and administration. The greater the statesman, the greater power he shows in just this capacity. It might be fun to try to do it in one's own life, to say: "Here are the materials of my life. How would the artist arrange them in order to make the composition the most significant? How would he subordinate lesser values to higher values? How would he manage to give everything its fullest value?" Or we might ask ourselves the craftsman's question, "How can I make of my life a whole whose beauty and use shall be one?" Organization is what separates mediocre endeavour from high endeavour. No one has a better opportunity than the business manager to take part in this the highest endeavour of the human race.

It occurs to me that you may think, because I have hardly mentioned the profit motive in business, that I have deliberately avoided it. I assure you I have not. We all want profit and as much as we can get. And this is as it should be when other things are not sacrificed to it.

When people talk of substituting the service motive for the profit motive, I always want to ask: Why this wish to simplify motive when there is nothing more complex? Take any one of our actions today and examine it. There probably have been several motives for it. It is true that if anyone asked you why you did so and so, you would probably pick out to present to the public the motive which you thought did you the most credit. But the fact of the actual complexity remains. We work for profit, for service, for our own development, for the love of creating something. At any one moment, indeed, most of us are not working directly or immediately for any of these things, but to put through the job in hand in the best possible manner, which might be thought of, perhaps, as the engineer's motive. But whatever these motives are labelled—ethical or service motive, engineer's motive, craftsman's motive, the creative urge of the artist, the pecuniary gain motive—whatever, I say, these various motives, I do not think we should give any up, but try to get more rather than fewer. To come back to the professions: can we not learn a lesson from them on this very point? The professions have not given up the money motive. I do not care how often you see it stated that they have. Professional men are eager enough for large incomes; but they have other motives as well, and they are often willing to sacrifice a good slice of income for the sake of these other things. We all want the richness of life in the terms of our deepest desire. We can purify and elevate our desires, we can add to them, but there is no individual or social progress in curtailment of desires.

COMMENTARY

Most Quoted—Least Heeded:
The Five Senses of Follett

Sir Peter Parker

I HAVE to begin with a confession: I have lived with Mary Parker Follett all my managerial life—she has mattered more to me than any other of the founders of modern management this century. When I was studying management in the United States at Cornell and Harvard in 1950–1951, I had the opportunity to learn something of the history of management theory. I found myself dividing it into the New and the Old Testament, in which of course Genesis was the doctrine of Frederick W. Taylor, his *Principles of Scientific Management* followed by hot gospels of efficiency from all over the Western world. By the 1920s and 1930s, reactions to Taylorism were building up slowly and inevitably. Hamlet described man as a perfect piece of work, but for scientific management he is not that well designed, not that reasonable, not that free and isolated a variable, not that reliable and predictable. The New Testament (or New Beginnings, as they were called) was founded on the work of the human relations school led by Elton Mayo and his Harvard team. I devoured the works of the new prophets such as Roethlisberger, Barnard, and Simon, but then found myself weighing the ambiguous blessing of the new approach of human relations. It was wise but somehow unengaged, understanding but temptingly manipulative too, consultative but not necessarily deciding and doing—with all its refreshing humanity, it seemed not to include the awkward reality of action and command. Wasn't it the slump that finally put paid to the Hawthorne research? My doubts grew. There was a no man's land to cross between the schools of Taylorism and Human Relations. Just at the right moment of doubt I found the right woman, Mary Parker Follett. I found in her work the coherence that integrated the great works of the other early pioneers and the prophets of Old and New Testaments.

The bony, plain, charming Bostonian had for me the most persuasive vision of them all. She transformed the ideas of modern management into human proportion, into terms of community. In the 1950s I discovered her *Creative Experience* (published in 1924); it explored the key issues of authority and leadership in a democracy, and the role of management in that subtle and human process. These same key issues confront us today. Her own findings and her analytical approach anticipated by 70 years the conclusions that are only now coming to be fully appreciated by business leaders and academics alike: that business and society are not discrete fields of human activity—they are so inextricably interwoven as to be conceptually and analytically inseparable. Business and society are infinitely interpenetrative, and neither can be usefully understood in isolation from the other.

That reciprocity was, I learned, the pattern of her own career. As a young woman, she undertook constitutional studies and work on government that raised her reputation high in academic and national affairs. Her imaginative energy led her into the practicalities of education. She saw for herself the deprivation of the poor families in Boston and developed there social and educational programs around her Roxbury Neighborhood House; the Boston centers had nationwide influence. Her interest in placement and vocational guidance drew her closer to industry; through wage arbitration in World War I she became fascinated by the vitality of business. And the confusion of bargaining relations, the judging and nudging, "each side hoping to win by keeping the whole problem vague." Human nature in action in business became the challenge that shaped the rest of her life.

"Industry is the most important field of human activity," she wrote in a 1926 paper, delivered at the Rowntree Lecture in Oxford, "and management is the fundamental element in industry." For me, this unity of vision of the economic and social worlds was her crucial contribution to management practice. Yet, alas, she has been, as Drucker put it, "the most quoted but probably the least heeded of all students of organization." Why have we been so slow to come round to her relevance? I want to explore that question and to suggest that she remains relevant specifically in five senses.

When we consider relationships of work and community in pre-industrial societies, we do not fall into the trap of false dichotomy. Relationships between peasant and lord in feudal society are not analyzed the one without the other; the farmer and his family worked and lived in the same place, among the same people. Yet with the advent of the industrial revolution, the nature of the inter-relationship of the social and the economic changed not only in form but also in content. The case for this new distance between work and social life was obvious.

The worker now left home to go to the firm or the factory, where he clocked in each morning and out each afternoon. He put on special clothes—overalls or suit, blue collar or white collar—to emphasize that, almost literally, he now had his "working cap" on. The relationship between employer and employed, it is argued, was now a purely economic one. The employer was no longer responsible for the welfare of the worker, as the lord was once (theoretically) responsible for the welfare of his peasants. The factory worker did not live in the same house as the factory owner, did not eat at the same table, was not part of his family. And, it was maintained, the worker increasingly ceased to feel a social (and political) deference toward his employer.

This model may seem tempting, but it is wholly misleading for two reasons. First, business still takes place within society. The firm employs people; and people are shaped by their society and upbringing, by a shared culture, customs, language, traditions, and received patterns of thought. Second, a business is itself a micro-society within the broader community; its members interact socially, not just outside office hours but all the time. Generally speaking, even in advanced industrialized societies most workers spend at least as many of their waking hours with their colleagues as with their families. The place of work, rather than the home, is the primary field of human social interaction.

Mary Parker Follett had this sense of the organic unity, the infinite interpenetrations of business and society. I find it not surprising that the Japanese "discovered" Follett in the early 1950s. Pauline Graham, Follett's passionate champion in this generation, has noted that "As we try to emulate their ways of managing, we get Follett secondhand." The phenomenal performance of post-war Japan is a reminder that the foundation of prosperity in any industrial society is in a harmony of purposes in its economic and social life. How long Japan will retain that integrity is another matter—so far, however, it has proved a vivid illumination of Follett's relevance to our times.

And there are four more senses of Follett's relevance to which we should be giving heed, academics and businesspeople together.

1. Her interdisciplinary approach. Mary Parker Follett synthesized the study of business with broader social and political studies. She was unhesitant in deploying evidence, concepts, and analytical tools from fields as diverse as political science, political theory, history, and social psychology. She enjoyed business (as I do) because "Here the ideal and the practical have joined hands. That is why I am working at business management, because, while I care for the ideal, it is only because I want to help bring it into our everyday affairs." She was even prepared to turn to the most liberal of arts for inspiration or instruction. In studying the concept of power, she declared, "I am making a list of all the different definitions I come across, by novelists or artists, or whoever, and I find this all helping me in my observation of power in everyday life."

In our time, the holistic approach, a defining characteristic of her work, is too often absent in management studies and schools. Management is about the interaction of human beings—of individual people. Whatever functions and expertise that enlarge its skills, management remains a human and social process.

2. Her humanity. In the introduction to *Dynamic Administration,* Metcalf and Urwick made a revealing remark. "Briefly stated, the Follett philosophy is that any enduring society, or continuously productive organization, must be grounded upon a recognition of the motivating desires of the industrial end of the Group." For her, organization was never a puzzle: puzzles have answers. Managing an organization was more human than that, more dynamic, more complicated, and less quantifiable than some accountants might like, less technical than some technologists might hope.

Unlike many, Follett refused to displace the human element from the focus of her political or her management theory—which were aspects of the same holistic approach and theoretical paradigm. A particular characteristic of Follett's work is the anecdotal nature of her evidence. One searches *Dynamic Administration* in vain for abstract tables and complex formulas of dubious applicability. Born in 1868, the year that Benjamin Disraeli first became prime minister of Great Britain, she seemed to share his opinion of statistics. But this should not be taken as evidence of unprofessionalism. By combining individual items of evidence with critical rigor, a knowledge drawn from a diversity of disciplines, and real life experience, she was able to construct a sturdy frame of argument in which evidence played its part but did not have to carry too much of the load. She never hid behind a bewildering display of statistics and abstract models, and she was prepared to draw conclusions.

Today, management theory is waking up to the key issue, which is not the utility of one particular rationalist model versus another, but the limits of rationalist models themselves. One might call it the Romantic revolution in management studies. For example, some very useful pathfinding in this area has been done at the London School of Economics' Business Performance Group, with which I have been closely involved for a number of years. The Business Performance Group has undertaken research that has synthesized classical business management theory with analytical models and techniques drawn from the social sciences, social psychology in particular. In so doing, it has been attempting to put the "human" back in human resource management.

Like Follett, the group has gone out into the field, as it were, to conduct its research; and it has found that rationalist models on their own cannot explain fully the performance of the firms that the group has examined. Consider, for example, the John Lewis Partnership, a major employee-owned retailer in Great Britain: Group research noted that traditional performance models, focusing on the absence of capital market discipline in the partnership and on the impact of employees on decision making, would suggest that the partnership would perform badly. In fact, it performed very well. The partnership was a major business success in the 1970s and 1980s, and research suggests that the role of the human side of the business has been of major importance. From the earliest days of the partnership, the company has been run on principles that enhance financial remuneration, improve the flow of information, and emphasize service as a key commercial goal. The principles rest on a conviction that justice in dealings with people is not only ethically correct, but also leads to enhanced business success.

W. B. Yeats described William Blake (1757–1827), the poet, painter, and prophet, as "the first rise of the soul," the Romantic who rose against the Age of Enlightenment with its overconfidence in reason and systems. It is in this spirit that Follett was a Romantic. And she had the experience and imagination to operate behind the enemy lines of the Rationalists, of scientific organizational theorists who exiled emotion and anecdote. Those of us in business who take too much comfort from the conventional organization charts of responsibility should ponder: "Strand should weave with strand and then we shall not have the clumsy task of trying to patch together finished webs." There are no successful business managers of small and medium enterprises who do not understand the human element in business. It is in the bigger corporations that managers tend to lose the human perspective. Because the bigger corporations are operating in a global economy these days, the lessons of the Romantic revolution are all the more telling.

3. Her international relevance. I have already mentioned the irony of the Japanese adaptation of Follett. But human and social factors are intensified in any global company that has to manage production and marketing across frontiers and cultures. The relatively short hop across the bridge between America and Europe has proven to be anything but a cakewalk; the hop, skip, and jump to cross Europe with Southeast Asia and China will call for a whole new set of muscles. As Albert Koopman put it in a recent work, "To manage effectively across cultures we will have to be able to match strategy with culture, or in other words, to match the values of a community with an appropriate form of management and organization." In short, I suggest that the language of international management will be that of Follett.

Global business is indispensable to the quality and growth of the living standards of the world. That reality will characterize the next century, and I recognize it as enhancing and encouraging—it will transcend, we hope, the competition of nationalism and the emergent regional blocs. The logic of the situation, in Follett language, is trade globalization—despite the horrors of tribalism we are witnessing in all parts of the troubled globe. Nevertheless, even presuming the best will in the world markets (and some presumption that is), there are inevitably sensitive issues of sovereignty and authority that arise. Follett's thinking on such issues, conceived in quite another context, has a bearing on the answers. Follett described authority as "vested power." Of course, there will be conflicts; conflicts are normal and can be constructive in any organization. ("Opposition is true friendship," was one of Blake's sayings.) But conflict resolution emerges best not from the domination of a boss, although sometimes there can be no other way, nor from compromise, which changes too little. Resolution should come from both sides following the logic of the situation toward something new to both, a gain for both. Certainly in the business of my life

I have tried to live by that. I have found it makes sense in internal relationships in organizations, profit-making and otherwise, and also in trying to interpret the role of an international enterprise to a host country overseas.

Today we are in an era in which multinational corporations command vast resources and wield consummate economic, social, and political power. Furthermore, the exponential advance in science, in fields such as technology and microbiology, is daily adding to the social responsibilities of business executives. Businesses make decisions about the development of rural areas, about investment in the third world, about a new drug, about the environment. In literal terms, it is nonsense to refer to business as "the private sector"—does anything have as much public impact as business? Just as there is an enlarging appreciation of how society influences business, so the effect of business on the wider national and global community has also started to come to the fore. I mentioned earlier the LSE's Business Performance Group's work on the John Lewis Partnership as an example of society's influence on business. Recently the multinational pharmaceutical giant Smith Kline Beecham Seiyaku K.K. joined with LSE to develop a new Master's program, "Corporate Business & Society"; the course will be taught by a new Institute for Business & Society, to be developed out of the Business Performance Group. It is 60 years ago at LSE that Follett gave her last lectures—and they still make relevant reading for any international merger.

4. Her concept of "reciprocal service"—what Adam Smith called the "hidden hand." Follett maintained that business had responsibilities to the wider community, but not simply in addition to its primary economic function; she argued that social and economic responsibilities were integral. Whereas others contrasted the work of business and the work of social agencies, she called the latter "extra-social agencies." "Business is, and should be considered, a truly social agency." She summed up her philosophy with characteristic frankness:

There was a notion formerly that a man made money for himself, a purely selfish conception, in the daytime, and remedied his service to the community by sitting on the school board or some civic committee at night. Or he might spend his early or middle life in business, in getting money, and then also his service later by spending his money in ways useful to the community—if he did not die before that stage arrived. The more wholesome idea, which we have now, is that our work itself is to be our greatest service to the community.

She was not merely hoping naively that one sphere, business, should voluntarily give service to another, "society," but that they were both part of a single, organic whole.

So in conclusion, I am more than ever aware of the single-mindedness of Follett's vision. It is hard to examine it in parts, it can only be understood as a whole—in her words, "the wholesome idea." While I have been analyzing five senses in which her legacy is relevant to business today—her unity of vision of business and society, her interdisciplinary approach, the sheer humanity of her concepts of management, her internationalism, her definition of "reciprocal services"—all are variations of her fundamental theme of reconciliation between order givers and order takers. She was of the Romantic school in management. But not all starry-eyed. She expected there to be conflict—managers and managed share their cussed human nature. And she relied on self-interest: a long-term view of it would respond to the law of the situation.

"When we become enlightened enough to realise that we individually get more out of joining with people than by competing with them, we do it." "That's a deal," I thought, when I met her years ago, and the deal still holds—reasonable and romantic.

Epilogue

PAUL R. LAWRENCE

ALL OF the commentaries in this volume, to a degree, have been epilogues; all were written with full hindsight. Contributors have spoken about many of Mary Parker Follett's insightful contributions to management literature. In particular, they highlighted her treatment of order giving, authority, conflict resolution, power, teamwork, leadership, and citizenship. All have recognized how remarkably she anticipated the work of later management writers, many of whom were apparently unaware of her contributions. They have speculated about why her pioneering work was not more widely recognized.

In my own case, I first encountered Mary Parker Follett in 1947 as required reading for a Harvard Business School human relations doctoral seminar that Fritz Roethlisberger had just taken over on the retirement of Elton Mayo. I found her work invaluable, but the truth is that I simply did not know enough about management to appreciate it *fully*. Rereading her again for the purpose of this publication has been a real pleasure. I call it a pleasure because that is how I experienced it—the pleasure of discovering, as if for the first time, the richness of her perceptions and the completeness of her coverage. Clearly, my understanding of Follett had been enhanced by years of studying management firsthand. Thus I humbly confess that her work was not more recognized by me because I was not that wise. Perhaps it was so with others.

How did she do it? It is very hard to see behavior so clearly and so simply. I believe it was her experience running charitable organizations that gave her a firsthand, intuitive familarity with management. She knew what questions to ask. Her understanding of her subject also must have helped her gain access to top management as a valued adviser. Her persistent curiosity led her to interact at all levels of organization with empathy and respect. Her tools of inquiry were the tried and true ones of interview and observation in the field. Her observations were interpreted with the help of concepts drawn from multiple scientific fields. She was not handicapped by the theoretical blinders of a single discipline; hers was an applied orientation. She was constantly searching for better ways to manage, referring to "leading" firms, the "better" managers. She believed in the betterment of society and blatantly used her references to "progressive" practice to intrigue her audience and sell her ideas. But history has proven that her selection, out of all the management practices of the early 1920s, of what she believed constituted "advanced thinking" was uncannily accurate. Examples are numerous.

One is her treatment of union relations and collective bargaining. She described clearly the power tactics involved in the customary collective-bargaining process with its secrecy, its threats, its bluffing, and, of course, its frequent use of raw power in the form of strikes and lockouts. But she also saw an evolution away from power bargaining toward joint councils and problem-solving bargaining that is only now emerging as a mutually advantageous way of conducting union-management relations. She saw the potential advantages of institutionalizing a continuing voice for labor in all important decisions about a firm. She saw the promise of enlarging the sense of industrial community and of seeking win-win, integrated answers, even as she recognized that some zero-sum issues would inevitably remain.

In her discussion of conflict, she conceptualized three modes of resolution (domination, compromise, and integration) that have proven so useful for subsequent researchers that they are truly classical categories. These three resolution methods (in different words) were the keystone of the work of Blake and Mouton and, later, of my work with Lorsch on conflict. Her description of the interweaving and interpenetration of ideas in the integration process was a major contribution to management practice. Her insight that integration actually added value anticipated much of the contemporary attention to value analysis.

In dealing with coordination Follett shows her links with classical organizational theory even as she foreshadows modern organizational theory. She enumerates four "principles" (the normative language of classical theory) of coordination:

(1) Co-ordination as the reciprocal relating of all the factors in a situation.

(2) Co-ordination by direct contact of the responsible people concerned.

(3) Co-ordination in the early stages.

(4) Co-ordination as a continuing process.[1]

Her first principle points at a process that Thompson subsequently clarified by distinguishing between reciprocal interdependence and sequential and pooled interdependence. Her second principle, coordination by direct contact, offers an alternative to the classicist insistence on adherence to coordination only by the chain of command. She also referred to this process as "cross-functioning" and discussed the merits of cross-functional business teams. Coordination by these so-called lateral relations was later developed in detail by Galbraith. Her third principle anticipated the widespread practice of using concurrent design teams that bring manufacturing and marketing specialists in at the very start of new product development. The fourth principle is suggestive of today's continuous improvement programs.

In her treatment of the individual in society, Follett takes great pains to examine the importance of respecting and cultivating the differences among the specialized contributors to organizational performance: "Difference shaping itself in exact conformity with the need of the work we do." She saw that the tension generated by these work-based differences could be the source of the creative ideas that add value: "Separateness must be coordinated." The conflict generated by these differences must, of course, be handled in a constructive way: "Differences develop within the social process and are united through the social process."[2] The differences need to be resolved by the integrative process in order to achieve a unity of effort: "It behooves us . . . to search diligently after the law of unity that we may effectively marshal . . . all the varying diversities of life."[3] By now it should be clear to readers familiar with my work on differentiation and integration just how much I am in Follett's debt. I might add that her stress on the importance of appropriate differences is still far too little understood by both management scholars and practitioners.

Throughout her writings Follett uses systemic analysis, what would now be called "systems thinking." She elaborated on the formal concept of function as a reciprocal two-way relationship. She constantly stressed the need to move away from thinking in one-way, cause-and-effect relations. She used such terms as "total situation," "total environment," "relativity," and "inter-relating." She saw the subject-object relationship as circular. She argued that purpose is constantly emerging from the social process and argued against teleological reasoning. Applying this systemic thinking to management was pioneering, and it blazed a trail for others to follow.

In writing about the classical scholars of organizational theory in 1967, Lorsch and I stated, "At that time [the 1920s and early 1930s] very few writers were even suggesting alternative ways of looking at formal organizations. About the only exceptions were Mary Parker Follett and Elton Mayo. . . . The general beliefs and mores of the time supported the classical position."[4] I think this is an accurate statement, but it needs some amplification. Mayo was really focusing on workers and their social system, while Follett was focusing on managers and their social system. But each contributed in a complementary way to the emergence of the human relations perspective on organizations. And our review of Follett's ideas clearly reveals what a remarkable contribution hers was. I am delighted that this publication will reach a younger, wider audience.

In conclusion, I want to address the question raised in Nohria's commentary. Was Follett's vision of the emerging, the "new" organization too optimistic or perhaps even naive—an ideal type? Nohria writes that in the years since Follett wrote, there have been four waves of discovery and even promotion of this "new" organization. He identifies the human relations movement that Follett helped launch as the first wave, followed by the participative management waves of the 1950s and 1960s, the quality-of-work-life movement of the 1970s, and now the networking wave (a.k.a. delayering, empowerment, reengineering, team working, and so forth). By and large I agree with this summary of history. I do not agree at all, however, with his point that after each wave the iron law of oligarchy takes over and moves organizations back to authoritarian, hierarchical bureaucracies. Rather, I see slow, episodic movement toward the new organization, with periods of plateauing between the waves of interest and enthusiasm. Given the sweeping nature of the change in question, nothing less than total cultural change, what else could reasonably be expected? Organizational inertia is enormous; change is painful. Furthermore, some people will continue to seek the enjoyment of exercising power over others, even if it is an ineffective way of running organizations. I would also point out that even if the new organization becomes dominant, there will still be a useful place for traditional organizations in the more stable sectors of society. For many reasons the change has been slow and halting. But it is still coming, and I am convinced it is picking up speed. It has helped greatly to have outstanding pioneers like Mary Parker Follett to light the way. But the real driver of the change is the drive to survive. The new organizational form is simply more effective.

NOTES

1. L. Urwick, ed., *Freedom and Co-ordination: Lectures in Business Organisation by Mary Parker Follett* (London: Management Publications, 1949), p. 78.
2. Mary Parker Follett, *The New State: Group Organization, the Solution of Popular Government* (London: Longmans, Green, 1920), p. 63.
3. Ibid., p. 64.
4. Paul R. Lawrence and Jay W. Lorsch, *Organization and Environment: Managing Differentiation and Integration* (Boston: Harvard Business School Press, 1986), p. 167.

Bibliography of Mary Parker Follett's Writings

Follett, Mary Parker. *The Speaker of the House of Representatives.* New York: Longmans, Green, 1896.

———. *The New State—Group Organisation, the Solution for Popular Government.* New York: Longmans, Green, 1918. Reprint, with an introduction by Lord Haldane, London: Longmans, Green, 1920.

———. *Creative Experience.* New York: Longmans, Green, 1924.

———. *Freedom and Co-ordination.* London: Management Publications Trust, 1949.

Fox, E. M., and L. F. Urwick, eds. *Dynamic Administration—The Collected Papers of Mary Parker Follett.* New York: Pitman Publishing, 1973.

Metcalf, H. C., and L. F. Urwick, eds. *Dynamic Administration—The Collected Papers of Mary Parker Follett.* Bath: Management Publications Trust, 1941.

Index

About the Contributors

Warren Bennis is Distinguished Professor of Business Administration and founding chairman of the Leadership Institute at the University of Southern California. He has held senior academic positions at several other universities, including MIT, Harvard, and INSEAD, and has consulted for many companies. As an author or editor, Dr. Bennis has produced over 900 articles and 20 books, the most recent being *An Invented Life: Reflections on Leadership and Change* (1994).

John Child is the Guinness Professor of Management Studies at the Judge Institute of Management Studies, University of Cambridge, and editor-in-chief of *Organization Studies*. Previously, he was dean and director of the European Community's Management Institute in China. He is advisor to leading companies, with particular attention to the management of foreign ventures in China. An author of many books, his most recent publication is *Management in China During the Age of Reform* (1994).

Peter F. Drucker has been writing on management since he published *The Future of Industrial Man*—his second book—in 1943. A frequent contributor to the *Harvard Business Review*, he has since 1971 been Professor of Social Science & Management at The Claremont Graduate School in Claremont, California. His latest book is *Post Capitalist Society* (1993).

Angela Dumas is an assistant professor in Design Management and the Director of the Centre for Design Management at the London

Business School. She has published several papers on the integration of design into new product development teams and on the role of middle managers in that process. She is a fellow of both the Royal Society of Arts and the Chartered Society of Designers.

Tokihiko Enomoto is a professor of business administration at Tokai University, Japan. In 1986, he and several colleagues established The Mary Parker Follett Association of Japan. With Tadashi Mito, he wrote *Mary Parker Follett* (1986), a study of Follett's life and theories; he has also written several books about business administration based on the theories of Mary Parker Follett.

Pauline Graham is a lecturer and consultant on management and marketing. Fomerly, she ran her own international accountancy practice and worked in general management in the retail trade. An authority on the management philosophy of Mary Parker Follett, she has written *Dynamic Managing—The Follett Way* (1987) and *Integrative Management—Creating Unity from Diversity* (1991).

Rosabeth Moss Kanter holds the Class of 1960 Chair as Professor of Business Administration at the Harvard Business School. Her many books include the best-selling, award-winning *When Giants Learn to Dance* and *The Change Masters*. An advisor to leading companies worldwide, she also served as editor of the *Harvard Business Review* from 1989 to 1992 and hosts "Rosabeth Moss Kanter on Synergies, Alliances, and New Ventures" in the Harvard Business School Video Series.

Paul R. Lawrence is the Wallace Brett Donham Professor of Organizational Behavior, Emeritus, at the Harvard Business School, where he served as chairman of the organizational behavior area and also as chairman of both the MBA and AMP programs. His most recent book, with A. Charalambos Vlachoutsicos, is *Behind the Factory Walls: Decision Making in Soviet and U.S. Enterprises* (Harvard Business School Press, 1990).

Henry Mintzberg is Bronfman Professor of Management at McGill University and former president of the Strategic Management Society. He is a two-time winner of the McKinsey Award for the best *Harvard Business Review* article, for "The Manager's Job: Folklore and Fact" (1975) and "Crafting Strategy" (1987). His most recent book is *The Rise and Fall of Strategic Planning* (1994).

Nitin Nohria is an associate professor in the organizational behavior/human resource management area at the Harvard Business School. With Robert G. Eccles, he is the co-author of *Networks and Organizations: Structure, Form, and Action* (1993) and *Beyond the Hype: Rediscovering the Essence of Management* (1994), both published by the Harvard Business School Press.

Sir Peter Parker is chairman of the London School of Economics. He has also been the chairman of British Rail, a member of the National Economic Development Council, a founding member of the Foundation for Management Education, and chairman of the British Insitute of Management. He holds the RSA Gold Medal for Design as well as several honorary degrees. His autobiography, *For Starters—the business of life*, was published in 1989.